top TV shows of the year

top TV
shows
of the
year
1954–1955

EDITED BY
IRVING SETTEL

COMMUNICATION ARTS BOOKS

HASTINGS HOUSE · PUBLISHERS · NEW YORK

Library of Congress Catalog Card Number: 55-7910

Published simultaneously in Canada
by S. J. Reginald Saunders, Publishers, Toronto 1

Printed in the United States of America

FOR KENNY AND JOANNE

ACKNOWLEDGMENTS

The great task of assembling, reading and choosing these scripts could not possibly be the work of one person. Credit must go to many who contributed their services and advice. Without their help, this book could never have achieved fruition.

First of all, I wish to express my profound gratitude to Trudy Settel, my wife, for her untiring devotion, unceasing encouragement and relentless work in the cause of getting this volume into covers.

I also wish to thank President Robert S. Pace, Provost Edward J. Mortola, Dean Joseph F. Sinzer, Dr. Jack S. Schiff and the members of the faculty of Pace College for their help and encouragement.

Grateful thanks are also due Susan Shire, Bill Todman, Mark Goodson, Ed Rice, Hope H. Taylor, Bernard Platt, Norman Glenn, Fred Friendly, Fred Coe, Mike Horton, Ernest Stern, Joan Thornbury, Jack Philbin, Stanley Poss, Elizabeth Haglund, Francis C. McCall, Ross Donaldson, Richard C. Bostwick, Jack Perlis, Lawrence E. Spivak, Dick De Pew, Jack Goldstein, Paul Lammers, Al Durante, Abel Green, Henry C. Brown, Sara Polin, Lynn Poole, Stockton Helffrich, Ben Lifton, Al Seaton, Joan Wilkins, George Rosen, Robert Lewine, Sylvia Lyons, Leonard Lyons, and to the many executives and producers of NBC, CBS, ABC and DuMont Networks.

For their advice and constructive criticisms, my sincere appreciation is extended to Mrs. Gertrude G. Broderick of Washington, D. C., Leon Levine, Rev. Charles H. Schmitz, Ralph Steetle, Washington, D. C., and Mrs. Clara S. Logan, Los Angeles, California.

Finally, deserving special mention is Russell F. Neale, publishing director of Hastings House *Communication Arts Books* who advised me throughout with patience, wisdom and discernment.

I. S.

INTRODUCTION

The task of gathering material for this, the first comprehensive anthology of current television programs, involved a multitude of activities undreamed of in its blueprint stage. I had entertained the innocent notion that the project was a comparatively simple one concerned mainly with problems of selection. As the job progressed, however, difficulties began to mount and when at last we went to press, it had become apparent that the completed work had reached far beyond my original expectations.

In retrospect, the result has been most gratifying. For one thing, it represents the best work of new and dynamic writers and producers in this vital medium. True, it was not possible to include all worthy programs. Legal tangles caused the omission of some shows. With others, we had difficulties on clearances. Still others had to be discarded because of a lack of space. It is a matter of sincere regret that I could not include them all.

However, I have this consolation. The programs here presented make fascinating reading and, at the same time, should serve as a stimulating basis for television study groups. The chosen scripts are representative examples of the best that television had to offer during the experimental year of 1954. As such, it is felt that this volume will provide an indication of future trends in a developing medium.

From the start of the project, many basic problems were encountered. The new and sprightly giant had been drawing upon the resources of Broadway and of Hollywood, salvaging the best, discarding the inappropriate. Most important of all, television was trying out new styles and novel ideas, working in earnest to achieve a form of its own.

All these factors were added complications in setting up standards for choice. Vital questions arose. What types of shows should be included? Should filmed programs be used? Should TV versions of Broadway hits be considered? Television time was being occupied to an increasing extent by programs of a "non-television" type.

With the cooperation of producers from the major networks and stations, and advice from a group of distinguished persons vitally interested in the subject, standards were devised to meet the various aspects of the problem. It was decided, for example, that television, being a new medium, must be judged as such. It was agreed that *true* television should be considered on the basis of *live* performance—with its sparkle, its spontaneity, its immediacy. This new medium had come into its own despite the tremendous influx of mass-produced half-hour "TV films," the complexion of which strangely resembled the "grade B" double-feature programs of the often criticized movies. One concession was permitted. The *live* program which utilized film portions to broaden its scope, would qualify, for this was a *true* television technique.

The next major question concerned the categories to be included. Thirty-two possible classifications were considered. From this list, by combining similar groups, twelve categories were finally determined. These seemed to include all the major types of television programming being performed before TV cameras.

Then the word spread that scripts were being considered for inclusion in this volume. At first, a trickle of material began to arrive. This gradually developed into a virtual flood; literally hundreds of scripts stacked up around my desk. The task of sorting alone took many days. Then came the reading, eliminating, grouping and regrouping, and then final selection for publication.

As previously mentioned, unexpected problems arose during this period. Many scripts had "played" better than they read. Others were outstanding by virtue of their performance alone. I felt, as did my advisers, that, to be chosen, a script should not only have played well but also must *read* well. This was to be a book and if the script did not "project itself" in type, inclusion was impossible.

The program scripts finally chosen gave me and all concerned a deep sense of satisfaction. The overall selection appeared to be a fine, representative group of contemporary television programs—dignified, inspiring and vital.

Happily, good scripts never die. Since the selection was made, as if to concur with it, many of the programs attained new honors. *Elisha and the Long Knives* by Dale Wasserman and Jack Balch is currently under consideration by Hollywood for a movie production. *The Thinking Heart* by George H. Faulkner is a stirring drama and may be considered a television classic, destined to be produced again and again.

The Johns Hopkins Science Review's *Toys and Science* was subsequently retelecast twice because of popular request—and is scheduled for still another showing. Lou Hazam's *Arthritis and Rheumatism* has been singled out by medical groups as one of the finest "layman's" medical programs ever presented on television. *Conquest of Pain* has been kinescoped for distribution to schools and educational associations throughout the country.

Edward R. Murrow's *Report on Senator Joseph R. McCarthy* made journalistic history and influenced the news long after it had been telecast. Jackie Gleason has chalked up new honors, and is currently rated as one of the greatest television comedians. Certainly in terms of finances he has reached a pinnacle, with one of the most lucrative contracts ever written for a TV show (see page 35).

It should be noted that television programming has been in a state of more or less continuous flux during 1954. The pendulum of public favor swung from "variety" comedy to "situation" comedy. "Live" dramatic plays, unfortunately, became increasingly scarce as hundreds of *canned* "grade B" films were turned out for television consumption. Half-hour films "made especially for television" flooded into the market, and onto our TV screens.

Panel shows, both of the political and quiz type, established their place on the scene and seemed to be here to stay. The "spectacular," born of the desire to capture the ever-elusive audience rating, made its appearance, sky-rocketed costs and produced new names and faces. The advent of color has brought new problems that greatly affect the industry and its programming.

High costs and limited time periods led to the development of "magazine" type programs, such as the *Home Show* included in this book. This format, based upon the popular mass-circulation magazines with "feature" articles and "special sections," permitted the sharing of costs through "participation" sponsorship. "Tight" evening network hours made daytime and late nighttime programming a necessity. As money poured into these fringe periods, program quality improved and audience listenership ratings went up. TV programming was generally on the move during 1954 and the first half of the 1954/55 season.

Of particular interest, therefore, are the statements regarding programming on the pages immediately following. These contributions, specially written for this book by two top network executives, provide a brief résumé of developments and trends during the year just past.

NEW YORK CITY   IRVING SETTEL
MARCH 1, 1955

"YOU'VE GOT TO KEEP MOVING"

A friend of mine who has done a good deal of mountain climbing once explained the sport in very simple terms. "Once you've started up," he said, "you've got to keep moving."

Now television, in this sense at least, is like mountain climbing. Having started up as a medium of tremendous excitement, television must keep climbing or it may be left clinging to a low ledge of mediocrity and dullness.

At the National Broadcasting Company we are making a strong effort to maintain the exciting pace of television and we are channeling this effort through four main concepts. These are the concepts of the "spectacular," of the television "magazine," of editorial control, and of "enlightenment through exposure," as we call it at NBC.

By now the term "spectacular," as it is used in television, is widely known. Our purpose in launching these 90-minute color shows was to bring new luster to television and to refresh it as a center of attraction. In this we succeeded beyond our hopes. We feel that the spectaculars have proved to be the most exciting entertainment event of the year and, as one reviewer pointed out, each of them has generated more editorial comment than a whole series of Broadway plays.

The NBC magazine programs—*Today, Tonight,* and *Home*—are endowing television with a new and important flexibility, we believe. They permit the variety of a newspaper, the "depth" of a magazine and the illumination and immediacy of television. Above all, they aim to break away from the old stereotypes and give television an exciting sense of living, minute by minute, with the times.

This leads to the broader concept of editorial control. To an ever greater degree, NBC is assuming responsibility for its program planning and production. In this way, we are trying to provide viewers with a better balanced program diet. Just as an editor must plan the contents of a magazine to hold a wide readership, so the network must plan its programs to attract the whole viewing public. At NBC we are planning our programs to appeal not merely to the heavy viewers who are easily satisfied, but to the discriminating viewers as well. For this reason, in our opinion, network control means better programs.

Underlying all our program planning is the concept of "enlightenment through exposure," which seeks to raise the level of program content and with it the level of audience appreciation. To this end it is our policy to inject informational and cultural elements into all programs, even those which are usually considered pure entertainment. Under this policy it is now routine to introduce a ballet sequence, an operatic passage, or a dramatic excerpt into the *Colgate Comedy Hour,* say, or one of the NBC spectaculars. Our audience has come not merely to expect these things but to want them.

These, then, are some of the concepts which are adding new excitement to television. But it is the nature of our task that these concepts themselves must constantly grow and change if television is to maintain its exciting pace and to achieve its full potential of service to the public.

THOMAS A. MC AVITY
VICE PRESIDENT IN CHARGE OF NBC-TV
FORMERLY VICE PRESIDENT IN CHARGE
OF PROGRAMMING OF NBC-TV

TELEVISION IS COMING OF AGE

One of the most significant facts for television in 1954 has been the emergence of another major network, ABC, into the programming picture.

The dynamic effect of television exerts itself tremendously on the public, on the theatre, on talent and on all forms of entertainment. Programming patterns are, therefore, particularly important and, it seems fair to add, are largely formulated by the major networks.

In past seasons, two networks—more or less—dominated the television scene. Now that picture is changing, with additional competition for the viewer's attention. As a result, we find an encouraging improvement in programming and a quickening sense of service to the public—television's greatest of friends and severest of critics. At last, television is coming of age. To a great extent, this maturing process has been spurred by the added competition among the networks.

At ABC-TV, as other networks, we anticipate still further advances in programming during the coming year. During the past season, such programs as the new *Disneyland* series helped to provide a distinctive pattern with the combined use of animated cartoons, films and "live" performances. Another significant growth in television programming was ABC-TV's use of the famed Theatre Guild as consultant in developing new programs and talent for the industry.

In October 1952, TV network programming in the evening hours totalled about 69 hours weekly, whereas by late fall of 1954, this increased to over 86 hours weekly—and with program percentages more widespread among the major networks. As the competitive pace accelerates, there should be improved television for all. 1955 will see even greater progress.

ROBERT M. WEITMAN
VICE PRESIDENT IN CHARGE
OF PROGRAMMING AND TALENT
ABC TELEVISION NETWORK

CONTENTS

TOP CHILDREN'S SHOW OF THE YEAR

THE JOHNS HOPKINS
SCIENCE REVIEW

Toys and Science

TOYS AND SCIENCE

The Johns Hopkins Science Review Presented by
The Johns Hopkins University and WAAM-TV in
Baltimore in cooperation with the DuMont Tele-
vision Network.

PARTICIPANTS:

MASTER TIMMY CORCORAN . . . as the boy

JOHN LOCKWOOD . . . as the toymaker

LYNN POOLE . . . guide through the toy shop

PRODUCER AND MODERATOR . . LYNN POOLE

IN ASSOCIATION WITH . . . . . ROBERT FENWICK
AND JOHN LOCKWOOD

DIRECTORS . . . . KENNARD CALFEE
AND HERBERT B. CAHAN

ART DIRECTOR . . . . BARRY MANSFIELD

NARRATOR . . . . JOEL CHASEMAN

WRITER . . . . ROBERT FENWICK

TELECAST: JANUARY 20, 1954

THE
JOHNS HOPKINS SCIENCE REVIEW

THE JOHNS HOPKINS SCIENCE REVIEW is a fine example of educational television. Lynn Poole and his associates at the Johns Hopkins University believe that television is the greatest of all teaching media—if the teaching is spiced with a modicum of entertainment, excitement and drama. In spite of the prediction when it started that the show would be scuttled as soon as TV hit its stride, the program has lasted for more than six years and is still going strong.

The usual presentations on the program series of the Johns Hopkins Science Review are of subjects related to the current advances in many fields of science, including such topics as *Conquest of Pain* (see page 201), *X-Ray, Where Does It Begin?, Life Seen Through A Test Tube, Man Will Conquer Space,* and others. Its *Toys and Science* was pitched to children although kept as adult as possible. The result was that this program captured one of the largest audiences of the series—made up of both children and adults—and is considered one of the best and most successful ever produced by The Johns Hopkins Science Review.

The Review is a three way partnership—between The Johns Hopkins University, the DuMont Television Network and Station WAAM-TV in Baltimore (from where it originates). It is prepared, written and produced by a staff of three under the direction of Lynn Poole at the University.

Mr. Poole has established for the program a number of rules which have been imitated and practiced throughout the television world. "The Johns Hopkins Science Review," he indicated, "must be kept simple enough for everyone to understand and must establish a viewer identification with what is done. There usually is a way to demonstrate any complex, complicated scientific fact. If so, demonstrate. If not, don't talk about it more than a few minutes."

The program is also an example of how much can be done in television on a virtual "shoestring." The Review spends less in an entire year than do most shows in one single telecast. The total budget is under $30,000 for a full series of 52 shows, including a good deal of research in the use of films and animation. Actually, the cast, made up of University people and friends, works for nothing and props are usually purchased at the five and dime store.

Despite all this economy, the quality of the program has been exceptional and has reached a weekly viewing audience of more than 500,000 men, women and children.

A brain-child of Lynn Poole, The Johns Hopkins Science Review took to the air in 1948, after Poole created the idea. Seeing the vast possibilities of educational television after being engaged by the University as a public relations man, Poole pushed and promoted his idea. With the approval of University Provost P. Stewart Macauley, he approached Station WMAR even before it began operating. Fortunately the station needed a "time filler" and permitted the presentation. Later WAAM, Baltimore's second station, took over the show and shortly thereafter it was put on the entire DuMont Network.

Lynn Poole, now a slightly built man of 43, was a Major in the Air Force prior to joining Johns Hopkins and, before his military service, lectured at the Walters Art Gallery in Baltimore. He is a graduate of Western Reserve University in Cleveland.

TOYS AND SCIENCE

MD on exterior of toy shop . . . toy-maker can be seen through window. Dolly in to window filled with toys and in tight on title.

JOEL: "TOYS AND SCIENCE"

Music Up and Under
JOEL: The Johns Hopkins Science Review, presented by The Johns Hopkins University and WAAM in Baltimore in cooperation with the DuMont Television Network.

FILM

Music Up and Under
This is The Johns Hopkins University, famed for seventy-six years for its contributions to science and the humanities. Here in its many laboratories Hopkins scientists are probing into the secrets of science, which, when discovered, will be translated into benefits to be enjoyed by you, the people of America. Each week we look over the shoulders of today's scientists and catch a glimpse of the results of their research.

Dissolve from film to title in window

On this, our 239th showing of The Johns Hopkins Science Review, we present TOYS AND SCIENCE.

Music Up and Under

Dolly back to show L.P. looking in window

And to introduce this week's program, here from The Johns Hopkins University is Lynn Poole.

VIDEO	AUDIO
Turns to camera	POOLE: I have been admiring some of the toys in the window of this toy shop here. I guess we never grow too old to get some enjoyment out of toys —particularly new toys. Perhaps, that's why Junior sometimes has difficulty getting his electric train away from Dad. . . . But what have toys to do with science? . . . It isn't often that we stop to think that toys are the result of complex scientific research . . . and embody principles discovered by Archimedes and Newton and many other scientists. Scientific principles or not . . . it doesn't interfere with our enjoyment of toys . . . although we may wonder how some of them work. . . . But let's go inside and see some of these toys.
	Bells On Door Ring
Enters door . . . MD shot interior as he enters . . . walks to counter *Pan toy shelves*	POOLE: As you know the stores are crowded with thousands of toys . . . there are the old standbys . . . and hundreds of new ones every year. Some of these toys are designed with science in mind . . . the chemistry sets . . . and the mechanical building sets . . . but many others operate on some scientific principle . . . and it can be fun trying to decide just what that principle is . . . for example . . . (*picks up top*). . . . Here is a very simple little top. . . . You wouldn't think the principle behind it would be very complex . . . and yet we've asked dozens of people what that principle

VIDEO | AUDIO

is . . . and had as many answers. . . . Watch it work. (*Spins top*) Do you know what causes it to stand up on the stem when it reaches a certain speed? Watch as I spin it again. (*Spins again*) When I spin it rapidly it doesn't turn over until it slows down to that particular speed again. If you think you can explain the principle of this little top we would like to hear from you.

MD shot . . . toymaker has moved to other side of counter

TOYMAKER: Can I show you some more?

POOLE: (*Turning*) . . . Not just now, thank you. . . . I'm expecting a guest. . . .

(*Boy enters*) . . . Oh, here he is now. . . . Hello—.

BOY: Hello, Mr. Poole.

POOLE: (*Turning to Toymaker*) Well, now we're ready to see some toys. Which would you like to see first,—?

BOY: (*Moving auto*) . . . Boy, this is a keen auto. But how does it work? There's no place to wind it up.

ECU on auto

TOYMAKER: (*Takes auto — spins wheels and lets it go*) . . . This auto has no spring . . . you don't wind it up. . . . Just give it a start like this . . . and it goes. (*Picks up auto— turns it over*) . . . They call these friction motors. Probably "kinetic energy" motors would be a better name. There is a heavy wheel inside here and when I spin these wheels they make it move too. (*Spins wheels again*) . . . The wheel inside is much

VIDEO	AUDIO
	heavier than the wheels you see here . . . and when I put it down (*puts down*) . . . the big wheel keeps turning and makes the lighter wheels turn and the car moves along the counter. . . . You try it.
	(*Boy makes car go*)
	(*Toymaker puts wind-up tank on counter*)
	TOYMAKER: Here's a wind-up tank. . . . It works differently. Push the little lever there.
ECU on tank	(*Boy pushes lever—tank runs along counter*)
	BOY: This works on a spring, doesn't it, Mr. Poole?
	POOLE: That's right,——. And that is another form of energy. It is called potential energy. When you turn the little lever like this (*turns lever*) . . . it locks the spring. Now when we wind it up (*winds up*) . . . the energy is stored in the spring. It can't get out until we release the lever again. The spring is wound up tight . . . it stores up potential energy . . . and when we release the spring the tank goes. (*Lets tank go*) When you change the shape of a spring by winding, stretching or squeezing it you store up energy in the spring. Springs also operate clocks, door closers, mousetraps and many other things . . . even your zipper fastener is a form of spring. It's made so that pairs of springs grip each other and hold your jacket together.
	BOY: But how does the spring turn the wheels of the tank?
ECU on car	POOLE: (*Picks up other wind-up*

VIDEO   AUDIO

car—*turns upside down*) When the wound-up spring uncoils it makes this wheel turn and it in turn makes these wheels turn. When they turn the car runs along the floor.

BOY: But why is the extra wheel in there? Couldn't the spring be connected to the wheels?

POOLE: The car wouldn't go very fast then. The wheel turned by the spring is a large one (*points*). This large wheel turns the smaller ones. One turn of this large wheel makes the smaller wheels turn several times and the car goes faster.

BOY: (*Picks up slinky*) This is a spring. . . . How does it work?

TOYMAKER: (*Takes spring in hands*) Well, like all springs, Slinky, when stretched, does everything possible to return to his original shape. See when I put one end in each hand the spring is stretched out of shape. There is a greater distance between the coils at the top than on either end. Now when I lower one hand gravity helps one force to pull on the other and the spring pulls back to its original shape. Watch when I put him up here and put one end down on the counter. . . . See he bounces down onto the counter and then to the floor . . . but he winds up with all the coils all bunched up again.

BOY: What's this Mr. Poole? (*Picks up gyro top*)

POOLE: That's a gyroscope top,—. Would you like to see how it works? (*Spins top*)

VIDEO	AUDIO
	BOY: How does it lean over that way and not fall all the way over? POOLE: They say it acts that way because of constant angular momentum. Maybe you can understand it better if I tell you that a rapidly spinning wheel still wants to go in the same direction even when you change its position. When you ride your bicycle and turn your front wheel to the right, the wheel tends to throw you off to the left . . . or if you turn left it tends to throw you right. You lean to right or left to keep your balance. BOY: Oh, yes . . . everytime I turn right, I lean to the right . . . and every time I turn left I lean to the left. POOLE: That's right and the gyroscope works much like that. (*Holds in hand*) . . . it feels like a live thing. If we try to make it turn one way . . . *like this* . . . it turns at right angles to what we expect. The principle of the gyroscope has been applied to many useful things. It is used in the gyro-compass and other instruments
CU on airplane gyroscopes	in our modern airplanes. . . . Here you see some gyroscopes used in modern airliners.
CU on drawing	Gyroscopes also are used to keep ships from rolling so much in a rough sea. The gyroscope wants to continue the way it is going . . . and when the ship starts to roll with a wave . . . the gyroscope pulls it back. It is this spinning movement that keeps the
ECU on toy gyroscope	gyroscope from tumbling off this little peg as it turns. . . . When the wheel

VIDEO

AUDIO

slows down the top will fall.

BOY: Gee, that's great! I'd sure like to have one of those . . . But what's this funny bird? What does it do?

TOYMAKER: He looks like the thirstiest bird you've ever seen. He keeps dipping his beak in that water all day long.

BOY: What makes it do that?

CU on drawing

TOYMAKER: On the inside he is made something like your mother's vacuum coffee maker. His head is like the top "pot" and the body like the bottom of the coffee maker . . . and there is a glass tube connecting the two.

POOLE: Yes, and inside there is a liquid called methyl chloride . . . that turns into a vapor very easily. You start him bobbing by wetting his beak with water. As the water evaporates it cools his head. The vapor in his head condenses into a liquid when the head cools.

TOYMAKER: When the vapor condenses into a liquid it leaves a lot of space in the head, because liquids take up less space than vapors. But down below in the body there is a great deal of vapor which pushes the liquid up through the glass tube into the head.

CU on drawing

POOLE: When the head fills with liquid the bird becomes unbalanced and the heavy head and beak cause the bird to tip over into the water. When he has tipped over far enough

Dissolve back to bird dipping

the bottom of the tube comes out of the liquid and then the vapor in the

VIDEO	AUDIO
	body rushes up into the head. This causes the liquid in the head to flow back into the body and the head becomes lighter. Then the bird tips back into an upright position. But now his head is wet from the dip into the water and the water starts to evaporate again. . . . The same thing happens all over again and he keeps dipping into the water.
	BOY: Gee, that's a little complicated . . . but I always wondered how those things worked. Here's something . . . a steam engine. . . . I know steam makes it work . . . but how?
CU on steam engine	TOYMAKER: There's water in this boiler . . . and when it is heated it makes steam just like the steam you see when the teapot boils.
CU on drawing	But this steam goes into this cylinder and pushes on a piston on the inside. Here is a drawing showing what the piston looks like inside the cylinder.
Dissolve back to engine	The steam pushes the piston back and it turns this wheel. Now a valve closes the opening in the front of the cylinder and opens one in back of the piston. . . . You can see that in this drawing.
CU on 2nd drawing	Now the steam pushes the piston forward and the wheel turns. This goes on continually . . . the piston being pushed back and forth by the steam and making the wheel turn continuously.
Dissolve to engine	BOY: . . . And if you put a belt on this wheel it would run whatever was on the other end of the belt, wouldn't it?

VIDEO	AUDIO
	TOYMAKER: That's right . . . it works exactly as a large one might work.
	POOLE: Steam engines and engines that burn gas or vapors are all called heat engines . . . (*picks up glass tube*) . . . You wouldn't think that this is a form of heat engine, too . . . but it is. Watch when I hold this tightly at the bottom. See the liquid in the top seems to be boiling.
CU on tube	
	BOY: Say, that looks like a coffee maker . . . or like that dipping bird. It has a little glass tube inside of it, too.
	POOLE: That's right . . . it does work on some of the same principles of the dipping bird . . . and also on the principle of the heat engines. When I hold my hand here at the bottom, the heat from my hand causes the gas in the tube to expand. When the gas expands there isn't room for all the gas and the liquid to remain in the bottom. The gas pushes on the liquid and forces it up through the little glass tube and into the top. Actually, the liquid isn't boiling. . . . What causes that bubbling is the gas passing up through the liquid. But now most of the liquid is in the top bulb which is cooler. Let's heat that with my hand and see what happens. See, now the gas in the top expands and all the liquid is forced to the bottom.
	BOY: May I try it?
	POOLE: Here . . . just hold it tightly around the bottom bulb.
	BOY: Look! It's bubbling up . . . it

VIDEO

looks as if it's boiling even if it isn't. (*Puts tube down—picks up engine with balloon*) This is a funny engine. Why does it have a balloon over the smoke stack?

TOYMAKER: Well, that looks like a steam engine. . . . Actually it works on the same principle as a jet engine in a modern jet airplane. Blow air in here (*points*) . . . and blow up the balloon. (*Boy blows up balloon*) Now put it down here on the counter. See, the air blows out the tube and pushes the locomotive along.

POOLE: That follows Newton's third law of motion. "To every action there is always an equal and opposite reaction."

BOY: I wondered how a jet plane could work if it was out in space. I see now . . . it doesn't have to have air to push on. I know the engine doesn't work the same as a jet . . . it has an electric motor, hasn't it?

CU on locomotive

Dissolve to CU on motor

POOLE: In an electric motor, an electromagnet causes a round-and-round motion of a piece of metal. Here the motor consists of an electromagnet and an iron disk which is on a shaft so it can turn. Now watch as it is plugged in. (*Motor is plugged in*) The electricity flows through the coil of the electromagnet. This is AC current or alternating current. The electricity flows in one direction, stops, and then flows back in the other direction. Every time the electricity starts flowing the coil of wire becomes magnetized. It happens so

VIDEO

AUDIO

Dissolve back to ECU of locomotive wheels

fast, sixty times a second, it sets up a whirling magnetism. The whirling magnetism pulls the metal disk around with it . . . and the disk moves the wheels of the locomotive.

BOY: Is that the same kind of electric motor that makes other things work?

POOLE: That's right. Electric clocks, washing machines, vacuum cleaners all work in much the same way.

BOY: I have an electric train . . . but I never knew how it worked.

TOYMAKER: How would you like to see some musical toys?

BOY: Swell . . . but there's nothing scientific about musical instruments, is there?

TOYMAKER: Well, musical toys also work on some scientific principle. Here's one that looks like a little clarinet. Actually it has no reed in it . . . it works more like a fife. (*Blows tune*)

BOY: What makes the sound?

TOYMAKER: When I blow into the instrument it makes a column of air inside vibrate and that produces the sound you hear. Here's a simple experiment to show you how it works . . . (*puts two bottles on counter*) . . . You've tried to blow across the top of a bottle like this (*blows*). . . . When I blew across the top of the bottle I caused the air inside to vibrate. Now listen as I blow across the mouth of this bottle which is shorter. (*Blows*) . . . That made a higher pitched sound, didn't it. The column of air is shorter

VIDEO

AUDIO

in this bottle than the other one. The longer the column of air the deeper the tone. Listen to the difference now . . . (*blows into each bottle in turn*)

CU on clarinet

. . . This instrument (*picking up toy clarinet*) . . . works in the same way. When I push this key and blow into it you hear a high pitched sound . . . (*blows*) . . . But when I push this key the column of air is longer and you hear a lower pitched sound. (*Blows*) . . . Now by pushing different keys and different times I alternately shorten and lengthen the column of air and we get a little tune. . . . (*Plays happy birthday or some other easily recognized tune*) A real clarinet also has a reed here which also vibrates and gives a greater variety of sound.

BOY: Well, if longer things make a deeper pitched sound, then this xylophone (*points to xylophone*) should make a deeper sound at this end.

TOYMAKER: That's right. Let's try it. (*Plays xylophone*) (*pointing out high and low bars*)

BOY: (*Picks out harmonica*) . . . What about this harmonica. . . . It doesn't work the same way, does it?

TOYMAKER: Yes, it works on the same principle. In fact, the harmonica contains a small xylophone . . . only we call the small strips of metal in the harmonica, reeds. Instead of hitting the reeds with a hammer . . . they are made to vibrate when I blow air across them, like this. (*Blows*) The short reeds in the harmonica are

VIDEO

AUDIO

the high notes and the long reeds are the low notes . . . just as in the xylophone or the clarinet.

BOY: (*Picks up guitar*) But what about this guitar. . . . All the strings are the same length. How do you know which makes the low notes?

TOYMAKER: In stringed instruments, each string is thicker or thinner than its neighbor. On the xylophone the longer bar has the lower pitch; the shorter bar the higher pitch. But heavy things when they vibrate make a lower pitch than light things. On stringed instruments the thicker, heavier strings make the lower sound, the thinner ones the high sounds. But this guitar is really a form of music box. You see, you turn this crank and it plays a tune. This guitar has a rubber belt in it with little knobs on it. When I turn the crank the rubber knobs alternately scrape across little metal prongs in the back of the guitar here. . . . They are of different lengths. . . . The knobs cause the prongs to vibrate and you hear a musical tune. (*Plays*)

ECU on opening in guitar

BOY: (*Picks up telephone*) Don't telephones work by vibrating, too?

POOLE: That's right. When you pull this string taut and speak into the mouthpiece, the string vibrates and in turn makes a little diaphragm vibrate in this earpiece and you can hear the sound. We used to make these by using two tin cans with a string fastened tightly in the ends. Real telephones work much the same way . . .

VIDEO

AUDIO

only the vibrations are set up by electrical impulses.

BOY: Gee, there are so many things here. . . . I'd like to have all of them. What's this? (*Points to kaleidoscope*)

POOLE: That's a kaleidoscope.

BOY: Oh, I've seen these. You see all kinds of things when you look in it. (*Looks in eyepiece*)

SHOT through lens fitted with kaleidoscope

POOLE: When you twist the bottom here, you see all types of patterns and designs. Those designs are made by small chips of differently shaped glass . . . and what you are seeing is reflections of those pieces of glass as they fall into different patterns.

BOY: That's great.

TOYMAKER: Here's something you can fool your friends with. (*Holds up straw grip*) . . . Put your finger in there. . . . That's it. Now take your other hand and try to pull it off.

BOY: Gee . . . it won't come off. Oh, now I see . . . when you pull it, it won't come off . . . but if you push it, it loosens up. That's a good trick.

POOLE: It's more than a trick. Metal grips that work on the same principle as that little toy, are used in industry to pull cables through pipes and for many other reasons.

BOY: I never thought before that all these toys worked just like other things . . . with scientific principles and all.

POOLE: Many of them do. . . . Here is one which works on exactly the same principle as the large ones. It is

VIDEO   AUDIO

a helicopter. . . . (*Picks up helicop-ter*) (*turns blades*) When these blades turn they push the air beneath them down and in that way the helicopter stays up.

The blades work exactly the same as those on a real helicopter. The difference is that a gasoline engine turns the blades on a real helicopter, while I set these blades spinning by pulling on this handle. Watch as it flies.

Follow as helicopter takes off

(*Holds near floor and pulls handle*) (*Boy recovers helicopter and brings it back into picture*) (*Hands it to Poole*)

ECU on helicopter

Do you see the way the blades are shaped and tilted. That helps to do two things. It pushes the air down under the blades and at the same time as they turn rapidly the pressure on the top of the blade is reduced and the pressure becomes greater at the bottom of the blade. This causes the wing to lift and when the lift of all three blades is great enough the helicopter rises into the air. If I spin it slowly, like this, the lift isn't great enough to raise it into the air.

BOY: That's great, just like a real one.

TOYMAKER: (*Places toy clown balancer on counter*) Here's a nice toy. See how he spins around there without falling off.

BOY: Why doesn't it fall off?

ECU on balancing clown

TOYMAKER: You see on each end of this little beam there are weights. They weigh more than the little clown. When he stands here on top of this

VIDEO	AUDIO
	little stand the weights hang down here and the weight is evenly distributed on each side. The center of gravity is below the clown and keeps him from falling. But if we turn the beam with the weights so that the center of gravity is not directly down and beneath the clown, he falls off. When the weights are adjusted properly he can stand on his nose (*balance in different positions*) . . . or on either leg with no danger of falling.
	BOY: The people who made that had to know about gravity and those scientific principles, didn't they?
	POOLE: That's right, they had to know the scientific principles. Sometimes they accidentally discover something which can be used.
	(*Picks up silly putty*) . . . This is called silly putty and I believe that the chemist who discovered this was looking for something else . . . and discovered it accidentally. You can mold this into any shape . . . but after a while it returns to its old shape.
	BOY: Silly putty . . . that's a good name. . . . But what's it really called?
	POOLE: It is a polymeric organic silicon compound . . . but I think it's easier just to call it silly putty.
CU on acrobat	BOY: (*Spots mechanical acrobat*) . . . Hey, look at this! What does it do?
	POOLE: Let's see. (*Winds up and starts acrobat*) . . . There . . . he almost looks human doing those tricks.
	BOY: But how does it work?
	POOLE: There are several scientific

VIDEO	AUDIO
	principles involved in this little fellow. His energy comes from a wind-up spring like the ones we talked about a little while ago. But also he is delicately balanced . . . and has a little balancing weight, something like the clown here.
	The spring makes his little trapeze turn around . . . but the actions he goes through are due to the balance and the direction of the motion.
	BOY: That's really great. . . . I could watch his tricks all night. (*Picks up top*) . . . I know what this is. It's a top. Watch me spin it. (*Spins top*)
	POOLE: We were trying that one before you came in. There's a scientific principle at work there, too. Maybe some of the folks out there would like to solve that one. (*Direct to camera*) If you think you know how this little top works, drop us a line. . . . We would like to have your ideas on it. We hope you've enjoyed our visit to a toy shop and we hope you will be with us next week. . . .

SEQUENCE OUTLINE OF PROGRAM

OPENING ON TOY SHOP EXTERIOR		15 sec.	
STANDARD OPENING	1 min.	30 "	
POOLE OPENING with top	2 "	30 "	(HAVE TOP)
Friction and wind-up autos	2 "		(HAVE auto and tank)
Slinky		30 "	(HAVE)

SEQUENCE OUTLINE OF PROGRAM (*Continued*)

Gyroscope	1 "	30 "	(Have toy—pick up airplane gyro at Physics Dept.)
Dippy bird and drawings	1 "	15 "	(Have birds—make drawings)
Steam Engine	1 "		(JOHN will bring engine)
Tube Bubbler	1 "		(HAVE)
Jet Locomotive		30 "	(HAVE)
Electric train and bicycle wheel, also jet plane		45 "	(Pick up train set at Physics. Buy jet)
Electric motor	1 "		(Pick up at Physics Dept.)
Musical toys	2 "	30 "	(Have clarinet, guitar, xylophones—pick up harmonica and 2 bottles)
Telephone set		30 "	(HAVE)
Kaleidoscope		45 "	(Have small one—Barry makes larger one for camera)
Straw grip		30 "	(HAVE)
Helicopter	1 "		(HAVE)
Balancing clown	1 "		(HAVE)
Silly putty		30 "	(HAVE)
Acrobat	1 "		(HAVE—Poole)
Top—close		30 "	(Have—same as opener)

Pad—not included—how a baseball curves—2 minutes

TOP COMEDY SHOW OF THE YEAR

THE JACKIE GLEASON SHOW

THE HONEYMOONERS

"A Letter to the Boss"

JACKIE GLEASON

JACKIE GLEASON, star of the *Jackie Gleason Show,* was born in Brooklyn, New York, on February 26, 1916 and his early "show business" experiences included such roles as barker in a carnival, dare-devil driver in an auto circus and an exhibition diver in a water follies show. From 1935 to 1938 he performed in and directed the floor show at the Miami Club in Newark, New Jersey, finally landing a job as disc jockey at Station WAAT.

Following a tour of the country playing in vaudeville and night clubs Mr. Gleason was offered an engagement at New York's then famous Club 18. It was here that movie mogul Jack Warner saw him and signed Gleason for pictures—he did five movies in Hollywood.

In 1945 Jackie Gleason played the "sailor-on-the-loose" in *Follow The Girls,* a smash hit starring Gertrude Niessen. He made his television debut in the lead role in *The Life of Riley,* followed by his very successful *Cavalcade of Stars.*

Mr. Gleason came to CBS-TV in 1952 with his *Jackie Gleason Show* in which he established himself as one of the nation's foremost comedians. His *The Honeymooners,* which started as a short skit in this variety show and eventually took over the entire program as a full hour situation comedy, has brought Jackie Gleason top ratings on most of the important polls.

More recently, Gleason signed one of the biggest TV deals in history. The Buick Division of General Motors signed the comedian to a $7,000,000 contract (which began in January, 1955) with an option after two years for a third year at $4,000,000. It calls for a half hour filmed show of Gleason **and** his staff, Art Carney, Audrey Meadows and Joyce Randolph in *THE HONEY-MOONERS*. To top it off, Gleason also got a 15 year contract from CBS, for $2000 a week after the Buick show ends.

Mr. Gleason himself chose *The Honeymooners*—"A Letter to the Boss" for TOP TV SHOWS OF THE YEAR as one of the most successful comedy shows he has ever done.

THE HONEYMOONERS
A LETTER TO THE BOSS

THE JACKIE GLEASON SHOW

CAST

Ralph Kramden . . . . . Jackie Gleason
Alice Kramden . . . . . Audrey Meadows
Norton . . . . Art Carney

EXECUTIVE PRODUCER . . . . JACK PHILBIN
PRODUCER . . . . JACK HURDLE
DIRECTOR . . . . FRANK SATENSTEIN
SUPERVISOR OF PRODUCTION . . STANLEY POSS
MUSICAL DIRECTOR . . . . . . RAY BLOCH
WRITTEN BY . . . . MARVIN MARX, WALTER STONE,
SYD ZELINKA, HOWARD HARRIS,
LEONARD STERN, BILL HACKETT,
BILL SHELLEY
CHOREOGRAPHY BY . . . . . JUNE TAYLOR
SCENIC DESIGNS BY . . . . . . RANDOLPH GUNTER
COSTUMES BY . . . . PEGGY MORRISON
SUPERVISION OF ENTIRE PRODUC-
TION BY . . . . JACKIE GLEASON

A Jackie Gleason Enterprise Production in Association
with the CBS Television Network

Sponsored by: Nescafe Instant Coffee
The Schick "20" Electric Shaver
Sheaffer's New Snorkel Pen

Telecast: March 6, 1954

LESCOULIE

And now it's time for another visit with two of your favorite characters, Ralph and Alice Kramden, better known to you as the Honeymooners. Usually our visit with the Kramdens is a short one depicting one brief incident in their daily lives. But tonight something has happened to Ralph and Alice that will take a little longer to tell you about. What is it? Well, suppose we look in on the Kramdens as played by Jackie Gleason and Audrey Meadows and see for ourselves.

PART I

APARTMENT

As travelers part the camera holds on establishing shot of the Kramden kitchen. Alice is seated in chair beside table. She is cutting a sleeve out of a suit of long underwear. She is cutting the sleeve at the shoulder. As she is doing this, Trixie enters carrying a cup.

TRIXIE

Hi'ya Alice.

ALICE (*turning head*)

Hello, Trixie.

TRIXIE

I came down to bring back that cup I borrowed from you.

ALICE (*still cutting*)

Thanks, Trix.

TRIXIE (*crosses to icebox and puts cup on top of it*)

Oh, Alice, do you have any extra cream? I ran short.

ALICE (*indicating icebox*)

Help yourself.

TRIXIE (*opens icebox and takes out cream container and holds it in her hand*)

I don't want to take the whole thing, Alice.

ALICE

Well, take as much as you want.

TRIXIE

Thanks. (*picks up cup she previously put there*)

31

Can I borrow this cup?

ALICE

Sure. You always return it.

TRIXIE (*pours some cream into cup. She then places cream back in icebox. She is crossing to leave when she notices what Alice is doing*)

What are you doin', Alice?

ALICE

Well, I just bought Ralph a suit of winter underwear, and I'm cutting off the sleeve.

TRIXIE

Why don't you buy the sleeveless kind?

ALICE

Cause Ralph only wants the right sleeve off. He says it's hot on the bus.

TRIXIE

Isn't it just as hot for his left arm?

ALICE (*holds underwear up*)

No. That's the one he sticks out the bus window when he makes turns!

TRIXIE (*puts down cup and holds up loose sleeve holding it taut between her hands*)

Gee, the leftovers would make wonderful sweaters for dachshunds!

ALICE

By the way, Trixie, since the boys are bowling tonite, how about you and me taking in a movie?

TRIXIE

Fine.

ALICE

I'll come up for you right after I finish feeding Ralph.

TRIXIE

Swell. See you later, Alice.

(*Trixie picks up cup of cream and*

exits. *Alice folds up underwear and crosses to bureau and puts it in drawer when Ralph enters. Ralph is dejected and puts his lunchbox on the table. He is also carrying newspaper.*)

ALICE

Hello, Ralph. I'll have your dinner fixed in a minute.

RALPH

Don't bother. I'm not hungry.

ALICE

You mean you're going bowling without eating?

RALPH

I'm not going bowling.

ALICE

But you and Ed always bowl on Tuesday nite.

RALPH

And I always go to work on Wednesday morning but I'm not tomorrow.

ALICE

What do you mean?

RALPH

I'll tell you what I mean. I been fired.

ALICE

Fired?

RALPH

Yeah. How do you like it? After nine years drivin' a bus for them I been fired. Tonite when I pull into the depot there's a guy from the supply room waitin' for me. He tells me to turn in my uniform tomorrow, because I'm not drivin' a bus for them anymore.

ALICE

I can't believe it.

RALPH

Neither can I. For nine years I been

slavin' for that company, Alice, and this is the thanks I get. Up every morning at five o'clock. No holidays off. Had to work three Sundays out of four. And in all kinds of weather. Blizzards, heat waves, hail storms. And the abuse I had to take. Old ladies yellin' at me. Drunks tryin' to get on without payin'. Cab drivers cuttin' me off. And when other bus drivers were sick, I had to take a double shift. . . . And this is the thanks I get!

ALICE

Don't worry, Ralph. You'll get another job.

RALPH

Yeah. But I'll never get one as good as this!

ALICE

Look, Ralph, don't upset yourself this way. You're young and healthy. And there are plenty of other jobs.

RALPH

That's what you think. I was reading the want ads comin' home tonite. Get a load of some of these jobs.

(*He opens newspaper and reads.*)

Here's one. "Drill press operator wanted. Seventy dollars a week. Learn while you earn." Here's another one. "Welder, no experience necessary. Sixty-five dollars a week." Listen to this one. "Tool and die worker. Good opportunity for right party."

ALICE

Well, what's wrong with any of those jobs?

RALPH

Nothing. Except that they're all listed under "Help Wanted. Women!" . . . I'm tellin' you, Alice, there's nothin' here for men.

ALICE

Look, Ralph, maybe until you get something for yourself I could get a job to help out.

RALPH

Oh, no you don't. When I married you I promised that you'd never have to work again.

ALICE

But it won't be for long.

RALPH

I don't care, Alice. I got my pride, you know. Before I'd let you go to work, I'd rather see you starve! . . . Just don't worry, Alice. We'll get along until something comes up. We'll just have to live on our savings.

ALICE

That'll carry us through the night, but what'll we do in the morning!

RALPH

Then we'll have to change our way of livin'. We'll get out of here and move to a cheaper apartment. . . . Then we can sell this furniture and buy some second hand stuff. . . . Wait a minute. I got a better idea. For the time bein' we can move in with your folks.

ALICE

Ralph, just a minute ago when I said I wanted to go to work you said you had too much pride.

RALPH

And that still goes. When we move in with your folks, I won't even let you help with the dishes!

ALICE

Ralph, how can you even think of moving in with my folks? You know, you haven't exactly gotten along with my father. Do you realize that not once in the last five years have you let me invite them over for dinner?

RALPH

Well, let's invite them tonite! . . . We can break it to 'em during dessert!

ALICE

The answer is no.

RALPH

Well, what are we going to do, Alice?

ALICE

Ralph, stop getting so panicky. You've only been out of work for a half hour. You'll get something.

RALPH

Yeah . . . but where, when, how?? . . . Let's face it, Alice, I haven't got the greatest background in the world for having my pick of jobs. After all I quit school in the sixth grade. I should have gone to high school and then through college . . . but, that wouldn't have done any good, it'd be even worse.

ALICE

What do you mean?

RALPH

Can you imagine how bad I'd feel. . . . A college graduate fired by the bus company!! . . . It's a terrible thing, Alice, after you've had the same job for so long and you lose it, you just don't know where to turn.

ALICE

Look, Ralph, you'll never get a job if you have that attitude. Remember

you've got a lot of friends. Tell them you're out of work, maybe they'll be able to help you get another job.

RALPH

Oh no. I'm not letting my friends know I'm out of work. And have them stand around saying, "Poor, Ralph." And getting their phoney sympathy. . . . Not me.

ALICE

Oh Ralph. That's carrying your pride too far.

RALPH

Never mind. That's the way I want it. Remember I don't want any of my friends to know I'm out of work. When I get another job I'll tell them I quit to get a better one. But in the meantime, I'm not tellin' anyone!

(*Door opens. Norton enters carrying bowling ball in carrying case*)

NORTON

Hello, Alice. . . . H'ya Ralphie boy!

RALPH (*unconcerned*)

Hi'ya Norton.

(*Almost in tears*) I lost my job today. I was fired!

NORTON

Ralph, you're kidding.

ALICE

No he's not. It's true.

RALPH

Yeah. They told me I'm through, washed up, finished.

NORTON (*seeing how downcast Ralph is puts arm around his shoulder for comfort*)

Come on, Ralph, you're not gonna let this get you down . . . where's the old spirit? At a time like this you gotta keep your chin up. You gotta smile. Come on, boy, let's have a little smile.

(*Ralph awkwardly tries to smile*)

There, that's my boy. . . . Bigger, bigger, that's it! That's the way you gotta stay even if it takes you a whole year to get another job. Even if you never get another job!

RALPH (*loses his smile and looks angry and throws Norton's arm away*)

How can you expect me to keep smiling with you talking like that!

NORTON

I was only trying to cheer you up.

RALPH (*bitterly*)

A fat lot I've got to smile about. Nine years on a job. Today I'm fired and by tomorrow I'm forgotten. They won't even remember what I look like.

NORTON

That's great. . . . Go right back tomorrow morning and ask for a job.

RALPH

Norton, you are a mental case.

NORTON

Well, look Ralph, we'd better get going or we'll be late for bowling.

RALPH

Are you crazy? How do you expect me to go bowling after what happened to me today?

ALICE

Wait a minute. Ralph . . . Norton's right. It'll do you good to go bowling.

RALPH

Maybe you're right. I'd like to take my mind off this.

NORTON (*picks up bowling ball*)

That's the way to talk, Ralph . . . but come on, let's get goin'. I want to get home early. After all, you can sleep all morning. You ain't working!

RALPH

Will you stop with that! Look, leave me alone. Go bowlin' without me.

ALICE

Ralph, you're acting silly. If only you'd . . .

RALPH

You leave me alone too, Alice. You don't know how I feel. You've never been through this. Do you realize what it's like working for a company as long as I have and then bein' tossed out on your ear? When I think of the president of that company, J. J. Marshall, boy, would I like to be alone with that guy for just five minutes. Do you know what I'd do? I'd grab him like this.

(*Ralph grabs Norton by his vest*)

Then I'd give him this.

(*He shakes Norton*)

Then I'd bend him back over his desk and I'd belt him.

(*Ralph bends Norton back over table and is ready to belt him when Norton speaks . . .*)

NORTON

Wait a minute, Ralph. Not so rough.

RALPH

Don't tell me how to treat my boss!

ALICE

Let go of him, Ralph. You're acting like a maniac.

RALPH (*lets Norton go*)

I'm sorry, Norton . . . but I'm so mad when I think of what he did. If there was only some way of letting that guy know what I think of him.

(*Ralph paces*)

NORTON

Why don't you phone him?

RALPH

With thirty secretaries I'd never get through to him. . . . Wait a minute. . . . Alice, get me some writin' paper.

ALICE

Ralph, you're not going to write him a letter.

RALPH

I certainly am. He's going to know exactly what I think of him.

ALICE

Look, writing him a letter isn't going to solve anything.

RALPH

I'm warnin' you, Alice. Butt out of this thing. I'll get the paper myself.

(*Ralph crosses to bureau and opens drawer looking for paper. When he opens second drawer he turns to Alice . . .*)

You know why I'm steamed, Alice. You want to know why I'm steamed . . . (*pointing in drawer*) There it is. After all those years of slavin' for that bus company, this is all I got to show for it.

(*He pulls out bunch of underwear sleeves from drawer and slams them to floor*)

Thirty-six underwear sleeves!

(*He then takes writing paper and pen out of drawer. He crosses back to table and sits down. He takes sheet of paper from box and poises pen*)

ALICE

Ralph.

RALPH

I told you to stay out of this.

ALICE

All right. I will.

(*Alice crosses to bedroom and enters. She then slams door*)

RALPH

Now let's see . . . Dear Mr. Marshall. . . . No. That's no good.

(*He starts writing. He crumples paper and throws it on floor*)

Look, Norton, I'm too nervous to write this letter. You sit down and I'll tell you what to say.

NORTON

Okay, Ralph.

(*Ralph gets up and Norton takes his place. Ralph starts pacing*)

RALPH

Now let's see. . . . Put this down, Norton . . . "You dirty bum."

NORTON

Wait a minute, Ralph. Don't you think that's a little strong for a starter?

RALPH

Maybe you're right . . . Take this . . . "Dear Mr. Marshall . . . (*Ralph pauses trying to think of something a little nicer to say but can't*) You dirty bum!"

NORTON

That's better, Ralph.

(*Norton starts writing. Ralph keeps pacing. All the while Ralph dictates Norton writes*)

RALPH

"After giving you the best years of my life, you fired me, you miserable low life. A man like you should turn in your membership card in the human race."

NORTON

That's a nice touch, Ralph.

RALPH

Thanks Norton . . . "After what you did to me, I can safely say that you are the meanest man in the whole world, you dirty bum" . . . uh . . . uh . . . I can't think of anything else to say.

NORTON

Maybe this is a good spot to hint around about getting your job back!

RALPH

Don't be an idiot. . . . Now look, while I get a stamp, finish writin' that up, and end it with somethin' like "Sincerely or Very truly yours, etc., etc." You know.

NORTON

Okay, Ralph.

(*Norton continues writing as Ralph goes over to bureau and starts looking through drawers for stamps. While Ralph is looking Norton finishes letter, takes envelope out of box, puts paper inside and seals envelope*)

Hey, what's the address?

RALPH (*turns while looking for stamp*)

Oh . . . "Mr. J. J. Marshall. In care of the Gotham Bus Depot, 225 River Street, New York."

(*Norton writes address. Ralph finds stamp and crosses back to table*)

RALPH

Here. (*Takes envelope. Licks stamp and puts it on*) There. Now that J. J. Marshall will think twice before he fires me again!

NORTON

Okay, Ralph, now that you got it off

your chest, how about goin' bowling?

RALPH

Nah. I just don't feel like it tonite. You go ahead and mail this letter on your way over.

NORTON

All right. And don't you worry, pal. Maybe I can get you a job with me in the sewer. All you have to do is pass the test.

RALPH

What test?

NORTON

Can you float?

RALPH

Forget it, Norton. I don't think I'm cut out for that kind of work.

NORTON

Just remember the old fight, boy.

(*Norton lightly clips Ralph on chin*)

Keep your chin up.

(*Norton exits. Ralph is now standing next to bureau where he had placed uniform hat when he came in. There is a small mirror hanging over bureau. He picks up hat a little sadly and looks at it. He then puts it on and sadly looks in the mirror at himself. As he is doing this Alice enters from bedroom*)

ALICE

Where's Ed?

RALPH

He went out to mail my letter.

ALICE

Ralph, you're going to be sorry you wrote that letter.

RALPH

I know what I'm doin'. Now let's drop the subject. You got no idea what it did to me inside when that bus company fired me. I worked for them for nine years, Alice. That's a big part of a man's life. In all that time I made a lot of friends on my run. And I'm going to miss 'em too. The kids especially. Do you know how many kids I've driven to school in the past nine years? Probably thousands. I seen 'em start from kindergarten and go right through high school. The little ones. They were my favorites. I'd take 'em up on my lap and let 'em pretend they were drivin' the bus. Let 'em blow the horn and open and shut the door. And I'd even let 'em punch transfers and make change if I wasn't too busy. I used to teach those kids everything about the bus. . . . Some of those kids today are young men ready to go out in the world . . . Wait a minute. I just thought of somethin'. It's probably one of those little brats that's takin' my job!

(*Knock on door*)

Come in.

(*Door opens and man enters wearing a bus dispatcher's uniform*)

FREDDIE

Hello Ralph. Hello Alice.

RALPH

Hi'ya Freddie. Now, look, I don't want any of your sympathy.

FREDDIE

What sympathy? I came over to tell you the news.

RALPH

I already got the news. They told me about it when I brought the bus into the depot tonite. I'm not driving for the company anymore. I've been fired!

(*Freddie laughs. Ralph reacts steamed*)

I don't see anything so funny.

FREDDIE

I'll tell you what's funny. Sure you're not driving a bus anymore but not because you were fired. Mr. Marshall told me about it in his office this afternoon. You've been promoted to traffic manager.

RALPH

Me . . . Traffic manager!

FREDDIE

That's right, Ralph. Congratulations. Well, I have to get home for dinner. Don't forget to bring some cigars down to the depot tomorrow. From now on you're an executive. Well, goodnight Alice . . . goodnight R.K.

(*Freddie shakes hands with Ralph and leaves*)

RALPH

Did you hear that Alice? I'm an executive. You know what we're going to do, we're going down and celebrate. I'll go in and change.

ALICE

But Ralph . . .

RALPH

Whatever it is, it can wait. . . .

(*Ralph goes into bedroom, stays in for a split second and comes out like an enraged bull*)

I got to get that letter back!! I got to get Norton before he mails it.

ALICE

You shouldn't have written it in the first place.

RALPH

One of these days, Alice . . . One of these days—pow . . . Right in the kisser.

(*Ralph exits. BLACKOUT.*)

PART II

LOCKER ROOM

(*As travelers part, camera holds on establishing shot of the locker room of a bowling alley. There is a center door on the back wall and both side walls are lined with practical lockers. There is a bench upstage center. As scene opens there is an attendant sweeping up. As he's sweeping Norton enters. Norton is dressed in same clothes as when he left Ralph's. He is carrying bowling ball in bag. As he enters he sings*)

NORTON (*singing*)

You. You. You. There's no one but you. You. You.

(*He puts his bowling ball on bench and then takes ball out of bag. He places ball on floor next to bench. He then takes bowling shoes from bag and places them on bench. He then picks up bowling bag and crosses to his locker. He opens locker and throws in bag. He then takes off top coat and hangs it up. After he hangs it on hook in locker, he looks in at it and removes letter from inside pocket*)

NORTON

How do you like that? I forgot to mail Ralph's letter.

(*He looks towards attendant*)

Hey, pal.

(*Attendant leans broom against lockers and crosses to Norton*)

ATTENDANT

What do you want?

NORTON

Is there a mail box around here?

ATTENDANT

Yeah. There's one right out front.

NORTON

Do me a favor. Mail this letter for me, will you?

ATTENDANT

Sure.

(*Attendant takes letter and stands there as if waiting for tip*)

NORTON

Don't worry. Don't worry. I'll make it up to you. I'll be careful not to litter up the floor!

ATTENDANT

Big deal.

(*Attendant starts to exit and Norton starts to put on bowling shoes. As Attendant just about reaches doorway, Ralph bursts through door*)

RALPH

Norton.

(*Ralph bumps into Attendant knocking letter out of Attendant's hand*)

I'm sorry.

(*Ralph bends down and unconsciously picks up letter and hands it to Attendant who reacts and exits*)

NORTON

Hi'ya, Ralph? Changed your mind

about bowlin', huh?

RALPH

No, I didn't change my mind . . .
Listen, Norton, that letter I gave you.
Did you mail it on the way down
here?

NORTON

Well . . . uh . . . no, I didn't, Ralph.

RALPH

You didn't?

NORTON

No, but I can explain everything. You
see . . .

RALPH

Norton, you don't have to explain
anything, you just saved my life. I
feel like celebratin'!

NORTON

You're happy, huh, Ralph?

RALPH

Happy. I'll show you how happy I
am. I'm going to bowl with you
tonite, and after we're done bowling, I'm taking you out and buying
you the biggest steak you ever had
in your whole life.

(*Norton and Ralph laugh*)

NORTON

I don't know what's making you this
way, Ralph. But as long as you're
happy, I'm happy.

RALPH

Now, give me the letter, Norton.

NORTON

How can I? I ain't got it.

RALPH

What do you mean you ain't got it?
You just told me you didn't mail it on
the way down here.

NORTON

That's right. I gave it to somebody
else to mail.

RALPH

You what!— Who did you give it to?
Who?

NORTON

Remember that guy you bumped into
on the way in here? You know that
letter he dropped?

RALPH

Yeah.

NORTON

That was the letter!

RALPH

Oh, no, and I gave it back to him.
Where's the mail box around here.
I've got to stop him.

NORTON

Right up stairs in front of the en-
trance.

(*Ralph rushes out door leaving Norton standing there looking after him*)
How do you like that guy? And he
calls me a mental case!

(*Norton now sits down and puts on
bowling shoes. He then gets up and
takes bowling ball in his hand. He
feels the weight of the ball in his
hand for a second and then breaks
into crazy practice step. He practices
a couple of different approach styles
to the alley. As he is doing this Ralph
reenters, winded*)
Did you catch him, Ralph?

RALPH

No—he was already gone.

NORTON

Hey, Ralph, you know that steak you
said you were going to buy me after

bowling? Look, I had meat for dinner. Let's have pizza instead. We'll
get one with the mushrooms and one
with the Italian sausages and then . . .

RALPH

Will you shut up?

NORTON

All right, so we'll have steak.

RALPH

What am I going to do? . . . I gotta
get that letter back.

NORTON

What happened, Ralph? Did you
think of something better to call the
boss? . . . Something stronger than
dirty bum or miserable low life?

RALPH

Will you stop that! . . . Look, Norton,
I'll explain it to you. I made a mis-
take. I wasn't really fired today. Mr.
Marshall promoted me. He made me
the new traffic manager.

NORTON

Congratulations!

RALPH

What are you congratulatin' me for?
Don't you realize if Mr. Marshall sees
that letter I sent him, he'll fire me.

NORTON

If he fires you, you know what you
do, Ralph.

RALPH

What?

NORTON

Send him another nasty letter.

(*Ralph reacts with a realization that
he's helpless against Norton's idiotic
reasoning*)

RALPH

What a rotten break. To get a chance

like this and then lose it.

NORTON

Wait a minute, Ralph. Maybe you're
looking at the dark side of things.
Maybe that Mr. Marshall won't fire
you.

RALPH

Are you crazy? After what I said to
Mr. Marshall in that letter he's bound
to get mad and fire me. If I called you
a dirty bum and a miserable low life,
wouldn't you get mad at me?

NORTON

Have I ever?

RALPH

Gee, I got to do something, Norton.
I can't take this thing layin' down. All
my life I wanted to be an executive.
You don't know what it's like. You
come in in the morning dressed up in
a business suit, a white shirt and tie.
And you know how great it is to have
your own private office. To have people doing things for you. You push a
button and a girl comes in and brings
you a pitcher of water. You press another button and a girl comes in with
your mail. Then you push another
button and a girl comes in and takes
dictation. Wouldn't you want a job
like that?

NORTON

Who wants the job? I just want the
buttons!

RALPH

Wait a minute, Norton. I'm going to
be an executive. We're going to get
that letter back.

NORTON

What's the plan, Ralph?

RALPH

I don't know yet. All I know is that Marshall can't get that letter. Let me think. We know that letter's in the mail box right in front of this place. Right?

NORTON

Right.

RALPH

So all we got to do is get into that mail box somehow and get that letter out.

NORTON

Hold it, pal. Fooling around with a mail box is a federal offense.

RALPH

Well, I got to take the chance. This is too important to me, Norton. Ever since I was a kid I wanted to be an executive. I wanted to be a boss with people workin' under me. Other guys obeyin' my orders.

NORTON

You break into that mail box and you'll probably get your wish. In prison they may make you a trusty!

RALPH

We gotta figure this thing out.

NORTON

Wait a minute. If I help you break into that mail box and we're caught, we both get sent to prison. But if I help you get the letter out and we don't get caught, you get the job as traffic manager. What do I get out of this?

RALPH

Well, you got a lot of nerve asking me that. You seem to forget what I

did for you last year. I didn't ask you what I was gettin' out of it.

NORTON

What was that, Ralph.

RALPH

The time you got that hot tip on a horse and you come down to borrow ten dollars from me.

NORTON

But you didn't lend me the ten.

RALPH

That's just my point. The horse lost, didn't he?

NORTON

You're right, Ralph. Boy, am I an ingrate!

RALPH

I'll forget it. Now let's sit down and think of a way to get into that mail box.

(*Ralph and Norton sit down on bench*)

RALPH

Now let's concentrate. We'll think of all the ways we can do it.

(*Both Ralph and Norton sit silently for a moment, trying to think of what to do. They are both sitting with chin in right hand and with right leg bent over left knee. After a split second they both sigh and simultaneously uncross legs and recross them this time with left leg over right knee and then both put chins in left hand. Upon completion of this, man enters who is dressed in blue police pants and plain tee shirt. He is carrying a bowling ball. He opens his locker and puts ball inside. He then takes his shirt out and starts dressing. The*

locker he is standing at is behind
Norton)

NORTON

Hey, Ralph, I got a great idea how to
open it . . . It's sensational . . . Dynamite.

RALPH

What do you mean.

NORTON

I just told you. Dynamite!

RALPH

Are you crazy? We can't use dynamite
to open a mail box.

(*Man who is dressing reacts slowly
to this. Both Ralph and Norton go
back to silent thinking. Man continues
dressing, but still keeping an eye on
them*)

NORTON

Hey, Ralph, I remember seein' a picture once where a guy had to get a
package out of a mail box. Maybe we
could do the same thing he did.

RALPH

What did he do?

NORTON

Well, he took a lot of tools and he
went down to the mail box. First he
hit it with a mallet and tried to spring
the lock. Then he tried to open it with
a hairpin. That didn't work, so finally
he tried forcin' it with a crowbar.

RALPH

Did he get his package?

NORTON

No. While he was forcin' it with the
crowbar, a cop shot him!

(*Ralph reacts*)

RALPH (*steamed*)

What do you have to tell me stories

like that for?

NORTON

I'm sorry Ralph. I didn't know you
were so chicken!

(*They both stop and pause to think
again. As they are doing this man
takes police jacket out of locker and
slips it on. He also puts on police hat.
He then goes and stands right in back
of Ralph and Norton*)

RALPH

Wait a minute. Maybe we can find a
skeleton key that'll fit the mail box.
Nah, they have special locks on them
things.

NORTON

Ralphie boy, I got it. I'll borrow my
brother-in-law's truck. We'll drive it
down here. Wait till there's nobody
on the streets, and then steal the box.

RALPH

I don't know. That sounds a little . . .

(*As Ralph says this line he turns a
little to the side and rear and sees the
cop. He reacts with bulging eyes*)

NORTON

Don't be crazy, Ralph. We gotta try
somethin'. I still think stealin' the
mail box is the best idea.

RALPH (*flustered speech—starts kick-
ing Norton*)

Uh . . . Uh . . . Norton . . . Uh . . .
Where's your bowling ball?

NORTON

Why? We'll never be able to open a
mail box with that.

RALPH

Norton.

(*Ralph makes motion with his thumb
for Norton to look behind himself*)

NORTON (*as he says this, he turns*)
Ralph, what's the matter with you?
You're acting as if you . . . EEEEEE.
EEEEEE.

OFFICER
Now would you two mind explaining
just what you were talking about?

RALPH
Well, uh, uh, uh, you see, uh, well,
uh. You tell him, Norton.

NORTON
It's very simple. We were just . . .
You tell him, Ralph.

OFFICER
Well, one of you better start to tell
me.

RALPH
Well, you see, officer, we're playwrights. Yeah . . . That's what we
are. We're writin' a play.

OFFICER
You're writing a what?

NORTON
A play. Like those things you have
when you're in the third grade, where
you're a tree or an alarm clock or an
apple.

RALPH (*trying to bail Norton out*)
My friend here has a sense of humor.
He writes all the jokes in the play.

NORTON
Yeah. I write all the jokes. Want me
to tell you the one about? . . .

RALPH
Shut up, Norton . . . I tell you officer,
you see this play is about a guy robbin' a mail box and we were just
testin' some of the lines.

OFFICER
It's about robbin' a mail box, eh.

NORTON
Yeah. You know a good way to rob
one?

RALPH (*reacting*)
We'll figure that part of the story out
for ourselves, Edward.

OFFICER
Well, I got to admit your conversa-
tion had me wondering for a while.
But I can see you two boys aren't the
criminal type. . . . Well, good luck
with your play.
(*As the Officer leaves . . .*)

RALPH
We'll send you tickets.

NORTON
Boy, that was a close call, Ralph.

RALPH
Yeah, but never mind that. We better
get out of here and start tryin' to get
that letter back.

NORTON
Yeah, but first we better catch that
cop.

RALPH
What for?

NORTON
You forgot to get his address to send
him those tickets.

RALPH
Will you come on.
(*Music up as they go through door
and BLACKOUT.*)

PART III

STREET

Scene: *Street at night. Prominent in scene is standing type U. S. mailbox. The light on scene comes from lamppost near mailbox.*

At rise: *Man and woman enter from stage left. They continue across stage. Ralph and Norton enter from stage right. As Ralph and Norton reach mailbox Norton stops but Ralph pulls him past it. A few steps further and Ralph looks back and sees man and woman leave scene.*

NORTON
Ralph, what's the idea of pulling me that way?

RALPH (*sotto*)
Don't be a moxie—did you want those people to catch us looking at the mailbox?

NORTON
Gee, if you're nervous about somebody catching us *looking* at the mailbox—how you gonna feel if someone catches us climbing in!!

RALPH
Quiet! Now look, we're gonna do this my way. You stay here—I'll go over to the box. If you see anyone coming, you let me know.

NORTON
Okay.
(*Ralph saunters nonchalantly toward box. Norton remains where he is.*

Ralph gets to box and starts going over it carefully. Just as he opens slot Norton speaks.)
(*suddenly*)
Hey, Ralph! Somebody's coming!!
(*Ralph jumps frightenedly away from box. Looks down street.*)

RALPH
Where? I don't see anyone.

NORTON
I was only practicing.

RALPH
Are you out of your mind, yelling like that?

NORTON
Gee, Ralph, I was only—

RALPH
Come over here.
(*Norton crosses to him*)
Now stand right here and if you see anyone coming just tap me on the shoulder.

NORTON
Okay, Okay.
(*Ralph faces box, begins examining it again. Norton standing to right of Ralph is looking from stage when man enters right with letter in hand. He approaches mail box but is unable to get to it because Ralph is blocking him. Man finally taps Ralph on shoulder. Ralph speaks without looking up*)

RALPH
Somebody coming?
(*Norton still looking stage left*)

NORTON
Nope. Nobody.
(*Ralph speaks angrily as he turns around*)

RALPH

Are you practicing again?

(*Ralph finds himself face to face with the stranger*)

MAN

If you don't mind I'd like to mail this letter.

(*Ralph, embarrassed, speaks unnecessarily. Man looks at him puzzledly a moment then leaves while Ralph keeps talking*)

RALPH

You see I just mailed a letter and I thought maybe I forgot to put a stamp on and I was just trying to see if I did or not because—

(*Man has now exited stage left*)

NORTON

You can quit now, Ralph—he's gone.

RALPH (*nervously wiping perspiration from face*)

What am I gonna do? My whole future is in the bottom of that mail box. What am I gonna do?

NORTON

Keep cool, pal. This is no time to lose your head, Ralphie old boy. You stand there, I'll look this thing over.

(*Norton goes over box slowly and carefully. Speaking with great assurance as he does so*)

If you can get a letter in, you can get it out—you just gotta use the old noodle. Just leave it to me. There's gotta be an answer to this problem and I'll find it.

(*Opens slot and closes it. He faces Ralph*)

I've got the answer.

RALPH (*anxiously*)

You have?

NORTON

Yeah. You can't get it out!

(*Ralph shoves Norton aside*)

RALPH (*angrily*)

I've *gotta* get that letter out!

(*Ralph opens mail box flap and looks in first, then sticks hand into opening. . . . He feels around a bit*)

RALPH (*hopefully*)

Maybe I can reach the letter.

(*suddenly*)

Hey, Norton!

NORTON

Ya get the letter out?

RALPH

I can't get my *hand* out!

NORTON

Are you sure?

(*Ralph is tugging now.*)

RALPH

Sure I'm sure! Do something!

NORTON (*looks into opening*)

Boy! Your hand is sure *in* there.

RALPH

What am I gonna do?

NORTON

This is a tough one . . . Hey, Ralph— are you a member of the automobile club?

RALPH

Norton, grab hold of my arm and start pulling.

NORTON (*grabs Ralph's arm*)

Okay, pal, are you ready?

RALPH

Ready.

NORTON

Let's go.

(*They both tug hard. As they are tugging, Norton suddenly stops*)

Hey, somebody's coming!

(*Norton walks a few steps away*)

RALPH (*in panic*)

Where are you going? What am I gonna do?

(*Man enters from left*)

NORTON

Just act as though your hand wasn't in it.

(*Ralph gives take but turns so that he has back to box with hand still in it. As man gets closer he tries to look nonchalant and starts whistling. Man gets to box, takes letter from coat pocket and puts it into slot. He tries to close lid*)

MAN

Doesn't seem to close.

RALPH

Heh-heh, yeah, maybe it's stuck.

(*Man tries to force it shut. Ralph is unable to give vent to pain he feels, just writhes and face shows pain . . . Man finally quits and shrugs*)

MAN

Yep. Guess it's stuck all right.

(*Man goes off. As he leaves scene, Norton speaks*)

NORTON

He's gone Ralph.

(*Ralph who has been using all his self control now lets out a bellow of pain*)

RALPH

Oohhhhhh, my hand!

NORTON

We'd better get it out, Ralph, before it starts swelling up. All right, let's go.

(*Norton grabs Ralph's arm. They both strain and pull . . . hand finally comes out. Ralph holds out hand*)

RALPH

Will you just look at that hand . . .

NORTON

You're lucky. If it was the other hand you couldn't bowl . . . Hey, maybe we could . . .

RALPH (*desperately*)

Norton, will you please be quiet a minute while I try to figure this out. I gotta find a way.

(*Ralph paces. Norton stands where he is*)

RALPH (*speaks while pacing . . .*)

Can't get your hand inside . . . Box is too strong to break open . . . If we could only get something to drop down and pull the letter out.

NORTON

How about one of those sticks with a nail in it . . . Like the guys use in the park?

RALPH

Where're we gonna get one of those now?

NORTON

Hey! How about a fishing rod with a hook on the end? I got one home!

RALPH

Norton, please, like I asked you . . . Be quiet and let me think.

NORTON

Okay Ralph, you're the boss.

(*Ralph resumes pacing. Norton remains still and takes package of Chiclets from pocket and pops one idly into his mouth*)

NORTON

Want a piece of gum, Ralph?

RALPH

Will you please leave me . . . Gum!
That's it! How many pieces you got??

NORTON

A whole box.

RALPH

Chew them all.

(*Ralph empties box into hand and gives them to Norton*)

NORTON

I wanna save some for tomorrow.

RALPH

Will you chew 'em up!

(*Norton puts all Chiclets into his mouth and starts to chew with difficulty*)

RALPH

Now when you get that all chewed up we'll stick the wad of gum at the end of something . . . Stick it down there and pull out the letter . . . What've we got to stick the gum on the end of?

NORTON

You got a long piece of wire?

RALPH

What would I be doing with a long piece of wire?

NORTON

Sticking it down in the box to get the letter out.

RALPH

Oh you . . . Never mind . . . Have you got that gum all chewed yet?

NORTON

Yeah.

RALPH

Okay. Stick it on the end of your belt.

(*Norton pulls off belt, takes gum from*

mouth and sticks on end*)

NORTON

I getcha Ralph . . . That's using the old bean.

RALPH (*opens slot of box*)

Now put it in here slowly and see if you can get it to stick onto some of the letters.

(*Norton lets belt into box slowly*)

RALPH

Now move it around . . . Easy . . . Easy . . .

NORTON

It's catching, Ralph. It's catching. I think I got something.

(*Woman enters stage left*)

RALPH

Hey, Norton, there's someone coming.

(*They both turn facing front with backs to mail box trying to look innocent. Woman passes them and exits*)
Okay. Start in again.

NORTON

I can't.

RALPH

What do you mean you can't?

NORTON

I dropped my belt in the box.

RALPH

What did you do that for?

NORTON

I guess I'm just a bundle of nerves, Ralph. . . . But you know something. . . . I was just thinking . . . this thing's made just like a piggy bank.

RALPH

So, what about it?

NORTON

So when you wanna get something out of a piggy bank, what do you do?

You just turn it upside down and shake it . . . All we have to . . .

RALPH

Well, what are we waiting for? Let's do it! Come on, you grab that side and I'll grab it here.

(*Business of turning over mail box. Struggle with it and grunt until they finally have it off the ground and are holding it a few feet off the ground. Mailman enters scene, stands a few feet from them without being seen by them*)

MAILMAN (*a la Percy Kilbride*)

Say, what's going on there?

(*Ralph and Norton freeze for a moment*)

RALPH

Well, er . . . Aba . . . Aba . . .

MAILMAN

What's the idea of turning that mail box upside down?

RALPH

Heh . . . Heh . . . that's the way we found it. We're just putting it right side up . . . Come on, Norton.

(*They turn box upright and set it on ground. Mailman stands looking suspiciously at them*)

We always do that whenever we see a mail box upside down. Good citizens, you know. We always throw papers in trash baskets too . . . Heh . . . Heh . . .

(*Ralph flicks imaginary dust from box*)

MAILMAN

Oh I see. But from where I'm standing it looks like you're tampering with the mail. Federal offense you know,

three years in prison or a thousand dollars fine.

NORTON

How about that Ralph? You get a choice.

RALPH (*earnestly*)

Look, Mister . . . I might as well tell you the truth. There's a letter in that box and it's mine . . . If you could . . .

MAILMAN

Sorry. Nothing I can do for you.

RALPH

But I don't want to gyp the government. Look, give me my letter and you can even keep the stamp.

MAILMAN

Bribing a government official, eh?

RALPH (*desperately*)

Honest, I don't wanna do anything wrong. All I want is my letter. If that letter is delivered it means I lose my job . . . I'm a married man, I support my mother, we'll be out in the street, we'll starve. I must have that letter. It's up to you, you can save my whole future. All you have to do is say the word.

(*While Ralph speaks Norton wipes tear from eye with handkerchief*)

MAILMAN

No.

(*Mailman bends down and opens box.*)

NORTON

That ain't the word, Ralph.

(*Ralph and Norton defeated, stand watching helplessly as mailman puts letters from box into his bag. All mail is out and he pulls out belt*)

MAILMAN

Awful the way people wrap things. Look at this . . . out of the package already.

(*He puts belt into mailbag with letters. Starts off and pauses*)

Sorry . . . Hope you find a job.

(*Mailman leaves scene*)

NORTON

Guess it's just one of them days, Ralph . . . What do you say we go home, pal?

RALPH

How can you talk about going home? I still have to figure how to get that letter.

NORTON

Okay, Okay . . . But I'd better go down to the drugstore and call Trixie. I wanna let her know we'll be late.

(*Norton goes off. Ralph paces disconsolately. Bowling alley attendant dressed with hat and coat comes out of alley. Takes pack of cigarettes out of pocket and walks toward Ralph*)

MAN

Got a match, pal?

(*Ralph paying little attention, preoccupied looks through pockets, comes up with book of matches*)

RALPH

Here.

(*Man lights cigarette gives back matches*)

MAN

Thanks.

(*Takes long puff. Ralph keeps pacing while man talks. Pays no attention to him*)

Would you believe it this is the first time tonight I've had a chance for a smoke . . . Boy, working in a bowling alley ain't no picnic. On the hop every minute. Ya know?

RALPH (*absently*)

Yeh, yeh . . .

MAN

If it ain't a guy yelling for a bottle of beer, it's a guy wanting to know where he left his sweatshirt. You sure get some beauts. Ya know?

(*Man is now next to mail box. Ralph is about eight feet away*)

RALPH

Yeh, yeh . . .

MAN

You start out to do one thing and someone asks you to do another . . . Half an hour ago a guy asked me to mail a letter . . . and this is the first chance I've had to mail it.

(*As man drops letter into box, Ralph gives take, springs at box just as flap closes. He let's out a bellow. Scene ends with him hitting top of mail box in frustration*)

RALPH

Oh, no!!

(*BLACKOUT.*)

PART IV

OFFICE

As travelers part, camera holds on establishing shot of the boss' office. As scene opens a secretary enters through door carrying a large batch of mail. She crosses to desk and places mail on upstage end of desk where couch is. She then examines flower which is on desk in vase. She takes water pitcher from desk and pours a little into vase. She replaces water pitcher and turns to exit. As she approaches open door, she notices picture on stage left wall upstage is crooked. She crosses and starts to straighten picture. She is now standing between open door and stage left wall. She first adjusts picture and then stands back a little to see if it is straight. As she is doing this Ralph comes by and pokes head in doorway. Since she is hidden by open door, Ralph cannot see her. Ralph has satisfied look on his face feeling that room is empty. His face registers cat-like satisfaction . . . secretary realizes that picture is still not straight and goes back to readjust it. Ralph starts to tiptoe towards desk in cat-like fashion. He is just about at desk when secretary gives a little cough. On hearing cough Ralph does eye-bulge take. He does a "Red Marshall" and starts tiptoeing back towards door. As he nears door secretary finishes adjusting picture and comes from behind door and sees him. Ralph stops in his tracks

SECRETARY

Ralph!

RALPH

Oh, hello Miss Wilson . . . Uh . . . Uh . . . I was just leaving.

SECRETARY

Leaving?

RALPH

Yeah. I came in to see Mr. Marshall, but since he's not here, I'm leaving.

SECRETARY

Oh. Mr. Marshall will be in in a few minutes.

RALPH (*looks pathetically toward desk*)

He will?

SECRETARY

By the way, Ralph, congratulations on your promotion.

RALPH

Thanks.

SECRETARY

You know, I was in here yesterday when Freddie Muller was discussing it with Mr. Marshall. You've certainly got a friend in Mr. Marshall. He said some very nice things about you.

RALPH (*again looks pathetically toward desk*)

I've said some nice things about him too.

(*Ralph continues looking toward desk as secretary does next speech*)

SECRETARY

Mr. Marshall really thinks you'll go far.

RALPH (*again looks toward desk*)

That's what I'm afraid of! Look, Miss Wilson, I know you're very busy and if you've got something to do outside in your own office go right ahead. I'll wait for Mr. Marshall.

SECRETARY

Oh, don't worry, Ralph. Until Mr. Marshall gets here, all I have to do is answer my phone.

RALPH

Oh . . . Didn't I just hear the phone ring in your office?

SECRETARY

I don't think so.

RALPH

I'm sure I heard it ring.

SECRETARY

That's funny . . . I'll go and check.

(*Secretary exits. Ralph looks after her. Then crosses over and closes door behind her. He then makes a beeline for the desk where the mail is. He picks up stack of mail in left hand and transfer it to his right hand, an envelope at a time as he is looking for his letter. He is about half way through when secretary reenters*)

SECRETARY

No Ralph, it wasn't . . .

(*Ralph is startled by her voice and by being caught and his hands go up and letters go flying up in air. She looks at Ralph in surprised manner as if wondering what he's doing by desk*)

Ralph, what are you doing?

RALPH

Oh, ah, ah, I just thought I'd tidy up Mr. Marshall's desk. I'm anxious to make a good impression.

(*Secretary looks around floor at letters strewn there*)

SECRETARY

I can see that.

(*Secretary gets down on one knee starting to pick up letters. Ralph realizes his opportunity to find letter on floor*)

RALPH

Let me help you with that.

(*Ralph gets down on hands and knees and starts crawling around picking up letters. Ralph is facing audience as he crawls around. Secretary is facing door. As Ralph picks up each letter he examines it. Finally all the letters are picked up. From the expression on Ralph's face, you can tell he hasn't found his letter and it is obviously in secretary's hand. Before either of them have a chance to get up Ralph speaks*)

RALPH

Here, Miss Wilson, I'll pick up those too.

SECRETARY

But I've already got them.

RALPH

Well, this way it'll be one neat stack.

(*Ralph reaches over and forcibly pulls them from secretary's hand*)

SECRETARY

Ralph, what's the matter with you?

(*Just then door opens and Mr. Marshall enters. Secretary sees him immediately and gets to her feet*)

Mr. Marshall!

(*Ralph is still on hands and knees on floor. He turns his head toward Marshall. Marshall looks at Ralph in amazement*)

RALPH

Oh, good morning, Mr. Marshall.

MARSHALL

What are you doing down there, Kramden?

(*As Ralph gets up he speaks . . .*)

RALPH
I was just helping Miss Wilson pick up these letters.

MARSHALL
Oh . . . Miss Wilson, you'd better get back to your office.

SECRETARY
Yes, Mr. Marshall.

(*Secretary exits. Mr. Marshall watches secretary leave. Ralph notices that Marshall's attention is elsewhere and starts going through letters. Marshall turns and starts crossing to desk. As he passes Ralph he takes letters from Ralph and says*)

MARSHALL
I'll take those, Kramden.

(*Ralph reacts like all is lost. Boss crosses and sits down at his desk. He places letters on desk in front of him. He takes first letter. Then takes letter opener and speaks to Ralph as he opens letter*)
Well, Ralph, I guess you're pretty excited about your promotion.

(*Ralph's eyes are riveted on letter fearing it might be his*)

RALPH
Yes sir, thank you, sir.

(*Mr. Marshall apparently doesn't hear Ralph's answer as he is reading letter. Ralph leans on desk and tries to peer into letter. Mr. Marshall looks slowly up from his letter and catches Ralph peering at letter*)

MARSHALL
Oh, Kramden, I suppose you probably want to know what your new duties are?

RALPH
That's right, sir.

MARSHALL
Well, you just go down to Bill Johnson's office and he'll show you the ropes.

(*Marshall goes back to letter and Ralph just stands there. Marshall opens a couple of letters and throws them into waste basket as if he thinks Ralph has left. He looks up and sees Ralph standing there again trying to look into letters*)

MARSHALL
Well, what is it, Kramden? Did you want to speak to me about something?

RALPH (*grasping at straws*)
Yeah, that's it . . . I wanted to ask you something.

(*Ralph sits down on couch.*)

(*Now that Ralph has sat down he doesn't know what to say. After a pause, the boss speaks*)

MARSHALL
Well, what is it?

RALPH (*groping*)
Ah, ah, nice day out, isn't it?

MARSHALL
Is that what you wanted to say to me?

RALPH
Well, that's only part of it . . . Ah, how's your wife?

MARSHALL
I'm not married. . . .

RALPH
Oh . . .

MARSHALL
Look, Kramden, you seem a little nervous this morning and I can

understand it. You just think over what you have to say while I go over my mail.

(*Marshall takes letter and starts to open it. Ralph gets up from couch suddenly . . . he shouts and points out window*)

RALPH

Look, Mr. Marshall . . . one of those new jet planes.

(*Marshall quickly turns toward window*)

MARSHALL

What? Jet plane? Where?

(*As Marshall looks out window, Ralph tries to look at mail on desk. He is going through it when he speaks*)

RALPH

You keep looking! It's right out there!

(*Marshall turns back toward desk. As he turns, he sees Ralph hovering over desk with letters*)

MARSHALL

I still don't see any . . . Kramden, what are you doing with my mail?

RALPH

Oh, there's a fly loose. I was just trying to get it . . .

(*Ralph swats desk a couple of times with handful of letters*)

I think I got him.

MARSHALL

Ah, thanks . . . Now may I have my mail?

RALPH (*hands mail to Marshall*)

Yes sir.

MARSHALL

Sit down, Kramden, I'll be with you

in a minute.

(*Boss opens several letters, quickly glances at them and throws them in wastebasket. As boss does this, Ralph leans hand on desk and moves hand toward pile of letters with walking fingers. Boss takes Ralph's letter from pile and opens it . . . He glances at it quickly and reads . . .*)

What? Dear Mr. Marshall . . . You dirty bum!

(*Ralph looks wild eyed as if looking for place to run*)

You know, Kramden, I never read these crank letters. I always file them in the waste basket.

(*As Marshall does "waste basket" line, he reaches over basket with letter as if to drop it in . . .*)

RALPH (*greatly relieved*)

You do?

MARSHALL

But on second thought, I think I'll read it to you to show you the kind of crank letters people send to us executives.

(*During this speech, Marshall returns hand from over wastebasket and brings letter back to desk.*)

(*Marshall laughs a hearty "boss to newly appointed boss" laugh. Ralph jumps in quickly to try to save himself*)

RALPH

Oh, don't bother, Mr. Marshall. I got to get to work anyhow. Just throw that letter away.

(*Ralph gets on his feet to leave. Marshall reaches over wastebasket with letter again as if he's going to throw*) *it away)*

MARSHALL

Well, if you feel that . . .

(At this point Marshall again brings letter back as from over wastebasket to desk)

Oh, so you're a few minutes late for your job. You'll get a good laugh out of this. Sit down!

(Ralph sits down on couch resigned to fate. Boss starts reading . . .)

"Dear Mr. Marshall . . . You dirty bum!" Can you imagine the mentality of a man who would write a letter like this? . . . "After giving you the best years of my life, you fired me, you miserable low life! A man like you should turn in your membership card in the human race." Well, that line at least shows a little more clever thought than the average crank uses. . . .

RALPH *(unconsciously)*

Thanks.

(Boss looks at Ralph a little bewildered and goes back to letter and reads remainder.)

MARSHALL

"After what you did to me, I can safely say that you are the meanest man in the whole world, you dirty bum," . . . Kramden, do you know how this is signed?

(Ralph is too weak to even answer) It says, "Sincerely yours, etc. etc." . . . He didn't even have the nerve to sign his name.

(Ralph does big reaction.)

RALPH

Sincerely yours . . . etc. . . . etc. . . .

Oh no. . . .

(Ralph falls on floor and faints. Boss looks down on him and calls out . . .)

MARSHALL

Miss Wilson! Miss Wilson!

(Boss comes from behind desk and bends over him and pats hand. Miss Wilson rushes in)

SECRETARY

Mr. Marshall, what happened?

MARSHALL

He fainted! I guess the excitement of his promotion was too much . . .

(Secretary takes bottle of water off boss's desk)

SECRETARY

This should bring him to.

(She empties contents of pitcher into Ralph's face. Ralph sits up spluttering and looks from secretary to Marshall with happy expression on face. BLACKOUT)

PART V

APARTMENT AGAIN

At rise, establishing shot of the Kramdens' kitchen. Alice is seated by table. She is darning socks. Door opens. Ralph enters happily. He is laden with packages

RALPH *(expansively)*

Hello, Honey, get out the dishes. I bought the best Chinese food in town. We're celebrating!

ALICE *(puzzled)*

But Ralph, when you left this morning you acted as though the world had come to an end.

RALPH

Not any more, Alice. Boy! Is that Norton a doll! His stupidity saved my life! Not only did I get my job back but I got the promotion.

ALICE

I still don't get it. What about the letter?

RALPH

That's just it. When Norton wrote it, all he put at the end was sincerely yours etcetera, etcetera. And he didn't put my name down at all.

ALICE (*excited*)

Then Mr. Marshall didn't know it was . . .

RALPH

He had no idea who sent it, thought it was some crazy crank! Come on, dish out the egg rolls and heat up the chow mein!

ALICE (*opening packages*)

Ralph, you bought enough to feed an army.

RALPH

Call in the neighbors . . . This is a night to cerebrate . . . Baby, from now on we're living. Nothing but the best for you. We'll move to the country and you'll wear the best clothes money can buy. I want you to get rid of that old coat you've been wearing. An executive's wife ain't gonna wear imitation squirrel. You're gonna wear imitation mink!!

ALICE

Ralph, I haven't seen you this happy in years.

(*Door opens. Norton enters. He sniffs as though smelling something*)

NORTON

Hey, what's doing here? From downstairs it smelled like the Hong Kong Gardens.

RALPH

If you were just a little prettier I'd kiss you for what you did for me!

NORTON

Wait a minute, Ralph, how did you know? I only saw your boss a half hour ago.

RALPH (*petrified*)

My boss?

NORTON

Yeah, I felt so rotten about you losing your job and everything, I thought about it all day. So when I finished work I went down to the bus company. I saw your boss and explained the whole thing to him.

RALPH (*takes deep breath*)

You explained the whole thing??

NORTON

That's right. I told him you didn't mean that stuff in the letter about him being a big bum.

RALPH (*sinks into chair*)

You didn't??

NORTON

Sure. And believe me you got nothing to worry about. He said he wantsa see you first thing in the morning.

(*Norton opens door and speaks from doorway . . .*)

And remember, if you're ever in trouble again, Ralphie old boy,

(*Indicates upstairs with finger*)

I live right upstairs.

(*Scene ends with close shot of Ralph's face showing utter despair.*
BLACKOUT)

TOP COMMENTARY SHOW OF THE YEAR

SEE IT NOW

REPORT ON
SENATOR JOSEPH R. McCARTHY

REPORT ON

SENATOR JOSEPH R. MCCARTHY

SEE IT NOW

PRODUCED BY . . . . CBS TELEVISION

COMMENTATOR . . . . EDWARD R. MURROW

SPONSORED BY ALCOA
TELECAST: MARCH 9, 1954
CBS TELEVISION NETWORK

SEE IT NOW

IN ITS TELECASTS DURING THE 1954 SEASON the famed CBS television program series, *See It Now,* has brought its large audience into intimate personal contact with world events, scenes and personalities—ranging from a midwest coal mine to the Korean battlefield, from Samuel Goldwyn to Sir Winston Churchill.

No program in its history, however, caused such a storm of public comment as the *Report on Senator Joseph R. McCarthy,* chosen for this volume. In the course of this presentation, *See It Now* offered films related to this very controversial political figure. Mr. Murrow made no observations, offered no opinions, but merely presented facts previously recorded by the camera. The result was a show that made the front pages of almost every newspaper in the land.

"See It Now," said Jack Gould, former Radio and TV Editor of the New York Times, "is a striking demonstration of the power of television as a journalistic tool, lifting the medium to a new high in maturity and usefulness . . . a foretaste to television's true glory."

See It Now has won every major award and citation given in the field of television, including the George Foster Peabody Award, the Polk Memorial Award and many others.

Edward R. Murrow, producer and commentator of *See It Now* for CBS, has himself achieved what may be a winning record—more than 100 major awards and honors during the past 16 years of broadcasting news of war and peace.

Mr. Murrow was born in Greensboro, N. C. on April 25, 1908. He was graduated Phi Beta Kappa from Washington State College in 1930, and traveled extensively in America and Europe until 1932 as president of the National Student Federation. From 1932 to 1935 he was assistant director of the Institute of International Education and directed its foreign operations in London, Paris, Berlin, Geneva and Vienna.

Mr. Murrow was appointed Director of Talks and Education for CBS in 1935. He began broadcasting in 1938, his first program coming from Vienna. Here, his historic report of the German Anschluss won him world-wide recognition. Returning to London, he built up the CBS Radio Network's roster of correspondents. During the London "blitz" and thereafter, Murrow broadcast war reports direct to the United States.

After the war, CBS appointed Murrow Vice President and Director of Public Affairs. Later, he narrated the *I Can Hear It Now* albums for Columbia Records from which stemmed the *Hear It Now* program on CBS-Radio. The show ran until 1951 and then went on television as the current *See It Now* program.

Mr. Murrow also does the *Person To Person* program on television and a daily radio news program. He is married to the former Janet Brewster and has one son, Casey, born November 6, 1945 in London.

Fred W. Friendly, associate editor and co-producer of *See It Now,* shares the laurels for the consistently fine performance of the programs. A virtual dynamo of ideas, he works mainly on allocating assignments to film editors, reporters and technicians on the staff. Murrow frequently goes out on an assignment; Friendly seldom does, but instead devotes his time to production. Murrow and Friendly have collaborated for six years since they presented the Columbia Record Album, *I Can Hear It Now.*

Fred Friendly's conception of the program series can be described in one sentence. "The idea behind *See It Now,*" he says, "is to take the world and dump it into the listener's living room, with our cameras going everywhere and bringing world events to the television screen."

MURROW: Good evening. Tonight SEE IT NOW devotes its entire half hour to a report on Senator Joseph R. McCarthy told mainly in his own words and pictures. But first . . . (*Commercial*)

MURROW: Because a report on Senator McCarthy is by definition controversial we want to say exactly what we mean to say and I request your permission to read from the script whatever remarks Murrow and Friendly may make. If the Senator believes we have done violence to his words or pictures and desires to speak, to answer himself, an opportunity will be afforded him on this program. Our working thesis tonight is this question.

"If this fight against Communism is made a fight against America's two great political parties the American people know that one of these parties will be destroyed and the Republic cannot endure very long as a one party system."

We applaud that statement and we think Senator McCarthy ought to. He said it, 17 months ago in Milwaukee.

MC CARTHY: The American people realize this cannot be made a fight between America's two great political parties. If this fight against Communism is made a fight between America's two great political parties the American people know that one of those parties will be destroyed and the Republic cannot endure very long as a one party system.

MURROW: Thus on February 4th, 1954, Senator McCarthy spoke of one party's treason. This was at Charleston, West Virginia where there were no cameras running. It was recorded on tape.

MC CARTHY: The issue between the Republicans and Democrats is clearly drawn. It has been deliberately drawn by those who have been in charge of 20 years of treason. The hard fact is —the hard fact is that those who wear the label, those who wear the label "Democrat" wear it with the stain of a historic betrayal.

MURROW: 17 months ago Candidate Eisenhower met Senator McCarthy in Green Bay, Wisconsin and he laid down the ground rules on how he would meet Communism if elected.

EISENHOWER: This is a pledge I make. If I am charged by you people to be the responsible head of the Executive Department it will be my initial responsibility to see that subversion, disloyalty, is kept out of the Executive Department. We will always appreciate and welcome Congressional investigation but the responsibility will rest squarely on the shoulders of the Executive and I hold that there are ample powers in the government to get rid of these people if the Executive Department is really concerned in doing it. We can do it with absolute assurance.

(*Applause*)

This is America's principle; Trial by jury, of the innocent until proved guilty, and I expect to stand to do it.

MURROW: That same night in Milwaukee, Senator McCarthy stated what he would do if the General was elected.

MC CARTHY: I spent about a half hour with the General last night. While I can't—while I can't report that we agreed entirely on everything —I can report that when I left that meeting with the General, I had the same feeling as when I went in, and that is that he is a great American, and will make a great President, an outstanding President. But I want to

tell you tonight, tell the American people as long as I represent you and the rest of the American people in the Senate, I shall continue to call them as I see them regardless of who happens to be President.

MURROW: November 24th, 1953.

MC CARTHY: A few days ago I read that President Eisenhower expressed the hope that by election time in 1954 the subject of Communism would be a dead and forgotten issue. The raw, harsh, unpleasant fact is that Communism is an issue and will be an issue in 1954.

MURROW: On one thing the Senator has been consistent . . . Often operating as a one-man committee, he has traveled far, interviewed many, terrorized some, accused civilian and military leaders of the past administration of a great conspiracy to turn the country over to Communism, investigated and substantially demoralized the present State Department, made varying charges of espionage at Fort Monmouth. (The Army says it has been unable to find anything relating to espionage there.) He has interrogated a varied assortment of what he calls "Fifth Amendment Communists." Republican Senator Flanders of Vermont said of McCarthy today:

"He dons war paint; he goes into his war dance; he emits his war whoops; he goes forth to battle and proudly returns with the scalp of a pink Army dentist."

Other critics have accused the Senator of using the bull whip and smear. There was a time two years ago when the Senator and his friends said he had been smeared and bull whipped.

MR. KEEFE: You would sometimes think to hear the quartet that call themselves "Operation Truth" damning Joe McCarthy and resorting to the vilest smears I have ever heard. Well, this is the answer, and if I could express it in what is in my heart right now, I would do it in terms of the poet who once said:

Ah 'tis but a dainty flower I bring you,

Yes, 'tis but a violet, glistening with dew,

But still in its heart there lie beauties concealed

So in our heart our love for you lies unrevealed.

MC CARTHY: You know, I used to pride myself on the idea that I was a bit tough, especially over the past 18 or 19 months when we have been kicked around and bull whipped and damned. I didn't think that I could be touched very deeply. But tonight, frankly, my cup and my heart is so full I can't talk to you.

MURROW: But in Philadelphia, on Washington's Birthday, 1954, his heart was so full he could talk. He reviewed some of the General Zwicker testimony and proved he hadn't abused him.

MC CARTHY: Nothing is more serious than a traitor to this country in the Communist conspiracy. Question: Do you think stealing $50 is more serious than being a traitor to the country and a part of the Communist conspiracy?

Answer: That, sir, was not my decision.

Shall we go on to that for a while? I hate to impose on your time. I just got two pages. This is the abuse which is . . . the real meat of abuse, this is the Official reporter's record of the hearing. After he said he wouldn't remove that General from the Army who cleared Communists, I said: "Then General, you should be removed from any Command. Any man who has been given the honor of being promoted to General, and who says, 'I will protect another general who protects Communists,' is not fit to wear that uniform, General."

(*Applause*)

"I think it is a tremendous disgrace to the Army to have to bring these facts before the public but I intend to give it to the public, General, I have a duty to do that. I intend to repeat to the press exactly what you said so that you can know that and be back here to hear it, General."

And wait 'til you hear the bleeding hearts scream and cry about our methods of trying to drag the truth from those who know, or should know, who covered up a Fifth Amendment Communist Major. But they say, "Oh, it's all right to uncover them but don't get rough doing it, McCarthy."

MURROW: But two days later, Secretary Stevens and the Senator had lunch, agreed on a memorandum of understanding, disagreed on what the small type said.

STEVENS: I shall never accede to the abuse of Army personnel under any circumstance including Committee hearings. I shall not accede to them being browbeaten or humiliated. In the light of those assurances although I did not propose cancellation of the hearing, I acceded to it. If it had not been for these assurances, I would never have entered into any agreement whatsoever.

MURROW: Then President Eisenhower issued a statement that his advisers thought censored the Senator, but the Senator saw it as another victory, called the entire Zwicker case "a tempest in a teapot."

MC CARTHY: If a stupid, arrogant or witless man in a position of power appears before our Committee and is found aiding the Communist Party, he will be exposed. The fact that he might be a General places him in no special class as far as I am concerned. Apparently—apparently, the President and I now agree on the necessity of getting rid of Communists. We apparently disagree only on how we should handle those who protect Communists. When the shouting and the tumult dies the American people and the President will realize that this unprecedented mud slinging against the Committee by the extreme left wing elements of press and radio were caused solely because another Fifth Amendment Communist was finally dug out of the dark recesses and exposed to the public view.

MURROW: Senator McCarthy claims that only the left wing press criticized him on the Zwicker case. Of the 50 large circulation newspapers in the country, these are the left wing papers that criticized. These are the ones which supported him. The ratio is about three to one against the Senator. Now let us look at some of these left wing papers that criticized the Senator.

The Chicago Tribune: McCarthy will better serve his cause if he learns to distinguish the role of investigator from the role of avenging angel.

The New York Times: The unwarranted interference of a demagogue— a domestic Munich.

The Times Herald, Washington: Senator McCarthy's behavior towards Zwicker is not justified.

The Herald Tribune of New York: McCarthyism involves assault on Republican assets.

Milwaukee Journal: The line must be drawn and defended or McCarthy will become the government.

The Evening Star of Washington: It was a bad day for everyone who resents and detests the bully boy tactics which Senator McCarthy often employs.

The New York World Telegram: Bamboozling, bludgeoning, distorting.

St. Louis Post Dispatch: Unscrupulous bullying. What tragic irony—the President's advisers keep him from doing whatever decent instinct must command him to do.

That is the ratio from three to one of the left wing press.

There was one other interesting quote on the Zwicker controversy, and it came from the Senator himself.

MC CARTHY: May I say that I was extremely shocked when I heard that Secretary Stevens told two Army officers they had to take part in the cover-up of those who promoted and coddled Communists. As I read his statement, I thought of that quotation "On what meat doth this, our Caesar, feed?"

MURROW: And upon what meat does Senator McCarthy feed? Two of the staples of his diet are the investigations (protected by immunity) and the half truth. We herewith submit samples of both. First, the half truth. This was an attack on Adlai Stevenson at the end of the '52 campaign. President Eisenhower, it must be said, had no prior knowledge of it.

MC CARTHY: I perform this unpleasant task because the American people are entitled to have the coldly documented history of this man who says he wants to be your President. But strangely, Alger—I mean Adlai . . . but let's move on to another part of the jigsaw puzzle. While you may think that there can be no connection between the debonair Democrat candidate and a dilapidated Massachusetts barn, I want to show you a picture of this barn and explain the connection. Here is the outside of the barn. Give me the picture of the in-

side of the barn. Here is the outside of the barn at Lee, Mass. It looks as though it couldn't house a farmer's cow or goat. Here's the inside. (Showing picture) A beautiful, panelled conference room with maps of the Soviet Union. What way does Stevenson tie up with that?

My—my investigators went out and took pictures of the barn after we had been tipped off what was in it. Tipped off that there was in this barn all the missing documents from the Communist front—IPR. The IPR which was named by the McCarran Committee —named before the McCarran Committee as a cover-up for Communist espionage. Let's take a look at the photostat of the document taken from the Massachusetts barn. One of those documents which was never supposed to see the light of day. Rather interesting it is. This is a document which shows that Alger Hiss and Frank Coe recommended Adlai Stevenson to the Mount Tremblant Conference which was called for the purpose of establishing foreign policy—post-war policy in Asia. As you know, Alger Hiss is a convicted traitor, Frank Coe is a man who has been named under oath before the Congressional Committee seven times as a member of the Communist Party. Why do Hiss and Coe find that Adlai Stevenson is the man they want representing them at this conference? I don't know. Perhaps Adlai knows.

MURROW: But Senator McCarthy didn't permit his audience to hear the entire paragraph. This is the official record of the McCarran hearings and anyone could have bought it for two dollars. Quote: "Another possibility for the Mount Tremblant Conferences on Asia is someone from Knox' office or Stimson's office." (Frank Knox was our wartime Secretary of the Navy; Henry Stimson our Secretary of the Army, both distinguished Republicans) Coe and Hiss mentioned Adlai Stevenson, one of Knox' special assistants and Harvey Bundy, former Assistant Secretary of State under Hoover, and now assistant to Stimson because of their jobs.

We read from this documented record not in defense of Mr. Stevenson, but in defense of truth. Specifically, Mr. Stevenson's identification with that red barn was no more, no less than that of Knox, Stimson, or Bundy. It should be stated that Mr. Stevenson was once a member of the Institute of Pacific Relations. But so were such other loyal Americans as Senator Ferguson, John Foster Dulles, Paul Hoffman, Henry Luce, and Herbert F. Hoover. Their association carries with it no guilt, and that barn has nothing to do with any of them.

Now a sample investigation. The witness was Reed Harris, for many years a civil servant in the State Department directing the Information Service. Harris was accused of helping the Communistic cause by curtailing some broadcasts to Israel. Senator McCarthy summoned him and questioned him about a book he had written in 1932.

MC CARTHY: Mr. Reed Harris, your name is Reed Harris?

ANSWER: That's right.

MC CARTHY: You wrote a book in '32, is that correct?

ANSWER: Yes, I wrote a book and as I testified in executive session—

MC CARTHY: At the time you wrote the book—pardon me, go ahead, I'm sorry, proceed.

ANSWER: —at the time I wrote the book the atmosphere in the universities of the United States was greatly affected by the Great Depression then in existence, the attitudes of students, the attitudes of the general public were considerably different than they are at this moment, and for one thing there certainly was no awareness to the degree that there is today of the way the Communist Party works.

MC CARTHY: You attended Columbia University in the early thirties, is that right.

ANSWER: I did, Mr. Chairman.

MC CARTHY: Will you speak a little louder, sir?

ANSWER: I did, Mr. Chairman.

MC CARTHY: And you were expelled from Columbia?

ANSWER: I was suspended from classes on April 1, 1932. I was later reinstated and I resigned from the University.

MC CARTHY: You resigned from the University. Did the Civil Liberties Union provide you with an attorney at that time?

ANSWER: I had many offers of attorneys and one of those was from the American Civil Liberties Union, yes.

MC CARTHY: The question is did the Civil Liberties Union supply you with an attorney?

ANSWER: They did supply an attorney.

MC CARTHY: The answer is yes?

ANSWER: The answer is yes.

MC CARTHY: You know the Civil Liberties Union has been listed as a front for and doing the work of the Communist Party?

ANSWER: Mr. Chairman this was 1932.

MC CARTHY: I know it was 1932. Do you know they since have been listed as a front for and doing the work of the Communist Party?

ANSWER: I do not know that they have been listed so, sir.

MC CARTHY: You don't know they have been listed?

ANSWER: I have heard that mentioned or read that mentioned.

MC CARTHY: You wrote a book in 1932. I'm going to ask you again at the time you wrote this book did you feel that professors should be given the right to teach sophomores that marriage "should be cast off of our civilization as antiquated and stupid religious phenomena?" Was that your feeling at that time?

ANSWER: My feeling was that professors should have the right to express their considered opinions on any subject whatever they were, sir.

MC CARTHY: I'm going to ask you this question again.

ANSWER: That includes that quotation, they should have the right to teach anything that came to their mind as being a proper thing to teach.

MC CARTHY: I'm going to make you answer this.

ANSWER: I'll answer yes, but you put an implication on it and you feature this particular point out of the book which of course is quite out of context, does not give a proper impression of the book as a whole. The American public doesn't get an honest impression of even that book, bad as it is, from what you are quoting from it.

MC CARTHY: Then let's continue to read your own writings.

ANSWER: 21 years ago again.

MC CARTHY: Yes, we shall try and bring you down to date if we can.

ANSWER: Mr. Chairman, two weeks ago Senator Taft took the position that I taught 21 years ago, that Communists and Socialists should be allowed to teach in the schools. It so happens nowadays I don't agree with Senator Taft as far as Communist teachers in the schools is concerned because I think Communists are in effect a plainclothes auxiliary of the Red Army, the Soviet Red Army, and I don't want to see them in any of our schools teaching.

MC CARTHY: I don't recall Senator Taft ever having any of the background that you have got.

ANSWER: I resent the tone of this inquiry very much, Mr. Chairman. I resent it not only because it is my neck, my public neck that you are, I think, very skillfully trying to wring, but I say it because there are thousands of able and loyal employees in the Federal government of the United States who have been properly cleared according to the laws and the security practices of their agencies as I was, unless the new regime says no. I was before.

QUESTION: Do you think this book you wrote then did considerable harm? Its publication might have had adverse influence on the public by an expression of views contained in it?

ANSWER: The sale of that book was so abysmally small, it was so unsuccessful that a question of its influence, really you can go back to the publisher, you'll see it was one of the most unsuccessful books he ever put out. He's still sorry about it just as I am.

MC CARTHY: Well I think that's a compliment to American intelligence. I will say that.

MURROW: Senator McCarthy succeeded only in proving that Reed Harris had once written a bad book which the American people had proved 22 years ago by not buying it, which is what they eventually do with all bad ideas. As for Reed Harris, his resignation was accepted a month later with a letter of commendation. McCarthy claimed it was a victory. The Reed Harris hearing demonstrates one of the Senator's techniques. Twice he said the Ameri-

can Civil Liberties Union was listed as a subversive front. The Attorney General's list does not and has never listed the ACLU as subversive nor does the FBI or any other government agency. And the American Civil Liberties Union holds in its files letters of commendation from President Eisenhower, President Truman, and General MacArthur.

Now let us try to bring the McCarthy story a little more up to date. Two years ago Senator Benton of Conn. accused McCarthy of apparent perjury, unethical practice and perpetrating a hoax on the Senate. McCarthy sued for two million dollars. Last week he dropped the case saying no one could be found who believed Benton's story. Several volunteers have come forward saying they believe it in its entirety.

Today Senator McCarthy says he's going to get a lawyer and force the networks to give him time to reply to Adlai Stevenson's speech. Earlier, the Senator asked, "upon what meat does this, our Caesar, feed?" Had he looked three lines earlier in Shakespeare's *Caesar* he would have found this line, which is not altogether inappropriate: "The fault, dear Brutus, is not in our stars, but in ourselves." No one familiar with the history of this country can deny that Congressional committees are useful. It is necessary to investigate before legislating, but the line between investigation and persecuting is a very fine one and the Junior Senator from Wisconsin has stepped over it repeatedly. His primary achievement has been in confusing the public mind as between internal and the external threat of Communism. We must not confuse dissent with disloyalty. We must remember always that accusation is not proof and that conviction depends upon evidence and due process of law. We will not walk in fear, one of another. We will not be driven by fear into an age of unreason if we dig deep in our history and our doctrine, and remember that we are not descended from fearful men, not from men who feared to write, to speak, to associate and to defend causes which were for the moment unpopular.

This is no time for men who oppose Senator McCarthy's methods to keep silent, or for those who approve. We can deny our heritage and our history but we cannot escape responsibility for the result. There is no way for a citizen of a republic to abdicate his responsibilities. As a nation we have come into our full inheritance at a tender age. We proclaim ourselves, as indeed we are, the defenders of freedom, what's left of it, but we cannot defend freedom abroad by deserting it at home. The actions of the Junior Senator from Wisconsin have caused alarm and dismay amongst our allies abroad and given considerable comfort to our enemies, and whose fault is that? Not really his, he didn't create this situation of fear, he merely exploited it and rather successfully. Cassius was right, "The fault, dear Brutus, is not in our stars, but in ourselves."

Good night, and good luck.

TOP DOCUMENTARY SHOW OF THE YEAR

MARCH OF MEDICINE

Arthritis and Rheumatism

ARTHRITIS AND RHEUMATISM

MARCH OF MEDICINE—PROGRESS REPORT No. 5

Presented by Smith, Kline & French
Laboratories and the American Medical
Association.

WRITER . . . . LOU HAZAM

DIRECTOR . . . . CHARLES CHRISTENSEN

PRODUCED BY . . . . MEDICINE TELEVISION UNIT,
SMITH, KLINE
& FRENCH LABORATORIES

NBC PRODUCER . . . . DORIS ANN

TELECAST: APRIL 29, 1954

WNBC-TV and the NBC TELEVISION NETWORK

ARTHRITIS AND RHEUMATISM

ONE OF THE OUTSTANDING ACHIEVEMENTS in television documentary programs, *March of Medicine* has attained an almost unbelievably high rating for this type of show—approximately 14 million viewers.

The series has covered such topics as heart disease, cancer, infancy and old age and, of course, arthritis and rheumatism. Some of the unusual subjects presented have been the televising of a stomach operation, a caesarean delivery, a visit to a mental institution, a dramatic cross-circulation heart operation. *March of Medicine* has been acclaimed by the medical profession, and by the public, as one of television's finest educational programs.

Lou Hazam, writer of *Arthritis and Rheumatism,* has been writing scripts ever since he graduated from Columbia College in 1933. His material has run the gamut from the "arty" *Columbia Workshop* to the popular plot construction of *Stars Over Hollywood.* More recently, Mr. Hazam has specialized in documentary scripts for radio and television and has achieved an outstanding success. His television credits include such prize-winning shows as *Background For Trouble, Battle Report, Washington* and the series, *March of Medicine.*

Mr. Hazam has also played a part in many top special events telecasts—NBC assigned him to cover the 1952 national political conventions in Chicago; he wrote the script for NBC's day-long presentation of President Eisenhower's Inauguration; and was sent to England as associate producer and writer of NBC's coverage of the Coronation of Queen Elizabeth.

AUDIO	VIDEO
NARRATOR: (*Off camera*)	
These are arthritics . . .	*Camera, starting with wide shot, dollies in on group of arthritic patients in studio*
People, no different than you and your neighbors,	
Stricken by the crippler	
Known as rheumatic disease . . .	
Disease that attacks more of us Americans	
Than cancer, heart disease, tuberculosis and diabetes combined . . .	
A disease that twists and disables	
The human body	
From childhood, at the curtain-rise of life,	*Switch to other cameras for CU's of child and old man successively*
On up through old age,	
At the curtain-fall.	
(*Change*)	*Dissolve to film of dinosaur. (This can be film taken at museum of natural history—skeleton or reconstructed animal—or slowly revolving model)*
This is a dinosaur . . .	
In the bones of the dinosaur,	
Who roamed the earth,	
Two hundred million years ago,	
Is written—in hard crust—	
The fact	
That arthritis is a disease	
That arrived on this earth	
Long before man did . . .	
Hence is an affliction older	
Than the human race.	
(*Change*) This is New York City . . .	*Film: Scattered shots NYC, starting with sky-line, then street shots that emphasize crowds . . .*
Largest city	
On the face of the American continent.	
We show you New York City	

AUDIO   VIDEO

That you may visualize
How many people
Have arthritis and rheumatism in the
    United States—
(*Deliberately*) As many
As *all the people who live in New
    York City*—
Over ten million people—
Two hundred thousand so twisted
And wracked by pain
As to be completely lost
To the support of their families
And the strength of this nation;
Almost five million
Partially disabled . . .
And the rest chronically afflicted.   *Dissolve to Narrator in studio*
(*Change: Concluding on camera*)
And this is Ben Grauer. . . .
Launching the March of Medicine's
Progress Report on the greatest crip-
    pler of mankind—
A report ranging from Massachusetts
    General Hospital in Boston,
To the Mayo Clinic in Rochester—
By inviting your attention first,
For the facts on the *nature*
    of arthritis and rheumatism,
To one of the Nation's foremost   *Switch to Dr. Walter Bauer in studio,*
    authorities in the field: *probably set up to one side of the*
Dr. Walter Bauer of Massachusetts   *arthritic group*
    General . . .
                (1:45)
DR. BAUER: The first thing I think   *Doctor Bauer . . . in limbo*
you'd like to know is that rheumatism
is not just *one* disease, but a *family*
of diseases. Like members of any
family each has its own particular
character.
The family includes seven important

AUDIO

groups—arthritis due to infections, rheumatic fever, rheumatoid arthritis, osteoarthritis, injury and gout, and the form which affects tissues other than joints, though they are all characterized by aches and pains in the joints and muscles—I hasten to add that not all such pains are due to arthritis.

The second thing I think you'll want to remember is that rheumatic diseases are not solely diseases of the joints. Quite the contrary. Most of them are what we doctors call "systemic" disease—disease of the whole person.

While some of the lesser forms can be cured—thanks to the advent of drugs like penicillin—we do not know the exact cause, or how to cure, the major forms.

Let's observe—through the generous cooperation of these afflicted individuals—three of the principal types of arthritis for which we have no specific cure.

Good evening, Mr. ———. (*Patient replies*) Mr. ——— has what we call gout . . . gouty arthritis. We recognize this, in part, from these nodules or lumps on his fingers, the tips of his elbows and ears. In this disease, uric acid accumulates in the blood because the body cannot excrete it. Instead, it lays it down in deposits like this, in and around joints and other tissues. Fortunately today, we have drugs that enable us to control this disease and relieve the patient,

VIDEO

Doctor moves from limbo to group as camera once again covers group

Doctor and 1st patient

AUDIO	VIDEO
but we still need a form of treatment that will *cure* gout.	
(*To patient*) Thank you.	
Good evening, Mrs. ——. This patient has osteoarthritis, otherwise known as degenerative joint disease. It is often called a disease of aging— almost all of us over 60 have it in some degree, but far less serious. It results largely from the wear and tear of the joint structures. These knobby fingers are the result of such changes. They take place in other joints, as well— Thank you, Mrs.—	*Doctor goes to 2nd patient*
How do you do, Mrs. ——. Mrs. —— has the misfortune of suffering from another type of joint disease— rheumatoid arthritis. Of the whole family of rheumatic disease, it's the *biggest* offender, causing more crippling and invalidism than any other type. As yet we do not know its cause or cure. It is a chronic inflammatory disease that has produced marked deformity in many joints, resulting in loss of motion. Together, rheumatoid and osteoarthritis account for 60% of all the misery caused by rheumatism.	*Doctor and 3rd patient*
(*To patient*) Thank you, Mrs. ——. Doctors suspect various causes for this group of diseases including infection; a change in metabolism—this is, the way your body uses food and carries on its work; a breakdown of the complicated hormone balance of the body; diseases of blood vessels, or the nervous system; or some kind of hypersensitivity or allergy. All are being explored.	*Turns from last patient to confront camera*

AUDIO

We do know that the common denominator of most of the members of this disease family is an inflammation of the connective tissue . . . the cobweb of fibers that hold our body together. In our fight against rheumatic disease, connective tissue appears today to be the battleground appointed by nature.

Let us join, now, one large group of scientists that is searching out the mysteries of connective tissue. Let us go to the cameras set up in the laboratories of the NYU-Bellevue Medical Center for a report on the work going on there from Dean Currier McEwen of New York University College of Medicine . . .

(4:15)

DEAN MC EWEN: Connective tissue research is research into the supporting framework of the human body. (It is what we call *basic* research, and it seeks to progress from the bottom up, toward an understanding of arthritis and rheumatism, instead of from the disease down.)

Of course, connective tissue is only *one* area of research into the rheumatic diseases. But even so, it divides into many separate endeavors. Look at this group, for example, drawn from our larger Study Group on Rheumatic Diseases. All of them are concerned in some way with connective tissue.

Dr. Maxwell Schubert's section, for instance, is at work on the abnormal constituents of connective tissue that

VIDEO

Dissolve to wide shot of NYU research group

Pan Dr. Schubert's section

AUDIO

appear during inflammation . . . on the breakdown of the products of this tissue that show up in the blood of an arthritic . . . and studies of the tissue under the electronmicroscope. This second group is concerned with the appearance of tissue from patients with arthritic disease . . . with the role of bacteria . . . and the relationship between the endocrine glands and connective tissue . . .

At the same time, Dr. Morris Ziff and his group are studying the whole patient—that is, evidence of connective tissue damage on patients hospitalized with rheumatic disease.

Obviously, there is not time for each of these investigators to describe his work. But let's begin with Dr. Ziff, who is in charge of the Clinical Research Section, who will give you some idea of what we know about connective tissue . . .

(1:30)

DR. ZIFF: First, we want to know what makes up *normal* connective tissue—where arthritis does most of its damage. We know that the answer lies in a variety of proteins and carbohydrates. They combine to form *different types* of connective tissue, best demonstrated with this drawing of a knee joint.

Our knee joint consists of *cartilage,* which is connective tissue that is rigid but still soft . . . *bone* which is dense connective tissue in which lime salts have been deposited . . . the synovialis or membrane that lines the joint . . .

VIDEO

Dissolve to Dr. Ziff

Camera on drawing as doctor points out features

AUDIO

VIDEO

joint fluid . . . and the capsule—all connective tissue that can become involved in arthritis.

Primarily, connective tissue seems to consist of a white, fibrous protein material called *collagen*. This ox-tail tendon, for example, is especially rich in these collagen fibers. Notice how they can be peeled away, one from the other?

Back on doctor who picks up ox-tail tendon

Peels fibers from tendon

These fibers, in turn, are cemented together by a sticky substance known as the *ground* substance.

Puts down tendon, moves to test-tube set-up

See what happens when we dissolve this substance in water? You get a sort of gluey solution like this. This is the material that in a sense, holds our *body* together.

Picks up test-tube and tilts to show slow-flowing solution

Now let's see what connective tissue looks like under the electronmicroscope, which magnifies 40,000 times. (*Points*) There are the fibers, with their characteristic banding . . . and this is the ground substance that holds them together.

Goes to electronmicroscope stills of tissue and points out features

Now, let me show you some connective tissue fibers after the ground substance has been extracted. Here you are—raw material of the supporting tissue of the body.

Back to doctor

It is here in connective tissue that arthritis strikes and does its principal damage.

And so the job that Dr. Maxwell Schubert and his team have appointed for themselves is the tough one of learning precisely what happens to connective tissue when it becomes inflamed.—Dr. Schubert—

Takes handful of fibers from jar and throws them on table, or continues to hold them in hand as camera dollies in for CU . . . dissolving through to Dr. Schubert

AUDIO (2:15)	VIDEO
DR. SCHUBERT: We are seeking to find out—at the level of the molecules that make up connective tissue—what goes wrong during inflammation. Let me see if I can explain it to you . . .	
To begin with, the molecules—that is, the units of matter—involved in the construction of these tissues are among the biggest and most complex of any that occur in the body. Some of these molecules we know, as yet, very little about. We call them *tissue mucoproteins*.	
To learn more about them, we are extracting these mucoproteins from the sticky material that holds together the fibers of the connective tissue. This shaker, for example, is extracting some from cartilage. There are reasons, for believing that it is the *changes* that occur in these materials we are extracting that are responsible for the tissue *damage* that occurs in rheumatoid arthritis.	*Dissolve to "shaker"*
Let me demonstrate an example of this change in the characteristics, let's say, of *joint* fluid. Here is a sample of normal joint fluid from a cow. It is very similar to normal *human* fluid. Notice how *slowly* it flows—this is as it should be.	*Picks up 1st test-tube . . .* *Demonstrates slow flow of normal joint fluid*
Now—here is a sample of fluid from the knee joint of a patient with rheumatoid arthritis. See how much more rapidly it flows? We believe it flows faster due to some damage that occurs with rheumatoid arthritis, and it	*Picks up 2nd test-tube of arthritic joint fluid and demonstrates rapid flow*

AUDIO

VIDEO

is the mechanism of this damage that we are studying by chemical means —here on the basement level of arthritis research.

(1:30)

NARRATOR:

Thus

While this group of scientists—

Augmented by others elsewhere—

Seeks literally to unravel

The basic framework of the human body,

Hoping ultimately to come face to face

With the causes of arthritis . . .

Here at the Nation's

National Institutes of Health in Bethesda, Maryland,

Researchers are seeking—

Among other things—

To perfect a *test*

That will establish early

Whether a person has rheumatoid arthritis

Or not—

Hence permit *specific* treatment at once,

Rather than after the disease has developed further.

To hear more of this,

Let's enter

The National Institute of Arthritis, and Metabolic Diseases,

Where we find its Clinical Director, Dr. Joseph Bunim,

In . . . er . . . strange company . . .

(45")

DR. BUNIM: Mary, you'll remember, had a little lamb that followed

Camera back on NYU-Bellevue group shot, panning . . . .

Switch either directly to film, or to Narrator before RS on which exterior, shots of NIH appear

Dr. Bunim, between lamb and rabbit, which are perhaps up on tables. He

AUDIO

her to school. Well, in a sense, *we* are getting a little schooling on arthritis with the help of this little lamb here —plus this rabbit. Let me explain it to you . . .

We are interested in perfecting a diagnostic test for rheumatoid arthritis that will be as good a test as the test your doctor now has for diabetes or tuberculosis.

Already this test—while it gives a wrong answer in the case of 1 or 2 people out of a hundred who do *not* have rheumatoid—this test is right in every three out of four patients who *do* have the disease.

How does it work? Well, that's where the sheep and the rabbit come in. First, we take a suspension of red blood cells from the sheep. Next, we add some serum from a rabbit that has previously been immunized against red blood cells from a sheep. And finally, we add a few drops of this mixture to a few drops of serum from a patient. We're using Danny's serum today in one part of this demonstration. Danny has had rheumatoid arthritis for 5 years, and is here for study at our clinical center.

Now over here are two test tubes in which the test ingredients have been resting in the refrigerator for 24 hours. What we must look for is a *clumping* of the sheep cells. Let's try the first one. . . . (*Picks it up and taps it*) No clumping. The sheep cells in this tube are apparently unaffected. Now let's try *this* one. (*Picks up 2nd*

VIDEO

might, as we come upon him, be stroking the neck of the lamb . . .

If boom-mike available, Dr. Bunim steps forward, as camera follows him, to test-tube rack set-up
If not, rack can be located alongside, and we can come in for CU here

At rack, putting together the ingredients. (If possible, each time he picks up a particular vial, we might frame in the BG, the animal concerned)

Cut-in shot of patient. (If we want Dr. Bunim, for action to proceed to a 2nd rack of test tubes, he might pass Danny as he walks to it, pausing with his arm around Danny's shoulders as he explains)

Doctor puts down tube in which he mixed elements, and indicates two other test tubes in the rack. Picks each up in turn and taps the tube. Cut-in CU shots of tubes

AUDIO   VIDEO

tube and taps it) There. See that
stringy, whip-like formation? That's
the characteristic clumping of the
sheep cells caused by the serum from
the patient with rheumatoid arthritis.
Well, you say, since it all seems so   *Back on Dr. Bunim*
clear cut, why not turn it over to the
routine labs, and go on to something
else?

For one thing, we're not satisfied with
a batting average of 75% . . . would
you be? Attempts are being made
here and elsewhere to improve the
sensitivity of the test so that better
than 90% of rheumatoid serums will
be positive. Also, the test is still not
effective in the first six months of the
disease when it would be most useful.
But perhaps even more important is
the answer to the question—what
causes this clumping? What is there
in the blood of a rheumatoid arthritic
that is not in the blood of a normal
person that is responsible for this reaction? Is the rheumatoid putting out
an abnormal protein as a consequence
of something injuring him?   *Doctor holds test tube out for CU*

That, then, is our next objective . . .   *shot of test tube with disc floating*
to identify this big "X" . . . to study   *in it*
its chemical nature. We want to trace
its source and find out what brings
on its formation. After that, we want
to learn *how,* if possible, we can *stop*
this factor from being produced. And
finally . . . finally we want to know
if *stopping* it has any effect on controlling or possibly arresting rheumatoid arthritis.

It is only by running down one little   *Back on doctor for wind-up*

AUDIO	VIDEO
lead after another, such as *this* one, that we may finally master, the curious and little understood disease.	
(3:15)	
NARRATOR:	*Narrator in studio on camera*
And so,	
In an increasing number of laboratories	
Throughout the country,	
Our medical researchers	
Continue to ask	
Questions they can't yet answer	
About the rheumatic diseases . . .	
But, with the persistent faith of the scientist,	
Assault the riddles they pose for themselves	
With every conviction	
That they will one day	
Overcome	
The disease that still confounds them.	
Meanwhile,	
Medicine is learning more each day	
About how to treat the rheumatoid arthritic,	
Applying rest . . . a nutritive diet . . .	
Aspirin to relieve pain . . . physical therapy . . .	
Injections of gold salts in certain cases . . .	
And finally	
What has been called:	*Dissolve to film*
"The miracle of *hormones*" . . .	
(45″)	
VOICE: (*Off camera*)	*Film: Dentist patient (from Mayo film) "running"*
Remember this scene? . . .	
This excited the medical world	
Back in '48—	
One of the first rheumatoid patients,	

AUDIO	VIDEO
Previously able to move only with pain,	
Who was treated	
With the hormone known as cortisone!	
Here, at the Mayo Clinic in Rochester, Minnesota,	*Cut to exterior shots Mayo Clinic (to come from Mayo)*
The hormone was discovered	
When Dr. Philip S. Hench	
Began to wonder what mysterious substance	
Nature produced	
In the body of the *jaundiced* rheumatoid patient,	
And also the *pregnant* rheumatoid patient,	
That temporarily freed them of the painful symptoms	
Of rheumatoid arthritis.	*Cut to lab shots of Drs. Kendall, Hench et al. (used in AMA film: original to come from Mayo)*
In this laboratory, his collaborator,	
Dr. Edward C. Kendall—	
Then Chief Biochemist at Mayo,	
And already researching in this field—	
Isolated, identified and synthesized Compound E,	
Later known as cortisone.	
He is flanked by Dr. Hench on the right	
And Doctors Slocumb and Polley on the left.	
Both Dr. Hench and Dr. Kendall	*Cut to film (Mayo film in our possession) of dentist patient. Begin with Dr. Hench examining him—*
Received the Nobel Prize for their work,	
And here—in this historic film—	
We observe Dr. Hench	
Examining the patient we saw previously.	*Then go to patient sitting with effort*
This is his condition *before* taking the drug.	

AUDIO	VIDEO
(*Pause*) Here he is —— days	*Sitting and rising easily*
After treatment with cortisone began.	
(*Pause*) Later still . . .	*"Running"*
(*Pause*) And once again when	*Sitting with effort*
The treatment was stopped.	
(*Voice off camera: On Narrator on camera*)	*(Stay on film if we have enough. Or else dissolve to Narrator. Or else to shot of Doctor in set in studio with camera slowly dollying in)*
Where do we stand today,	
Five and a half years after that historic occasion,	
With cortisone	
As an effective treatment	
For rheumatoid arthritis.	
Listen now	
To a member of the Mayo team	
That gave cortisone to the world—	
Dr. Charles H. Slocumb	
(*Title*) . . .	

(1′ 45″)

DR. SLOCUMB: (*On camera*) To begin with, as we pointed out at the start, cortisone—and other hormones like ACTH and hydrocortone—which are used in treating the arthritic, are not a *cure* for rheumatoid arthritis. Rather, they *suppress* the disease, and somewhat as in the case of insulin used for diabetes, the good effects last only as long as the hormone is taken regularly. This is as true today as it was in the beginning.	*Doctor seated in studio office set: medical chart of human body directly in BG*
How effective is cortisone? It is effective in over 50% of the cases—often making it possible for the people so helped to lead comparatively normal lives, when it is properly applied in conjunction with other useful therapy. In short, hormones such as corti-	

AUDIO	VIDEO
sone have already accomplished a good deal.	
Meanwhile, there is every reason to expect that their use will become *more* effective. You see (*Rises and goes to medical drawing*) unlike gold salts and certain other remedies, these hormones are "naturals" which our body itself makes . . . makes because it needs. (*Points to places on drawing*) Right here is the body's "manufacturing plant," so to speak, for the hormones . . . this adrenal gland here over *this* kidney, and this adrenal gland here, atop the other kidney. We call this the adrenal cortex. And because the hormones they produce are natural substances they will always be useful in medicine, and particularly in research.	*Camera follows doctor to chart and we get closeups of the sections indicated*
(*Returns to desk, perhaps to sit on one corner*) Now, then, we are still not as familiar as we'd *like* to be with how cortisone works . . . what parts of the body absorb it . . . how they use it . . . what's excreted. But we're all conducting further studies toward this end. And perhaps, when we learn more of the hormones' basic action, how they really work, we might be able not only to use them more effectively, but find a short-cut to treatment—some way of accomplishing the same effect by other means.	*Camera follows doctor back to desk*
(*Moving to original position behind desk again*) Although there seems to be no certainty of finding a substitute soon, much work along this line is being	

AUDIO

done in medical centers all over the world. Too, we mustn't overlook the possibility that the mysterious substance of jaundice and pregnancy may not be cortisone—or ACTH or hydrocortone—at all. If this is the case, then apparently the body is capable of making still *another* powerful antirheumatic substance that we have not yet discovered. If so, then perhaps some day we'll find *it,* and like cortisone put it, too, to work for the benefit of humanity.

(2′ 30″)

NARRATOR: (*Off camera*)
This woman
Is Mrs. Mary McMorrow . . .
Age—45 years . . .
Problem—Rheumatoid Arthritis,
The most vicious of all rheumatic
   diseases.
She has joined us in our studio tonight
As a living "symbol of hope"
For *all* arthritics.
For she is an example
of how a medical "team attack" on
   her arthritis—
Using not only drugs such as cortisone,
About which Dr. Slocumb has just
   reported to us,
But a combination of drugs and therapy—
Literally brought her back
To life as the normal person knows it!
Let Dr. Edward W. Lowman,
Assistant Professor of Physical Medicine and Rehabilitation

VIDEO

Down to black

Camera on Mrs. McMorrow, live, seated in studio

Dissolve to Dr. Lowman in studio

AUDIO	VIDEO

At New York University College of Medicine

Continue her story. . . .

DR. LOWMAN: (*On camera*) Mary McMorrow was one of 43 rheumatoid arthritics—selected from over 200—that were strictly the *worst* cases we could find in the New York City area.

They had had their arthritis for an average of 9½ years. We accepted these patients—and later others not so severely disabled—for a special two-year project at the Institute for Rehabilitation and Physical Medicine, to see what we could do for them through a new "total teamwork" approach . . .

This was Mary's condition when she first came to us . . . remember Mary? . . .

Dissolve to film of patient in bed, showing difficulty of moving . . . doctor examining her and taking notes

MARY: (*Replies,* i.e., "I sure do" . . .)

DR. LOWMAN: Bedridden 5½ years . . . she was carried out of her home in a chair only once during that time to see her son graduate from high school . . . Before we could decide on just how far we could expect to rehabilitate her, our first job was to *evaluate* her condition *medically* through a series of tests—lab. exams. . . . x-rays . . .

Super test reports

test her muscle power . . . her joint range . . . and particularly determine what we called her "functional capacity"—that is, her ability to carry out the many activities of her daily

AUDIO	VIDEO
living, such as washing her face, feeding herself and so on. Do you remember how deficient you were in this respect, Mary?	Hold up further reports but stay on film
MARY: (Replies, i.e., Yes, Doctor . . . I couldn't even get out of bed.)	
DR. LOWMAN: Yes, Mary was physically able to meet less than half the normal demands of daily life.	
In addition to the physical tests, we were interested in her psychological attitude toward her disease . . . her social problems . . . her mental outlook . . . her vocational skills . . .	Super additional reports
The sum total of all this data—gathered from internist, rheumatoid specialist, therapist, psychologist, social worker, vocational expert—was then used to determine just what Mary's goal should be in rehabilitation, as different from any other patient. Once	Dissolve from film to doctor in studio, standing next to pile of reports
established on cortisone, a program was then begun to reach that particular goal. It was a lot of hard work for her.	Dissolve to film (average 8″ each sequence)
Mary's treatment included the Hubbard Tank—to relax the taut muscles of her body—	(1) Hubbard tank
Hotpacks applied to her ankles and knees to relieve her joints . . .	(2) Hotpacks
Stretching exercises to get back some motion into the knees, shoulders, elbows and hips . . .	(3) Stretching exercises
Resistive exercises, like this one for the knees, to strengthen muscles . . .	(4) Resistive exercise
She also worked in occupational therapy using the loom to strengthen her hands and shoulders. . . .	(5) Occupational therapy at loom
Perhaps one of her biggest steps for-	(6) Parallel bars

AUDIO	VIDEO
ward was using the parallel bars . . . Gradually, what once seemed impossible ever again came true. Mary was walking—with a cane, to be sure, but walking . . .	*(7) Walking with cane*
Then came the monumental task of once again learning to climb stairs . . .	*(8) Stair climbing*
And finally, training to get Mary ready for travel in the world we were sure she was one day to join again outside the hospital . . .	*(9) Training for travel on street (entering mock bus?)*
	Dissolve to Dr. Lowman in studio
In all, Mary spent sixteen months under treatment but now Mary McMorrow and most of the patients have been dismissed. A third of these once-called "derelict" arthritics who stuck it out are back on the job, completely rehabilitated and independent. Two others are partially independent. In short, our project to see what total medical teamwork could do for the severely disabled is completed, a source of hope to all. As for Mary, instead of being 53% deficient in carrying out the activities of daily living, she is now down to 3%. And what's more, Mary now has a job . . .	
MARY: (*Tells of job in one sentence,* i.e., "I'm going back to work as a telephone switchboard operator again."	
DR. LOWMAN: Wonderful! (*Then*) Would you mind letting us see you walk, Mary?	
MARY: Not at all. (*Gets up and walks across studio and back, perhaps into camera.*)	*Camera follows Mary in her walk across studio*
(4:00)	
NARRATOR: (*Off camera*)	

AUDIO	VIDEO
A woman walking . . .	
What's so thrilling about that?	
Plenty, America . . .	
For in a simple little thing	
Like this woman walking	
Is reflected the progress	
Our doctors have made	
Against the greatest crippler of all—	
Rheumatoid arthritis,	
Behind every step she takes	
Are days, months, years of research and study	
That in the last five years alone	
Have seen more accomplished	
In our attack on the rheumatic diseases	
Than in all the many millions	
That man has been on the face of this earth.	*Dissolve to narrator*
We still	
Do not know the causes of arthritis	
Or how to cure it . . .	
But never before has such an attack been massed	
To relieve the suffering	
And conquer the crippling diseases	
As medical science is massing today.	
You can be part of that attack	
By supporting this work	
Through the Arthritis and Rheumatism Foundation . . .	
And well might you take hope	
That the rheumatic diseases—	
Like others once on the medical horizon—	
Will, in God's good time,	
Fall	
Before the doctors	
Who fill the ranks	
Of—the March of Medicine!	

TOP DRAMATIC SHOW OF THE YEAR
ONE HOUR PROGRAM

KRAFT TELEVISION THEATRE

Elisha and the Long Knives

ELISHA AND THE LONG KNIVES

BY

DALE WASSERMAN AND JACK BALCH

KRAFT TELEVISION THEATRE

DIRECTOR . . . . FRED CARNEY

SCENIC DESIGNER . . . . . . JAMES TRIPPIPO

CAST

Paiute Braves . . Andrew Gerado, Juna Luska

Chief Nebo . . . Lone Bear

Mr. Peabody . . Jerome Kilty

Mrs. Peabody . . Anne Seymour

Mace . . . . . Jared Reed

Brack . . . . . Royal Dano

Jeb . . . . . Dan Morgan

Elisha . . . . Van Dyke Parks

SPONSORED BY KRAFT FOODS COMPANY

TELECAST: FEBRUARY 4, 1954

NBC TELEVISION NETWORK

ELISHA AND THE LONG KNIVES

THE *Kraft Television Theatre* PRESENTED MORE than 100 full hour "live" television dramas, of which *Elisha and the Long Knives* is one, during 1954— a feat unrivalled in the history of telecasting. These productions have attained high standards of excellence and have won numerous awards.

The success of this series is indicated by its enthusiastic weekly audience, an estimated 27 millions of people—the largest drama audience of all time. Since May 7, 1947, *Kraft Television Theatre* has offered a full hour live drama every Wednesday evening over the NBC Television Network; and on October 15, 1953 a second weekly full hour show, completely different and presented on Thursday evenings, was begun over ABC Television Network. It is, incidentally, the longest running show *of any kind* on television, since it has never taken time out for a summer break.

One of the persons most responsible for the success of *Kraft Television Theatre* is Edmund C. Rice, of J. Walter Thompson Company and script editor of *Kraft,* who has helped to mold *Elisha and the Long Knives* and all the programs in the series. As this is written, *Elisha and the Long Knives* is being seriously considered as a full-length motion picture by a major Hollywood studio.

Dale Wasserman, co-author with Jack Balch of *Elisha and the Long Knives,* was born 36 years ago in the north woods of Wisconsin. He gravitated to

California in later years guided, in his own words, "by an itching foot and living off a limited quota of wits and various questionable employments." These included such diversified occupations as oil field roughneck, donkey engine operator in a lumber camp, a carnival shill and bookkeeper in a Nevada house of ill fame. By dint of this extended exposure, he became a "quasi expert" in the history and topography of the West, the material out of which *Elisha* was born.

"For no particular reason," he turned to the theatre and began acting, producing and directing. Joining Katherine Dunham as stage director and lighting designer, Wasserman toured with her company and, on arriving in New York in 1944, promptly won the award for the best lighting on Broadway. Soon after, Wasserman produced *Beggar's Holiday,* at the time the highest budgeted musical seen on Broadway. He continued his success with more than 30 productions and direction jobs in various theatrical capitals of the world. The 1954 engagement of the *Azuma Kabuki* Company from Tokyo carried his credit line.

After staging his last Broadway musical in 1952, Mr. Wasserman turned to writing because he felt it was a "more personal form of creative activity." The result—a play with Jack Balch, two movies, two dozen stories and several TV scripts, all of which, to his great amazement, sold.

Wasserman has recently completed the screenplay of a multi-million dollar movie, *The Viking* and is under contract as writer-director on another. He is also planning to do the librettos for a series of TV folk-musicals in collaboration with composer Tom Scott and also intends to do a major opera for TV with Gottfried von Einem. About the future, Wasserman says, "I plan to disengage myself at some point for further profitless wandering. Japan and southern Mexico are prominent on the itinerary."

Jack Balch has worked mainly in the newspaper and television fields. His ten years' newspaper experience included seven years with the St. Louis Post Dispatch. During four of these years, Balch held what he considered his most important job, drama editor and critic. In television, Balch was a staff director and producer for New York's station WPIX, handling all types of TV programs.

Mr. Balch is a prolific writer. During his after hours, he has turned out a tremendous amount of successful manuscripts. He is author of a published novel, *Lamps At High Noon*; has written a full-length play, *Me The Sleeper* which was produced in New York by ANTA; has written a full-length movie and numerous short stories.

Currently, Balch is writing his second novel; he is also working on a number of dramatic scripts for television.

ELISHA AND THE LONG KNIVES

ACT I

*A cabin off the Santa Fe Trail in the year 1840.
It is the home of three mountain men—"Long
Knives," as the Indians called them. They are
the trappers Jeb, Mace, and Brack. Jeb, at the
end of this working day, stacks pelts. Brack is
preparing the evening meal. Mace lazes on his
bunk, singing to the playing of his own guitar
(or banjo). His head is pillowed on a large and
incongruous object—an ornate quarto volume
of Shakespeare.*

MACE (*singing*)
  "The girls of St. Louis
    Won't let a man be;
    I'll give them my money,
    I won't give them me."
JEB (*as Mace comes to the end*)
Need more furs than these here tuh
raise dust in St. Louis. Durn ketch
keeps gittin' less and less every year.
MACE
Count 'em again, Jeb.
(*Strikes a chord*)
Mebbe countin' em once more will
make us think we got twice as many.
(*Strikes another chord*)
Effen we think we got twice as many,
mebbe that ol' tradin' company will
too.
JEB
I don't need to count twicet or even

oncet tuh know what's chasin' the fur
out of this country.
MACE (*singing*)
  "A snake on the water,
    And bufflers on hoof,
    Are safer than women,
    An' that is the truth."
JEB (*not interrupting, but just going
on*)
Them durn settlers from the East,
that's who.
(*His anger rising . . .*)
'N they ain't even settlers, far as I
kin see. They're more like passers-
throughers, but the animals don't
know that.
What they figure is, "Lissen at all that
noise 'n fuss comin' in over the rivers,
look at them human beings litterin'
up the mountains and dodgin' in and

out of the trees!"

MACE (*strumming and singing*)
  "A town's warm in winter,
    I'll not tell you lies,
  But mountains, dear mountains,
    Have got such clear skies."

JEB
Yuh know something? I counted two wagon trains o' them mis'able greenhorns passin' through here jes' in the last three weeks. *Two whole trains!* And they got women with 'em. *Women!*

MACE (*still strumming*)
Mebbe we ought to hunt us people 'stead o' bear and beaver.

JEB
Ol' Chief Nebo and his Paiute war parties'll take care o' that. But that ain't gonna help keep the animals here, I reckon. Once them animals start movin', there's trouble.

MACE
Reckon that's so.
(*Jeb, crossing to the cache of furs with another pelt in his hand, stops short as he catches sight of Mace's "pillow"—the book. He stares at the unfamiliar object. Points to it*)

JEB
In the name of creation—what's that?

MACE (*elaborately casual*)
What's what?
(*squirming to look*)
Oh, *that.*
(*lightly*)
That there's a book.

JEB (*astonished*)
A *what?*

MACE
Got writin' in it. 'N pictures.
(*Proffers it*)
Yuh want tuh look at it?

JEB
Yuh gone clean out o' yer mind? Yuh know I can't read.

MACE
Neither kin I.

JEB
Then what yuh doin' with a book?

MACE (*defensively*)
How'd I know I couldn't read til I tried it?

JEB
What kind o' book is it?

MACE (*picking up the volume tenderly*)
Feller I got it offen said it was somebody name o' Shakespeare.
(*quoting*)
Called it "The complete works o' The Immortal Bard."

JEB
Shakespeare, huh?
(*explosively*)
Foofaraw, I calls it!

MACE
Foofaraw!

JEB
Yah, foofaraw!
(*His eyes narrow as he adds it up. Suddenly he snatches the volume from Mace*)
Feller yuh got it offen, huh? Give it to yuh, did he? Jes' like that?
(*dangerously*)
What feller?

MACE (*on the defensive*)

Feller from the wagon train that went through yestiddy.

JEB

A greenhorn!

MACE

Said there was enough readin' in there tuh last me a lifetime.

JEB

That ain't the p'int! What did yuh give *him*?

MACE

Nuthin' we couldn't do without. Little flour—little meat.

(*There is thunder on Jeb's face. Ashamedly:*)

He were hungry, Jeb. Him and his whole fam'ly.

They all stood there at the door. Reg'lar poordevils. Had nary cash ner pelts tuh trade.

(*in protest*)

Leastways I got somethin' fer the provisions.

JEB (*an angry roar*)

Why, yuh thick-headed idjit! Yuh still don't git the p'int! Don't yuh know better'n tuh have anythin' tuh t' do with his kind? What d'yuh s'pose the Injuns'll do to *us* iffen they find out we been helpin' *them*?

(*Tosses the book back, contemptuously*)

Shakespeare. Gonna git all our hair raised, *that's* what.

BRACK (*interceding, calmly*)

Yore mouth raises more dust than a wagon wheel. Effen yuh don't both of yuh stop talking—

(*an expressive scalping gesture with his knife*)

—*I* raise leetle hair.

MACE (*pointing banjo at Brack and pulling string, plink*)

Next one puts you under, Injun.

BRACK

Half-injun.

(*lets out a bloodcurdling whoop*)

Come and git it.

(*Helps himself to food and sits down to eat. Mace wanders over to Jeb and helps him finish stacking the furs. Jeb lifts a fine fur for inspection and Mace takes it from him*)

JEB (*as Brack, eating, watches them*)

Purty, huh?

MACE

Purty, all right. Yuh know what I see, Jeb, when I look at that purty thing?

JEB

I know what I taste—

(*He licks his lips*)

Whiskey!—hot and runnin' fast like a river rassled over onto its side—!

MACE (*dreamily*)

Lookin' glasses and all kinds o' color cloth—and girls to look at their selves in the one and put the other on their backs—that's what I see.

(*He strokes the pelt with his hand*)

Purty girls—with blue eyes and brown eyes, and black hair and mud-yaller hair and red hair and—

JEB (*breaking in with a great laugh*)

Jes' like a river—that's the way I taste that stuff runnin'—raw nasty ol' St. Louis firewater tuh—

BRACK (*on his feet suddenly*)

Sssh!

(*Mace and Jeb freeze, watching the Halfbreed*)

We got visitors.

(*Mace leaps for his rifle as Jeb spins about to face the open door*)

JEB

Easy, Mace.

(*relaxing*)

Jes' a couple o' Nebo's boys. Musta heard us mention firewater.

BRACK (*an almost-smile on his taciturn face*)

Or mebbe Shakespeare.

JEB (*as Mace tries to find a retort, roaring:*)

Ha, ha!

(*Two Paiute Indians appear in the doorway. One carries a wrapped bale. Jeb motions to them.*)

Come in, boys, come in!

(*He turns back to his work. One of the Indians advances into the room. The other, with the bale, remains in the doorway. They are quite expressionless*)

Toss 'em some meat, Brack. Like as not they're hungry.

BRACK (*he is studying the Indians narrowly*)

They ain't up to no poordevilin', Jeb. Them's tradin' Injuns, not beggin' ones.

(*He points to the bale at the feet of the Indian in the doorway*)

Look.

JEB (*surprised, as he, too, looks*)

Tradin'? Then why ain't ol' Nebo here, hisself? We ain't never done no tradin' 'cept with him directly.

MACE (*softly*)

I ain't sure I like the looks o' this, Jeb.

JEB (*gesturing toward the silent Paiute in the cabin*)

Ask him, Brack. Ask him how come ol' Nebo didn't come hisself.

BRACK (*to the Indian*)

Inch-katz-ne-ate no-re-ah Nebo?

(*The Indian shakes his head in refusal to answer. Then he brusquely motions his partner inside. The second Indian brings the bale in, lays it on the floor, and undoes its wrappings. Laid bare is a stack of fine beaver pelts. Jeb and Mace are drawn to it, doubts forgotten*)

JEB

Holy jumpin' mountain tops!

MACE (*equally awed, softly*)

St. Louis, here we come!

(*joyfully*)

Effen they ain't brung every beaver in the country right into this cabin.

JEB (*in a roar*)

What are yuh waitin' fer? Break out the goods!

(*Mace plunges for the bags of trade goods*)

This is goin' tuh be the biggest trade since the greenhorns started comin' in!

(*Brack watches the Indians silently, his eyes narrowed in thought*)

Wait'll yuh see what we got fer you. Oh, there's goin' tuh be a heap o' happy squaws in your camp tonight!

(*Mace comes forward to the table loaded with small mirrors, cloth, trinkets, and beads. Jeb holds a mirror before the Indians' faces*)

How d'ye like *that* fer a starter?

(*The Indian contemptuously shoves*)

it aside)

MACE (*modeling a gewgaw necklace*)

How 'bout this?

(*The Indian shakes his head impatiently*)

JEB (*snatching up a roll of gaudy cloth*)

Here's the one that'll fetch him.

(*He drapes it on himself, hopefully. The Indian glares in disgust*)

Ain't havin' any, huh?

(*he examines the Indians a moment*)

All right. I know what yuh will take. Get it, Mace.

(*Mace understands instantly. He fetches the jug of whiskey. Jeb slams it down on the table*)

There yuh are. Best drinkin' whiskey yuh ever set yer teeth in. 'N it hurts me to see it go, too.

(*The Indians stare at it, licking their lips. Then, with resolve, the leader shakes his head. Jeb is staggered*)

No . . . firewater? Then what in thunderation *do* yuh want?

(*For answer the Indian strides across the cabin to where a powder horn hangs over one of the bunk uprights. He taps it significantly*)

Gunpowder! Whyn't yuh *say* so?

MACE (*eagerly*)

We got plenty!

JEB

Break it out!

(*Mace does so, piling tubular buckskin bags of gunpowder one by one on the table as he watches the Indian. Finally the Indian gives a satisfied grunt. He steps forward, tosses some of the bags to his partner. When they*

have them all, they go.

As he and Mace leap for the bale of pelts, going through them feverishly . . .)

Prime! Every one of 'em. Never *seen* primer.

MACE

Ain't they the little beauties, though?

(*holding up one*)

Look, Jeb. Must be four hours o' drinkin' and raisin' dust in this one alone!

(*Brack has been silently getting into his jacket. Now he picks up his rifle and crosses toward the door. Jeb looks up, surprised*)

JEB

Where yuh goin'?

BRACK (*halting in doorway*)

Ever know a Injun tuh turn down firewater before?

JEB (*struck by the thought*)

Come tuh think of it—never did.

BRACK

Ever know Nebo tuh send somebody else tuh do his tradin' fer him before?

JEB

Could be he's busy with somp'n else?

BRACK

That's what I figgered—but with *what*?

(*Neither Jeb nor Mace has an answer*)

'N furthermore, when all an Injun wants is gunpowder—and lots and lots of it—then it's time fer to go take a look-see. Which is what *this* child aims to do right now.

(*He turns and leaves.*

Fade to black)

The cabin, three or four hours later that night. Mace is seated at the table, poring with great interest over pictures in the open Shakespeare volume. Across from him Jeb sits, cleaning his rifle. He glances surreptitiously across the table from time to time, trying to make out the pictures upside down, but wishing not to reveal his interest to Mace.

JEB (*restlessly, arising and crossing to door*)
Where do yuh s'pose that dern Brack has got to?

MACE (*absently, his attention on the book*)
Can't tell about that half-breed. Effen he takes the notion, he'll git to St. Louis afore we do.

JEB (*crossing to peer sidelong over Mace's shoulder at the pictures, trying not to reveal his interest*)
Never seen a man git suspicious so fast.

MACE (*turning page, to Jeb's annoyance*)
Had cause tuh be. Brack's kind kin smell a mixed trail like you kin smell bad meat.
(*wistfully shaking his head*)
Shore wish I knew what these pictures mean.
(*pointing to illustration*)
Looka here, Jeb. Who d'ye s'pose is this tall black feller with the turban on his head?

JEB (*angrily*)
How should I know? S'a lot o' foofaraw, I tell yuh!

MACE (*disregarding his outburst*)
Hey, Jeb—look, look! Look at these fellers in the nightshirts pigstickin' the one in the middle. What d'ye s'pose that's about?

JEB (*his interest captured, despite himself*)
Danged if I know. Some kind of lynchin', ain't it?
(*He bends over the book with Mace, intrigued now*)

MACE
Now here's a varmint appears to be in the calaboose. Wonder what *he* done?

JEB (*stabbing a picture with a huge forefinger*)
Hold on there, Mace! Not so fast. Lookit this squaw with the drippin' knife in her hands!
(*shakes his head knowingly*)
Now that's what comes from lettin' women handle weapons.

Dissolve to a clearing on the mountainside overlooking Paiute Pass. In the foreground is the bole of a gnarled live-oak tree. In the background, the serrated profile of the mountain. Brack enters, treading softly, his eyes fixed on movement below and out of range.
He stands there tensely a moment. Then, clear on the night air but in the distance, comes the sound of a single gunshot. Immediately follows a savage but human yapping, and mingled with it heavy gunfire and screams of terror. Brack whispers:

Right: Lynn Poole, Director of Public Relations, The Johns Hopkins University and Producer of The Johns Hopkins Science Review.

Below: A scene from "Toys And Science".

Left: Jackie Gleason, star of
The Jackie Gleason Show.

Below: Ralph Kramden (Jackie Gleason)
argues with his wife, Alice
(Audrey Meadows), in a scene from
The Honeymooners'
"A Letter to the Boss".

J. Peter Happel

Edward R. Murrow and Fred Friendly review a filmed scene from See It Now.

Left: Lou Hazam, creator and writer of March of Medicine's "Arthritis and Rheumatism".

Below: A TV camera picks up a scene from "Conquest of Pain", The Johns Hopkins Science Review.

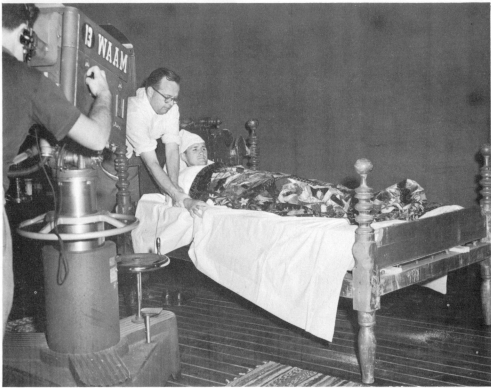

*Dale Wasserman, co-author of
Kraft Television Theatre's
"Elisha and the Long Knives".*

Suzy Harris

*Jack Balch, the other half of
the team who wrote
"Elisha and the Long Knives".*

Phillips St. Claire

*Left: Edmund C. Rice, Script Editor of
J. Walter Thompson Company, advertising
agency, which produces the
Kraft Television Theatre.*

*Below: Shooting a scene from
"The Thinking Heart".*

Right: Fred Coe, NBC-TV's Executive Producer of the Television Theatre.

Below: David Shaw, writer, on the set of "Native Dancer".

*"Glad we could get together". John Cameron Swayze
signs off his Camel News Caravan.*

Mark Goodson, of the production
team which makes up
Goodson-Todman Productions.

Bill Todman, co-owner and co-producer
of the many Goodson-Todman shows,
one of which is What's My Line?

James J. Kriegemann

What's My Line? panelists.

Dorothy Kilgallen

Victor Borge

Steve Allen

Arlene Francis

MR. DALY

John Daly, Moderator of What's My Line?

Right: Lawrence Spivak, creator and producer of Meet The Press.

Below: Governor Herman Talmadge of Georgia "meets the press".

MEET THE PRESS WITH
GOVERNOR HERMAN TALMADGE
JUNE 6TH, 1954

Reni Photos

Arlene Francis, Emcee
of The Home Show.

Below: The Home Show — "Growery" in upper
left corner, cooking area upper right.
TV monitors far right, center turn
tables, camera men, models, floor
manager, and Arlene Francis.

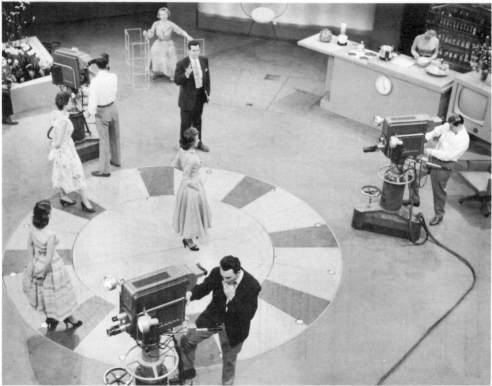

Crew and cast all set for an "on-the-air" signal. Note "mike boom".

*Eve Hunter, Fashion Editor of The Home Show, and
Hugh Downs, Man-About-Home, with children of
Home's staff during a tot's fashion show.*

BRACK

Nebo.

(*A faint flickering from a fire below grows and is reflected on Brack's face. He takes a step forward.*)

The wagon train. Great Jumpin' Jehosophat—lookit it burn!

He grips his rifle and starts moving.

Dissolve to:

The cabin. Mace and Jeb are now completely absorbed in the book and at the moment are laughing uproariously at a picture.

MACE

Say—this Shakespeare feller don't seem tuh be quite so holy as that greenhorn who give him to me.

JEB (*grabbing the book with a great guffaw*)

Haw! Here's a crazy blood got nothin' else t'do but be talking to a skull in his hand. Mebbe he's mad 'cause there's no hair on its head to raise. (*turns page, eagerly*)

'N look—here's one for you, Mace. Yes, sir, this one's for you. Feller got a girl over his knee, spankin' away at where she sits. Purty girl, too.

MACE (*grabbing at book*)

Let's see.

JEB

Careful, ya danged idjit! Yuh wanta ruin it?

MACE

Yeah, she's purty all right. Not many like that in St. Louis.

JEB

Looks like the feller's mad, Mace.

What yuh s'pose he's mad about?

MACE

I wisht I knew. She don't look mad.

JEB (*surrendering to the book, wistfully*)

Shore wish somebody around here cud read. Bet that Shakespeare knows whether she's mad or not.

(*A long peculiar whistling is heard from outside. The two men spring to alertness. The whistling is repeated in a moment, with a slight variation*)

That's Brack.

(*Jeb turns the lamp down and up again in a signal. Brack enters. He is carrying something over his shoulder, rolled in a blanket. He stands there silently*)

Somethin's happened all right. What is it, Brack?

(*Brack merely jerks his head toward the open door*)

(*Jeb springs to the door, peering out. Intensely, to Mace:*)

Fire. Up in the pass.

(*to Brack, almost accusingly:*)

That's Injun work, and you know it.

BRACK (*nods affirmation, placidly*)

Big war-party, under Nebo. Caught the wagon train in the pass. She burnt like a long snake.

MACE

(*pityingly*)

Why don't them greenhorns stay home?

JEB (*snatching up his rifle*)

Come on, Mace. Let's go have a look-see.

(*Mace grabs up his rifle. Brack leisurely unloads the burden from his shoulder, lowering it to the floor as he speaks*)

BRACK

Save your powder. Ain't a soul of 'em left alive.

(*In one moment, he spills out the blanket's burden on the floor. It is a boy, about 10 years old. His face is ashen, his eyes large pits filled with unfathomable horror and shock. He seems stupefied by the experience he's been through*)

BRACK

Less'n you count this.

JEB (*softly*)

Great Guns on the Mountain!

(*to Mace, wonderingly*)

It's a whelp!

MACE (*in soft amazement*)

It's a sure-enough young'un.

(*to Brack*)

Where'd you find him?

BRACK

Rolled up like this 'longside the trail. Musta bin flung off a wagon when the Paiutes hit.

MACE

That it, boy? Yuh Maw and Paw throw yuh off 'fore the Injuns got 'em? (*In rough kindness he reaches out hand toward the boy's shoulder. Swiftly, the boy strikes at him and jerks back. Mace recoils in amazement as Jeb roars with laughter*)

JEB

Nigh got yuh, Mace! Acts like a Injun hisself, don't he?

(*to the boy*)

What's the matter, boy? You skeert of us?

BRACK (*in admiration*)

Not skeert o' nothin', that one. When I laid hold o' him, he scratched at me like a panther.

(*Rubs his thigh, ruefully*)

Kicks, too.

JEB (*delighted*)

Good for him! Looks like we ketched ourselfs a wolf-cub.

(*Scratches his head*)

Only, what'll we do with him?

MACE (*likewise puzzled*)

Seems like at least we ought to be more hospitable.

(*An inspiration seizes Mace. He crosses to a shelf and returns with the jug which he warily offers the boy*)

JEB (*striking it away, angrily*)

Naw, you danged fool! He's too young for whiskey.

(*doubtfully*)

Leastways, I *think* so.

(*to the boy*)

You hungry, boy?

BOY

Yes, sir.

JEB (*a roar of triumph*)

Well, now, you *can* wag your tongue! Mace!

MACE (*testily, already on his way to the kettle*)

I reckarnize it when I hear man talk.

JEB (*beaming, he regards the boy*)

You're right, Brack. He sure ain't skeert o' nothin'.

(*to the boy*)

Now that yore maw and paw's dead, yuh got any kinfolk livin'?

BRACK

Shut yore face, Jeb!

JEB

What's the matter? All I'm askin' him is—

MACE (*returning with food on plate*)

He jes' don't want tuh talk about it, that's all.

(*hands the plate to the boy*)

Try that on yore teeth, boy. Antelope meat.

(*The boy falls to, hungrily, but keeps his eyes on the men*)

JEB

Look at 'im pack it away! Does a man good to see.

(*happily, as the men grin at each other*)

What's yore name, boy?

BOY (*mouth full of food*)

Elisha.

JEB (*in dismay*)

What?

BOY

Elisha, sir.

JEB (*roaring*)

Stop sirring me! Us Long Knives don't sir nobody!

(*He arises indignantly, pacing a few steps*)

Kin y'feature loadin' a name like that onto a pore defenseless young'un?

(*loudly, to the boy*)

Do you know what would happen to you around here if you was a growed man with a name like that?

BOY

No, sir.

JEB (*lamely*)

Well—wouldn't be nothin' good.

(*sitting on table, looking down at boy as he eats*)

We can't have nobody 'round here named "Elisha." Goin' tuh change it, boy. Goin' tuh give yuh a new handle. Goin' tuh give yuh a real mountain name like—like—

MACE

How 'bout callin' him "Boone"?

JEB

Like Boone!

MACE

Ain't no better name than *that*.

JEB

Right! From here on in, boy, yore name is Boone.

BOY

Yes, sir.

JEB (*magnanimously*)

Go on eatin', Boone.

(*The boy does so. Jeb is absently turning the pages of the volume of Shakespeare which lies beneath his hand. An idea lights his face. He looks at the boy, then to Mace. Mace has caught on. His face too, lights up and he nods, imperceptibly, at Jeb. Brack is merely puzzled by the interplay. Jeb, casually, leafs through the book, then speaks:*)

JEB

Wouldn't do no harm to find out somethin' 'bout yore eddication, Boone. Now, for instance, do you know how to read?

BOONE (*surprised*)

Yes, sir.

MACE (*keenly*)

Writin' or printin'?

BOONE

Both kinds.

(*with scorn*)

*Any*body knows how to read.

JEB

Natcherly. Jes' makin' sure.

(*He hands the volume, open at random, to the boy*)

But jes' tuh find out fer sartin, read me somethin' out of this.

(*The boy puts down his plate and takes the book. He throws a puzzled glance at Jeb, then turns the book right side up reading*)

"I will not yield
    To kiss the ground before young Malcolm's feet,
    And to be baited with the rabble's curse . . ."

MACE (*joyfully*)

By Jingo! He's readin' it!

JEB (*a joyful roar*)

Follerin' like a hunter on the trail! Mace—give this whelp some more meat!

(*Mace snatches the boy's plate and hurries to refill it. Jeb picks the boy up, drags a stool to the table, seats him at it*)

Set right down, Boone. Yuh comfterble?

(*He snatches the lamp and moves it to a better position. Mace hurries back with the refilled plate and sets it before Boone. Then he, too, seats himself at the table. Brack watches in bewilderment*)

Go on.

BOONE (*chewing as he reads*)

"Yet I will try the last. Before my body

"I throw my warlike shield. Lay on, Macduff . . ."

JEB

That the beginning?

BOONE

No, sir.

(*he looks*)

Almost the end.

JEB (*feverishly, stabbing at the pages with a huge forefinger*)

Back to the beginning, Boone. We want the whole thing—lynchin's, scalpin's, blood, *everythin'*. Don't yuh skip a word!

BOONE (*complying, turning the pages, then reading:*)

It starts like this. "Thunder and lightning. Enter three witches. The first witch speaks.

    "When shall we three meet again,
        In thunder, lightning, or in rain?
(*Brack, who has picked up his rifle and is polishing it, approaches the table amazed*)

    "When the hurly-burly's done,
        When the battle's lost and won."

BRACK

Everybody here gone crazy?

JEB AND MACE

Sssssh!

(*Brack, laying his rifle across the table and continuing the polishing, eases himself down on a stool, listening*)

BOONE (*reading*)

    "Fair is foul and foul is fair,
        Hover through the fog and filthy air."

(*slowly Brack's polishing motion comes to a halt*)

    "What bloody man is that?"

BRACK (*in amazement, pointing*)

What trail's he follering?

JEB (*roaring*)

Shakespeare, you danged idjit! Anybody'd know *that*!

(*Gestures imperiously to Boone to go on*)

BOONE (*reading:*)

". . . He can report,
    As seemeth by his plight, of the revolt
    The newest state . . ."

(*The three men are completely rapt, as we fade to black*)

ACT II

Early morning, several days later. Brilliant sunshine against exterior doorway and front walls of cabin. From nearby can be heard Mace's happy carolling to the accompaniment of splashing water as he goes about his morning ablutions.

MACE (*singing*)

    Oh whiskey, rye whiskey,
    I know you of old;
    You rob my poor pockets
    Of silver and gold.

(*He appears, about to enter cabin, then stops in doorway to shout at the other two men who are off camera*)

And come St. Louis, I figger I'll be robbed o' plenty!

(*Starts putting on his shirt as he sings*)

    Oh whiskey, rye, whiskey,
    How do I love thee;
    You killed my poor pappy,
    Now, durn you, try me.

(*Mace has entered the cabin. Jeb pops into view. He leans into the doorway to shout after Mace*)

JEB

Stop it, yuh bellerin' idjit! Boone's still sleepin'.

MACE

Not no more he ain't! And I kin prove it to yuh.

(*He appears in the doorway with the sleepy Boone in tow. Boone rubs his eyes as Mace drops a hand on his shoulder*)

Here he is, hisself. And rarin' tuh help us with our huntin'. Ain't that right, ol' hoss?

JEB

Let's get ready, Boone.

MACE

Hold on, there! You took him along yesterday. My turn today.

(*A bird's whistle sounds clear and cheerful on the morning air. Boone lifts his head alertly*)

BOONE

What kind of bird is that?

MACE

That's plain ol' curlew.

(*He whistles the same notes*)

BOONE (*intrigued*)

Can I learn to do that?

MACE

Nothin' to it, ol' hoss. Jeb kin do it better than me. Show him, Jeb.

JEB (*pleased, but embarrassed*)

Aw, I ain't so good. Brack, now—he's got Injun blood. He kin do it better than the bird hisself kin.

(*The curlew's whistle sounds again. Jeb looks about*)

In fack—that *is* Brack.

BOONE (*calling to Brack who is off camera*)

Good morning, Brack.

BRACK (*off camera, responds with curlew's whistle—then, coming into group:*)

Mornin', Boone. Sleep all right?

BOONE (*looking up at him with a trace of the old terror in his eyes*)

Brack—are you really an Injun?

BRACK (*a little uncomfortably*)

Half-Injun, boy.

(*smiling*)

Bird-whistlin' half, I reckon.

BOONE

Do it again.

MACE (*to Boone*)

We best be amblin', I'm thinkin'. Them beaver ain't gonna trap theirselves.

(*With Boone, he disappears into the interior of the cabin*)

JEB (*detaining Brack at the door: quietly*)

Any sign, yet?

BRACK

Nary sign. It's quiet—too quiet, I'm thinkin'. Yuh kin never tell about ol' Nebo. May know about the kid— may not.

(*Interior of the cabin. Boone is standing on the table as Mace holds a jacket against him for size*)

MACE (*doubtfully*)

Hmm. Leetle big, mebbe. Have tuh chop it down some.

(*Jeb and Brack enter the scene*)

JEB

D'yuh want tuh drownd him in that?

(*to the boy*)

Don't yuh fret, Boone. Brack, here, he'll make you some new duds. Get rid o' them greenhorn trappin's.

MACE

Leave 'im alone! He's gonna grow right into this here, ain't you, boy?

BOONE (*in his sober way*)

I'll try.

JEB (*grinning with pleasure*)

Beginnin' to look like a mountain man already, ain't he? Think you can hold a rifle today, Boone?

BOONE

I don't know, sir. I'll try.

JEB (*angrily*)

Them greenhorns don't teach a man nothin' useful, do they?

(*snatching up his rifle, which is nearly six feet long and weighs 30 pounds, he holds it in position for Boone*)

Here. P'int this out through the door and aim steady. This time—keep both eyes open.

(*Boone attempts to comply. Jeb takes his hands away and the weight of the rifle knocks Boone flat. Mace grabs the gun and Brack catches Boone as he falls off the end of the table*)

MACE (*angrily*)

Yuh blinkin' fool!

JEB (*ashamedly*)

He don't larn very fast, do he?

BRACK (*setting Boone on the edge of the table*)

Ain't big enough for a rifle-gun. Now, here's the weepon fer him, I'm thinkin'.

(*He unstraps his belt with knife and sheath and buckles it around Boone's*) middle. *As he is doing so:*)

JEB (*scratching his head*)

Mebbe the whelp's just wore out. We bin haulin' him around a lot the last few days. Think it'd be safe tuh leave 'im here alone while we're out huntin'?

BRACK

With Nebo still on the warpath?

(*buckling the belt, as Boone stiffens at Jeb's words:*)

Hold still, boy.

MACE

'Course he's a nuisance tuh have underfoot, but I don't mind takin' 'im—

JEB

Jes' what I was thinkin'. He kin come along with me and—

BRACK

Today he learns how to ride. *I* teach him.

JEB AND MACE (*heatedly*)

Hold on there! . . . Now, jes' a minute!

(*But Brack, who is facing the doorway, lifts his head alertly*)

BRACK

Sh-h-h!

(*In the silence a wagon and team can be heard coming to a sudden stop. A flurry of activity in the cabin. Mace and Jeb dive for their guns. Brack only has time to sweep Boone off the table and conceal him behind him, holding him in place with a firm hand. They are frozen in these positions when there is a knocking at the door*)

JEB (*startled at the unexpected sound*)

What tha—!

(*Another knock. The men stare, guns in hand*)

(*Then the door opens and there appear the Reverend Peabody and his wife. They are exhausted and under great strain*)

MR. P. (*looking about, dazed*)

They're dead. Every one of them.

(*no response from the men*)

The wagon train. There's been a massacre.

JEB

Who are you?

MR. PEABODY (*stammering, taken aback*)

My name is Peabody. Jonathan J. Peabody. I am a missionary. My wife and I—

JEB (*sharply*)

You with that train?

MR. PEABODY

We *were* with them but we'd fallen several days behind. You see, we stopped at Fort Bent to—

(*he halts, looking at the hostile faces*)

Gentlemen—we need help.

JEB

No help here. Fer mis'able greenhorns, anyway.

MR. P.

I—I don't understand. You—you're what they call Long Knives, aren't you?

JEB

That's right. Mountain men. What about it?

MR. P.

We're strangers in your country. We appeal to your generosity and—

JEB (*wonderingly, to Mace*)
We done tol' him no help here, didn't we? Reckon you kin figure out what this poordevil white is makin' more talk about?

MACE
Talks like a hoss that's got his back p'intin' somewhere else than his feet.

JEB
Knocks at the door 'fore he comes in. Real perlite.

MACE
Reckon it's clear which side o' sun-up *he* got lost from.

JEB
Mace, wouldn't you think a critter like this woulda had sense enough tuh stay home?
(*walks around the paralyzed Mr. P., inspecting him*)
Know somethin', Mace? He don't even carry a gun!

MACE (*lifts flap of Mr. P.'s jacket*)
That's right! Nor a knife. Why, he's mother-nekkid as the day he was whelped!

JEB
'N it don't look like he ever had 'em. Mace—he must be fixin' tuh lose his hair.
(*to Peabody*)
You fixin' to lose your hair? Or don't they tell yuh about Injuns back East?

MRS. P. (*breaking in furiously*)
You're savages! Nothing but savages!

MR. P.
Don't antagonize them, Martha.

JEB
Savages, are we? We ain't savaged you yet, did we?

MRS. PEABODY (*pointing at their rifles*)
There are other ways to talk with people than with guns.

JEB
Not around here, there ain't. Yore in Injun country now, ma'am. You aimin' tuh handle Injuns with *words*?

MRS. PEABODY
We intend to civilize them.

JEB (*in astonishment*)
Civilize the Injuns? You gonna civilize ol' Nebo?
(*He roars helplessly with laughter. Mace joins him*)

MR. PEABODY (*desperately*)
You don't seem to understand. We found the wagon train, and all the men—and women—and children dead. There has been a massacre!

JEB
Massacre? That's a matter of opinion, ain't it, preacher? I calls it a battle.

MRS. PEABODY (*her eyes flashing*)
Battle! Our poor people never wanted a battle. They weren't prepared for a battle.

JEB
No, ma'am. They was out-thought and they was out-fought.
(*hardening his tone*)
Of all the people who didn't invite yuh here, ma'am, most of all it warn't the Injuns. When yuh push in where yuh ain't wanted, yuh take yore chances. So why don't yuh hightail it back East while the hightailin's good?

MRS. PEABODY
We are going to California.

MACE
That's a real long way, ma'am. We bin there. It's a long way even fer birds.

JEB
Hold on a minute!
(*narrowly*)
How'd you git back down here 'thout bein' seen?

MR. P. (*as Mrs. P. is about to flare out again*)
Martha! *Please,* dear.
(*he turns to Jeb*)
Why, we hid last night and drove down this morning.

JEB
You done *what?* You drove down here by *daylight?*
(*furiously*)
Yore even worse fools than I give yuh credit fer!

MRS. P. (*scornfully*)
You're afraid. You're just afraid for your own precious skins.
(*she advances on Jeb, head up*)
Heathens. That's what you are. Heartless, cowardly heathens. There's neither love nor mercy in you. You're like this whole cruel country, except possibly you are worse. The Indians may be forgiven, for they know not what they do, but *you!* What is *your* excuse!

JEB
Yes, ma'am. And now mebbe you'd best be gittin' while you can still git. If I know ol' Nebo, you ain't got any too much time.

MR. PEABODY (*there's dignity and courage in him*)

Come, Martha. We have fallen among Philistines.

JEB
Philistines—!

MRS. PEABODY
And worse. All right, Mr. Long Knife. We'll be going now. And I hope that your own consciences will—
(*She stops short as Boone, hidden behind Brack, makes a sudden movement which catches her eye. Sharply*)
Who is that?
(*Before any of the men can prevent her, she darts across and pulls Boone into view*)
Why, it's—it's Susan Anderson's little boy!
(*Boone pulls away*)
You're Elisha Anderson!

MACE (*sharply*)
We call him Boone, ma'am.

MRS. P. (*just as sharply*)
His name is Elisha. All alone in the world now.
(*She tries to embrace him*)
Oh, you poor orphan.

JEB (*a roar, as Boone escapes her grasp*)
Don't you poor orphan him! He don't need no sympathy. He's tougher'n a rawhide strap, he is, and right now he's in plenty good hands!

MRS. P. (*with withering contempt*)
Good hands!
(*She looks the men over. The look is a scorcher.*)
He *will* be, you mean.
(*She takes Boone by the hand*)
Come, Elisha.

JEB (*stepping forward menacingly*)
What d'ya mean, "Come, Elisha"?
He ain't goin' nowheres—cep'n with
us.

MRS. P. (*not flinching in the least*)
I have my duty.

JEB
Your duty don't buy no goods in this
country. Boone's stayin' right here.

MR. P. (*who is near the door*)
Gentlemen, my wife speaks wisely. I
don't believe you have the right to—

JEB (*turning on him*)
Right! I'll show you who's—
(*he stops abruptly as a shadow falls
across the doorway*)
Ssst! Brack!
(*Like a flash, Brack understands,
seizes Boone and rolls him into one
of the bunks, hastily flinging blankets
over him. Then he swings upright and
lounges, easily*)

MR. P.
I don't understand. Is something—?

JEB (*quietly*)
Jes' stand easy. Don't do any talkin'
and don't make any sudden moves.
(*His eyes are focused on the doorway, waiting. All other eyes follow
his. There is an Indian standing
there. It is Chief Nebo, old, wrinkled,
but carrying calm authority. He is
unarmed, but behind him appear two
Paiute warriors carrying rifles. They
remain just beyond the door, relaxed,
but watchful. After a long moment
of tension, Nebo advances into the
room, his eyes missing nothing. Then
he raises both hands, palms turned
up, in the peace sign, to show he*
carries no weapons. With something
like an audible whoosh of relief, Jeb
responds by raising his left arm, palm
down, and gliding his right hand
down it from elbow to fingertips*)

NEBO (*he speaks only in Paiute*)
Tam-my ash-en-ty pesuds em inl-nel-
kah nah-eo-queay.

JEB
Brack.
(*Brack moves forward. Mace casu-
ally moves to where he covers the
bunk*)
What does he say?

BRACK
He wants to know why the Long
Knives have turned their faces agin'
him.

JEB
Tell him we ain't.

BRACK
Katz-i-a-no tam-my nah-no-nah!

NEBO
Tam-my ipeds me-poodge qweo-
gand.

BRACK
Then why are we shelterin' his ene-
mies?
(*Pointing to the Peabodys*)
He means them.

JEB
Tell him we ain't.

MR. P.
Martha.
(*She comes to him and they stand
together defiantly, but in fear*)

NEBO
Wino-att tam-my mah-no-na poon-e-
kee t-shuker at-tambar o-wish.

BRACK
Says in that case there ain't agoin' to be no trouble and he'll jus' be takin' them along.

JEB
Tell 'im there ain't goin' t' be no trouble and he's more'n welcome to 'em. (*He starts turning away*)

MRS. P. (*flying at him like a fury*)
You—you coward, you! You mean you're going to send us to a horrible death without lifting a finger? What kind of men are you, anyway?

JEB (*as angrily*)
The kind o' men, ma'am, that respects the Injuns' rights and don't cross their land withouten they say all right. Which is more than you folks done.

MRS. P.
He's a murderer!

JEB
I told you he don't consider hisself no murderer! That wagon train he put under has now got the name of a battle—not a murder. And be careful what yuh say to 'im—even in English.
(*pointing to the stack of pelts in the corner*)
Y'see that stack o' beaver plews? Well, we got more'n half o' them from ol' Nebo, here. Traded fair and square, and he didn't cheat us none, either. We've studied how to git along with him and no greenhorns is goin' to spile it now!

MR. P. (*quietly*)
There are times when a man has no choice but to abandon the ways of peace. If one of you gentlemen will hand me a rifle—

JEB (*stares unbelievingly*)
Yuh mean your goin' to *shoot* at him? At ol' Nebo?
(*a great guffaw*)
Preacher man, you must be real tired o' livin'!

MR. P.
But he's going to kill us anyway!

JEB (*angrily*)
How do you know he is?

MRS. P.
Isn't he?

JEB (*shrugging*)
I dunno. Mebbe he is. Brack—ask him, would yuh?

BRACK
Pa-in sha-unts oo-wo-on-e ipeds?

NEBO (*looking the Peabodys over like a horse trader—with a wicked glint of humor*)
Shab-no-ach or one-e nar-ri-ent mo-ap. Tammy-naw inch katz-ne-ate T-shuker-boin.

BRACK
Haw!

MR. P.
Well?

BRACK
Says he's goin' t'hold yuh fer ransom. Says yuh look like important people to him even if the white squaw talks too much.

MRS. P.
But—nobody will ransom us!
(*Brack shrugs indifferently*)
You mean you're just going to hand us over to these bloodthirsty savages? To be slaves in an Indian village?

MACE (*coming forward*)

You was comin' out this way tuh civilize the Injun, wasn't yuh?

(*a wave of the hand*)

Wall, there he is. Go right to it, ma'am.

MRS. P. (*her eyes, narrow, thoughtfully*)

All right. We will.

(*Before any of the men can discern her purpose or stop her, she darts to the now-unguarded bunk and snatches the blanket off Boone*)

But Elisha comes with us!

(*In dismay the men start toward her but they stop short at Nebo's voice*)

NEBO (*barking angrily*)

Tam-my mah-no-nah in-mel-ka!

JEB (*a look for Mrs. P. who stands triumphantly over Boone*)

Ain't no need to translate *that*.

(*to Mrs. Peabody, in sad accusation*)

Misery shore must love company— tuh take a innocent little fella along with it.

MRS. P.

Better for him to come with us than to stay among men who trade for people!

JEB

So that's how it's goin' tuh be, huh?

MR. P.

Mrs. Peabody is perfectly right. The boy will be better off in the hands of savages who *don't* know better than with savages who *do!*

MRS. PEABODY (*she has Boone by the hand*)

Let us go, Elisha.

(*She drags the unwilling Boone for-ward. There is panic in his eyes as he stares at the Indians*)

MACE

Jeb!

JEB

Hold on, thar!

(*Mrs. P. stops . . . to Brack—in angry frustration*)

Ask him what he wants fer the whole passel of 'em.

MRS. P.

I will not be bought or sold!

JEB (*a roar*)

It ain't no longer up to you! Jes' keep shut o' this! Ask him, Brack.

BRACK

Mah-ba no-quint, ipeds tsai inch tso.

NEBO (*Does not answer for a moment. His eyes rove around the cabin, then halt on the stack of beaver pelts in the corner. A gleam of humor lights his face and is reflected by anticipatory dismay in the men's. Pointing*):

Ker-mush to-buck ko-mong co-quets.

BRACK

He'll take beaver pelts, he says.

JEB (*apprehensively*)

How many?

BRACK

The whole kit'n kaboodle.

JEB (*an outraged roar*)

All of 'em?

MRS. P. (*equally outraged*)

Do you mean that he considers us worth no more than a bunch of smelly animal hides?

JEB

Ma'am, you are most cantankerous, crotchety, hard-to-git-along-with female I have *ever* met!

(*in a bellow*)

That there stack o' plews is nigh onto one whole year's trappin' and tradin'. Tradin' with that self-same Injun standin' before you!

MACE

And don't he know it, though! Look at him.

(*Nebo's face is split in a wide grin of enjoyment. He shrugs, deprecatingly*)

JEB

All right.

(*to the Peabodys*)

But, mind you, it ain't being done for you—

(*bitterly*)

—why, great balls o' fire, the two of you ain't wuth one o' them pelts in the wust market there ever was.

(*With a bitter gesture he indicates to Nebo that the pelts are his. Nebo waves to his two warriors who enter and carry off the entire stack. The men watch them sadly. Then Nebo, enjoying himself, turns to exit. He pauses at door for a final shot*)

NEBO

Tu-ege-shump em pucki nin-ny ipeds!

(*Exits*)

JEB (*wrathfully*)

Now what was *that*?

BRACK (*sadly*)

He says *that* was the worst tradin' the Long Knives ever done.

JEB (*starting for the door*)

Why, that ol'—

(*And the rest is lost in silent mouthing as he checks himself.
Fade to black*)

A few hours later. Boone is reading to the men who lounge about, relaxed and lost in the story. Nearby sits Mrs. Peabody. She is placidly sewing on Boone's new clothes as she listens.

BOONE (*reading*)

"Methought I heard a voice cry 'Sleep no more!
    Macbeth does murder sleep'—the innocent sleep,
    Sleep that knits up the rav— rav—"

MRS. P.

Ravelled. And speaking of sleep, it's time little boys were in bed.

(*a stir of annoyance from the men*)

BOONE

"—ravelled sleeve of care,
    The death of each day's life, sore labor's bath,
    Balm of great minds, great nature's second course,
    Chief nour-nour—"

MRS. P.

Nourisher. And in respect to nourishment, may I say that I find your cooking utensils filthy and your larder positively disgusting. Why, you've nothing but stale meat and—

JEB (*in tones of thunder*)

Madam—would you be so kind as to shut up?

(*Mrs. P. shrugs, disdainfully*)

You're nigh as bad as this here Lady Macbeth. Talk too much—the pair of yuh!

BOONE (*reading*)

"Still it cried 'Sleep no more!' To all the house:
    'Glamis hath murdered sleep, and therefore Caw—Caw—"

MRS. P.

Cawdor. And I still say it is past his bedtime.

(*Jeb crashes a huge fist on the table*)

BOONE (*reading*)

    'Cawdor shall sleep no more. Macbeth shall sleep no more.' "

MRS. P. (*to Boone, firmly, rising*)

But you *shall*. Come, Elisha. You'll stay with us tonight, out in the wagon.

JEB

His name is Boone—and he's stayin' right here till he's finished with his readin'!

MRS. P. (*sweetly*)

Why don't *you* read for a while, Mr. Jeb? Or you, Mr. Mace? Or you?

JEB

'Cause it's Boone who needs eddication, not us!

MRS. P.

Indeed? And do you think that *that* book is proper education for a child of Elisha's age?

MACE (*flabbergasted*)

What's wrong with it? It was one o' yore kind give it to us.

MRS. P.

Why, it will inflame the child's mind! It's full of blood, and murders, and . . . and highly improper things.

JEB (*cunningly*) What was one o' *you* doin' with it?

MRS. P.

Why—why—

(*Mr. P. enters. He wears partial night clothes*)

Mr. Peabody, would you please explain to these *savages* that Shakespeare is *not* proper reading for a young child?

MR. P.

Why, I don't believe it will do him any harm, Martha.

MACE (*crowing*)

Yuh see?

MRS. P.

Well, I *do*!

(*She snatches the book from Boone and slams it shut*)

And now, young man, it's long past your bedtime.

JEB

Set right where you are, Boone.

(*dangerously, to Mr. P.*)

Jes' when was it yuh said yuh was leavin', Reverend? Tomorrer mornin'?

MR. P.

Why, I didn't, but—

JEB

That's fine.

MACE

Yeah. Get a nice early start thataway.

MRS. P.

Don't argue with them, Jonathan. The sooner we put distance between ourselves and these uncouth specimens the better we'll feel. All three of us.

JEB

It can't be none too soon for—

(*it hits him*)

Jes' a minute! I don't see but *two* of yuh.

MRS. P.

You didn't imagine for a moment that we were going to abandon this poor child?

JEB (*with fine restraint*)

This here child ain't been abandoned, ma'am. Jes' to settle any remainin' doubts, Boone is stayin' right here. But you and him—you ain't.

MRS. P.

After all, you can't . . .

JEB

And in case yore feelin' rambunctious, ma'am, don't fergit that you two is our proppity—bought and paid fer.

MR. P.

We are not chattels!

JEB

We bought yuh fair and square! Paid a heap more'n yuh was wuth, too! But don't let it worry yuh none, folks, 'cause right this minute we're handin' yuh back the deed t'yerselfs. You're free as the wind.

(*in a roar*)

Only git started and go where yuh was goin'!

MRS. P.

Not without the boy.

MACE

Ma'am—what iffen Boone don't *want* ta go with you?

MRS. P.

Why . . . why that's ridiculous. Of *course* he will want to go with us.

(*bitingly*)

After all, Elisha is not an unintelligent boy. He recognizes the differences between—

JEB

Here he sets, Ma'am. Why don't we jest *ask* him?

MRS. P.

What? Ask a child to decide whether—

MACE

Why not, Ma'am? Didn't yuh jes' say how he was a intelligent boy? Well—why don't we jes' find out how intelligent he is?

MRS. P.

All right. I'm sure Elisha will see the advantages which we—

JEB

That's enough, Ma'am. We don't need no speechifyin'. Boone'll make up his own mind without it.

(*to the boy, gently*)

How 'bout it, Boone? D'yuh want tuh go with the Reverend and his wife, or do yuh want tuh stay with us?

(*Boone is silent, his sober eyes on Jeb's face*)

Take yer time, boy. Ain't nobody pressurin' yuh.

(*Boone is still silent, searching their faces*)

MRS. P. (*nervously, stridently*)

For heaven's sakes, Elisha, say something!

BOONE (*in a burst, to the men*)

Don't send me away! I don't want to go!

(*There is an answering roar of triumph from the men. Jeb scoops Boone off his stool and swings him high on his shoulder as Mace and Brack crowd in to shake hands with him. When ad libs die down:*)

JEB

That good enough for yuh, Reverend?

MACE

Are yuh satisfied, ma'am?

MRS. P. (*tightlipped, furious*)

No. I am not satisfied.

JEB (*confidently*)

Well, that won't stop yer from hitchin' up in the mornin' and bein' on yore way, now, will it?

MRS. P.

I'm afraid it will, indeed. I don't know what sort of pressure you have exerted on the child, but it won't matter. We are not budging from this place until Elisha changes his mind.

(*Fade to black*)

ACT III

Early morning of the following day. The yard in front of the cabin and the doorway-wall of the cabin itself. Boone is being taught to knife-fight, his opponent, Brack. The "knives" are sticks of wood. The scene is lively with yips and yells of encouragement and caution as Mace and Jeb coach from the sidelines.

JEB

Circle 'im, Boone, keep circlin'! *Away from his knife!*

MACE (*excitedly, jumping about*)

Don't get pulled in, Boone! Wait 'im out! Make 'im come to yuh!

JEB

Make 'im swing, then come in low!

(*Mrs. Peabody appears in the cabin door, a plate in her hand. She stands, horror-struck by the proceedings*)

Watch 'im . . . watch 'im . . . *now!*

(*Boone moves swiftly. Bullseye. Right under Brack's left ribs*)

BRACK (*this one isn't feigned*)

Yow-w-w!

(*There is an echoing shriek from Mrs. Peabody which genuinely startles all four, particularly since the plate, which she has dropped, shatters*)

JEB (*regaining some composure*)

Whatever on airth ails yuh, ma'am?

MRS. PEABODY (*faintly*)

Is he . . . is he hurt badly?

MACE (*confused*)

Who? Brack?

(*He bursts into laughter.*)

BRACK (*morosely, rubbing his side*)

Shet up yer guffawin'! Kid like to dug a hole clean through me.

BOONE (*anxiously*)

Did I really hurt you, Brack?

BRACK

Looks like yuh didn't put me under that time.

(*tousling his hair*)

But I'm real glad that wasn't a sure-'nough knife.

JEB (*admiringly*)

Ain't he a borned killer, though!

(*They turn toward the cabin door and are frozen in their tracks by the storm-clouds on Mrs. Peabody's face*)

MRS. PEABODY

And you consider yourselves fit guardians for a young boy!

MACE

Why, what's the trouble? We was only—

MRS. PEABODY

I saw what you were doing! Making a ruffian out of a well-brought-up child. Teaching him to fight like an animal!

MACE (*genuinely puzzled*)

Beggin' yore pardon, ma'am, but 'round these parts a man don't *live* long less'n he fights.

MRS. PEABODY (*withering them*)

A gentleman does not fight.

MACE

Are you sayin' I ain't no gentleman?

MRS. PEABODY

Exactly.

(*turning away*)

Breakfast is ready.

(*She exits into the cabin. In a moment the men follow. Inside the cabin Mrs. Peabody moves about serving breakfast as the men seat themselves at the table*)

BRACK (*picking up a chinaware plate*)

Great snakes! Lookit the fancy platters.

MRS. PEABODY

You will please be careful with those.

(*as she serves*)

I didn't bring them all the way from New Hampshire to have them smashed by clumsy fingers *here*.

JEB (*grinning*)

No, ma'am. We didn't figger you did.

MRS. PEABODY (*dishing up; disgustedly*)

Antelope meat! For breakfast. Don't you eat anything but *meat?*

BRACK (*puzzled*)

Whut else is there?

(*Mr. Peabody enters*)

MR. PEABODY (*cheerfully*)

Good morning, everybody! It's a simply glorious day.

JEB

Like any other day 'round here.

MR. PEABODY

Then the good Lord has favored you.

(*seating himself*)

I've been up and down the trail some distance. All seems clear.

JEB (*sarcastically*)

Didja think the Injuns'd be campin' on it? Ol' Nebo's a man of his word.

(*Mr. Peabody has bent his head to say grace, but the men are already wolfing their food*)

MR. PEABODY

If you don't mind waiting a moment.

JEB

Fer what?

MR. PEABODY (*gently*)

I should like to say grace.

(*He bends his head and murmurs the prayer. Only Mrs. Peabody and Boone follow suit. The men look at each other, then, uneasily, at Boone, but are too discomfited to imitate him. They resume eating, tearing at their meat. Jeb looks up to find Mrs. Peabody frowning at the way he's eating. He throws his meat back onto the plate and stands up*)

JEB (*flaring up*)

Whyn't you bring yore noses down out o' the air and hightail it outa here?

MRS. PEABODY

Gladly! Elisha!

(*Boone doesn't answer*)

Elisha! I'm speaking to you. Have you forgotten your manners already?

BOONE (*in a low voice*)

My name is Boone, ma'am.

JEB

Now are yuh convinced?

MRS. PEABODY (*furiously*)
I'm only convinced that—
MR. PEABODY
Just a moment, my dear. *I* should like to talk to the gentlemen.
MRS. PEABODY (*flustered*)
Well. It looks as though *no* one is going to eat much. I'll just clear away.
JEB
Jest a minute, ma'am.
(*picks up huge chunk of meat*)
Wouldn't want to put yuh to all that trouble.
MR. PEABODY (*to Boone*)
Child, perhaps you'd like to finish your breakfast outside in the sun.
(*Boone looks questioningly at Jeb*)
JEB
Go ahead, ol' hoss. Won't be but a shake.
(*as Boone takes his plate and exits*)
Maybe we kin have some more readin' then. I keep wonderin' how ol' Macbeth makes out!
(*Jeb turns back to Mr. Peabody, grimly*)
All right, preacher man. Say yore say.
MR. PEABODY
The boy is not old enough to know what is best for him.
JEB
If he'd thrown in with you, would yer *still* be of that mind?
MR. PEABODY
He needs education, which you cannot give him. He needs religious instruction, for which you are not—uh —fully qualified.
JEB (*grimly*)
He needs to learn how to shoot a

rifle. He needs to learn how to use a knife. And set traps for beaver.
MR. PEABODY
Trapping beaver is not the highest aim in living.
JEB (*drily*)
I don' know how you can low-rate it so, preacher man, considerin' that a stack o' beaver-skins jest saved *your* hide.
MR. PEABODY (*embarrassed*)
I'm sorry. I didn't mean to belittle your activities. And I am not ungrateful.
(*earnestly, leaning across the table*)
But I must keep appealing to your reason. Elisha's people intended him for a larger way of life than you can give him. That's why they were going West.
JEB
Thought you jest *left* the 'larger way o' life' yore talkin' about.
MR. PEABODY
But there will be *new* cities. New ways to serve God—and man. New—
JEB (*suddenly angry*)
That's enough. Yore jest runnin' in circles like a wolf with a crooked leg.
MR. PEABODY (*simply*)
Elisha needs parents.
JEB
He's got parents—three of 'em!
MRS. PEABODY (*ironically*)
Which one of you is his mother?
JEB (*furiously*)
All of us, ma'am!
(*more quietly*)
Boone don't need what yore talkin' about. And I reckon anything else

you kin do fer him, we kin do better.

MR. PEABODY (*at a loss*)

I know you are wrong. Perhaps I haven't found the right argument. What *is* the thing that will convince you? What is—

(*He sees Boone standing in the doorway. Acknowledging defeat:*)

It's all right, Elisha. You may come in now.

JEB

Sure—come on in, ol' hoss, and let's get on with the readin'!

MACE (*as they shift positions*)

Can't hardly wait tuh find out whether Macbeth kin put ol' Macduff under!

BRACK

I'm layin' *my* money on Macduff. He's shore 'nough whupped everybody so far!

(*Boone, at the table, is opening the book*)

MR. PEABODY

I'll get things stowed away, Martha. There's no use in delaying longer. You'll be ready?

MRS. PEABODY (*thoughtfully*)

I think I'll just finish sewing up this jacket for Elisha.

(*with an edge*)

That is, *if* the gentlemen don't mind?

JEB (*magnanimously*)

Help yourself, ma'am. Only I wouldn't lose too much daylight gettin' rollin'.

MRS. PEABODY (*to the Reverend*)

I'll only be a few minutes.

(*Mr. Peabody exits. Mrs. Peabody gets the buckskin jacket, seats herself, and begins working on it. The men continue eating as they listen to Boone*)

BOONE (*reading*)

"Another part of the field. Enter
    Macbeth.

Why should I play the Roman
    fool and die

    On mine own sword? whilers I
        see lives, the gashes

Do better upon them."

MACE (*enthusiastically*)

Ain't he jest right, though!

BOONE

"Enter Macduff."

BRACK

I tole yuh so! Watch *that* Injun raise hair!

BOONE

"Turn, hell-hound, turn!"

JEB

Now ain't *that* langwidge!

(*sighs happily*)

That Shakespeare beats a Comanche medicine-man fer layin' it on grand an' solemn, don't he?

BOONE

"Macbeth: of all men else I have
    avoided thee:

    But get thee back; my soul is too
        much charged

With blood of thine already"

(*Mrs. Peabody, as she sews, has begun to hum something; very softly at first, then more assertively. As Boone reads he becomes conscious of her humming, and his attention to the reading begins to falter*)

BOONE

"Macduff: I have no words:

    My voice is in my sword, thou
        bloodier villain

Than terms can give thee out!
They fight."
(*Simultaneously with this, Mrs. Pea-
body is singing the words below. She
is smiling to herself as she sings the
children's song*)
MRS. PEABODY
  "Intra, mintra, cute-ra corn,
    Apple seed and apple-thorn,
    Wire, brier, limber lock,
    Six geese in a flock—"
BOONE (*his attention torn, he falters
more in his reading*)
  "Macbeth: Thou losest labor:
    As easy mayst thou the intrench-
      ant air
    With thy keen sword impress as
      make me bleed:
    Let fall thy blade . . ."
MRS. PEABODY (*lilting her song, smil-
ing to herself*)
  "Sit and sing by the spring,
    O-u-t, out; up on yonder hill
    There sits old Father Wells—"
(*Boone is unable to continue*)
  "He has jewels, he has rings,
    He has many pretty things—"
(*She stops singing now, and talks,
smiling down at her sewing*)
Your mother used to sing that to you.
Do you remember, Elisha?
(*Boone, his eyes closed, is suffering
the pain she evokes. This is a new
Mrs. Peabody—warm, motherly, an
uninsistent softness in her voice*)
How did the next line go? I don't seem
to remember. Was it—Whip-John?
(*Boone, in a small voice begins sing-
ing it. After the first word or two,
Mrs. Peabody joins in*)

BOONE
  "Whip-jack, two-nails, blow the
    bellows out, old man."
MRS. PEABODY (*delightedly*)
That was very nice, Elisha. And do
you remember the next verse?
(*they sing it together*)
MRS. PEABODY AND BOONE
  "Six geese in a flock,
    Seven sit by the spring, O-u-t, out,
    Hang mother's dishcloth out,
    Fling, flang, flash it off!"
MRS. PEABODY (*to the men, who are
aghast at what is happening but
powerless to cope with it*)
Gentlemen, would you believe that
Elisha's mother played the organ in
the church and that Elisha sang in
the choir with all the other big boys?
Oh, he had a beautiful voice . . . yes,
he did . . . and he still has! And one
day when he was being naughty and
was out playing hopscotch when he
should have been in church, why his
mother didn't get angry at all. She
just kept her temper, and she made a
little song on the organ that sounded
like hopscotch. It went something like
this:
(*she hums*)
  Bumpety bump, bumpety bump,
    Bump, bump, bump.
(*Boone's eyes are closed, but his face
begins to contort in grief and he moves
from side to side as though unable to
escape*)
She loved her boy very much, and his
father did, too.
(*Boone gives way suddenly, racked
by his pent-up grief. Sobbing vio-*

lently, he runs to Mrs. Peabody and buries himself in her arms. She rocks him, soothingly)

There, there, child. You go on and cry now. You don't have to keep it to yourself any longer. Let it all come out. Cry, child, cry . . .

(The three men are on their feet, shocked and dismayed beyond words. Mrs. Peabody looks up at them with a warm smile.)

Would one of you gentlemen be so kind as to fetch me a handkerchief?

(FADE TO BLACK)

Fade up on exterior, the rear end of the Peabodys' Conestoga wagon. The Reverend Peabody is finishing stowing articles in the wagon; he raises the tail-gate and drops the link-pin in place. Then he turns toward the cabin, stops short, his face expressing surprise and curiosity. From the doorway of the cabin, one by one, are emerging the three men. Their attitude is hang-dog, ashamed. They avoid looking at one another. They lounge or sag against the cabin wall. Mr. Peabody hurries to them. He examines them worriedly.

MR. PEABODY

Gentlemen—what *is* it?

(For answer, Mace waggles a thumb toward the cabin door. Mr. Peabody turns and hurries into the cabin. There is a silence, then:

MACE *(in soft wonderment)*

Who'd'a thought he had all that sorrow in him?

JEB *(explosively)*

How was *we* s'posed tuh know? We ain't had no truck with young'uns!

BRACK *(almost to himself)*

More like a bird, he was, with broken wings. 'N we thought he was a wolf-cub.

JEB *(more quietly)*

Mebbe he is, at that. Think o' him holdin' all that grief to hisself, never lettin' on to nobody.

(shakes his head, sadly)

It were jest too much fer him.

MACE

Y'know somethin'? Right now *I* don't feel like I'm too much.

(Mr. Peabody emerges from the door and joins the group.)

JEB

Looks like we shoulda known about that boy all the same.

(to Peabody)

Don't you think so, Preacher?

MR. PEABODY

I don't know—it simply isn't given us to know everything.

(reflectively)

For instance, I knew my wife wanted a son—but I never knew how badly until I saw the look on her face just now.

MACE

Yeah—she got to be a right purty woman 'bout ten minutes ago.

JEB

(embarrassedly)

I don't 'magine yuh'd like tuh rest here a spell, would yuh, Rev'rand? The three of yuh?

MR. PEABODY *(gently)*

I'm afraid not, Jeb. We'd best be

pushing on just as soon as they are ready.

JEB (*hopelessly*)

Yeah—best to get back East while the weather holds.

MR. PEABODY

East? But we're going West.

JEB

West? Why, man, you'll never make it!

MACE

The trail's crawlin' with Apaches other side o' the mountains!

BRACK

There's a thousand miles o' desert twixt here and there!

MR. PEABODY (*firmly*)

California's where we started for, and California's where we're going.

(*the scene fades*)

Fade up on the rear of the Peabodys' Conestoga wagon. Mrs. Peabody, arranging things within, leans out as she shouts her instructions.

MRS. PEABODY

Don't forget to bring me my dishes, Jonathan! And be careful you don't drop them.

MR. PEABODY (*off camera*)

I've got them.

MRS. PEABODY (*fussing about*)

All the way from New Hampshire. I will *not* have them broken now.

(*Mr. Peabody enters scene; hands her the dishes which she stows away*)

Where has Elisha gotten to?

JEB (*off camera*)

He's coming, ma'am.

(*He enters, carrying Boone. Mace and Brack are just behind. Jeb swings Boone (who wears his buckskin jacket) into the wagon. To Mr. Peabody:*)

Don't fergit, now, Rev'rand—lay over at Santa Fe. You'll pick up a west-bound train there, fer sure.

MR. PEABODY

Never fear—I'll do just that. Well—that seems to be about it—doesn't it? (*tactfully*)

I'll just get set up front.

(*He exits around wagon*)

BOONE (*shaking hands*)

G'bye, Brack.

BRACK (*taps the knife which hangs at Boone's belt*)

Keep it sharp. An' don't fergit, if yuh git into a fight—circle!

(*Mace suddenly snaps his fingers and dashes back to the cabin*)

BOONE

I'll remember. G'bye, Jeb.

JEB (*shaking hands*)

G'bye, ol' hoss. Keep yore hair on.

BOONE

I will.

(*Mace re-enters, carrying his rifle and powder-horn*)

MACE

Durn near fergot it. Here y'are, whelp. Reckon there'll be good huntin' in Californy.

(*He slides the rifle into the wagon and hangs the powder-horn about Boone's neck*)

BOONE

Thank you, Mace.

MACE
Don't mention it, boy.

MRS. PEABODY
Put the rifle up where it will be safe,
Elisha.

JEB
Mrs. Peabody.

MRS. PEABODY
Yes, Jeb?

JEB
Would yuh do us one big favor? Fer
our sakes and hisn?

MRS. PEABODY
Of course.

JEB (*a bellow*)
Don't call him Elisha!

MRS. PEABODY
All right.
(*calling, up front*)
All right, Jonathan.

(*From off camera is heard Mr. Peabody's "Gee-up!" The departure of
the wagon is mirrored in the men's
faces as they watch it off to the ac-
companying sound of wheels and
hooves*)

The interior of the cabin. It is empty
for a moment, then the men enter one
by one. Mace picks up his guitar, but
after one ineffectual plunk discards
it. Jeb slouches by the table, brood-
ing, and Brack gazes disconsolately
out the window. Suddenly Jeb leaps
to his feet, and with a roar of disgust
kicks the stool across the room.

JEB
Yer mopin' around like a passel o'
grievin' squaws! What've yuh got tuh
be cryin' about?

BRACK (*flatly*)
Plenty.

JEB (*subsiding*)
Yeah. Reckon yer right.

MACE
We got no beaver, which means we
got no St. Louis. We got no boy—'n
furthermore, *I* don't think they'll
make it even so far as Santa Fe.

BRACK
Not nearly, they won't.

JEB
Me neither.
(*staring down at the open Shakespeare on the table*)
'N yuh know what's the worst of all?

MACE (*dully*)
Somp'n else?

JEB (*in an anguished roar*)
Now we ain't never goin' tuh know
how the story come out!
(*general dismay*)

BRACK
Now ain't *that* the bottom o' the
bar'l.

JEB (*sizing up his partners*)
Onless . . .

MACE
Onless what?
(*Catching on, excitedly*)
We could do it! Jes' long enough
tuh—

JEB
Ain't nothin' tuh keep us here.

BRACK
What in tarnation—?

MACE
We could ride with 'em a ways—'n
Boone could read us the rest of it!

BRACK (*lighting up*)

I still got my money on Macduff!
JEB
Hit's a big book—might take Boone
clear to Californy to finish readin' it.
MACE
We're wastin' time!
(*In an explosion of activity the men
grab rifles and odds and ends of
equipment. Brack is out the door first,
then Jeb. Mace is out and back in-
stantly to retrieve his guitar. Jeb pops
back in to shout at him, angrily*)
JEB
Fergit the foofaraw! Let's go!
(*Mace exits, Jeb after him, leaving*

*the cabin door wide open. Off camera
is heard sung, in dreadful trio*)
    "Way up on this mountain
        We're leavin' our home,
    There's nuthin' to bind us,
        We're goin' fer to roam."
(*And, receding*)
    "We eat when we're hungry
        And drink when we're dry,
    And if nuthin' don't kill us
        We'll live till we die."
(*The camera stares across the abandoned cabin toward the open door*)

The End

TOP DRAMATIC SHOW OF THE YEAR
ONE HALF HOUR PROGRAM

GOODYEAR TELEVISION PLAYHOUSE

Native Dancer

NATIVE DANCER

BY

DAVID SHAW

GOODYEAR TELEVISION PLAYHOUSE

PRODUCER . . . . FRED COE

DIRECTOR . . . . VINCENT DONEHUE

ASSOCIATE PRODUCER . . . . . GORDON DUFF

CAST

Shirley Kochendorfer . . . Gwen Verdon

Dr. Max Binder . . . . . Jack Warden

Mama . . . . Anna Appel

Oscar Miller . . . . . Ben Astar

Frances . . . . Mary Grace Canfield

SPONSOR: THE GOODYEAR TIRE & RUBBER COMPANY, Inc.

TELECAST: MARCH 28, 1954

NBC TELEVISION NETWORK

NATIVE DANCER

DAVID SHAW, AUTHOR OF *Native Dancer,* is a 38-year-old native New Yorker who originally studied to be an illustrator but switched to writing. His first play, *They Shoulda Stood In Bed,* opened on Broadway on February 13, 1942. Three and a half years in the Army gave Shaw the background for an original story, *Foreign Affair,* which was made into a movie starring Marlene Dietrich, Jean Arthur and John Lund. More movie stories followed until 1949, when Shaw returned to New York to do television dramatic scripts.

Since that time, Mr. Shaw has been extremely successful as a television writer, with more than 100 hours to his credit. He is currently one of the regular "stable" of writers of NBC-TV *Playhouse.*

Fred Coe, producer of the *Playhouse* which included *Native Dancer,* joined NBC in 1945 as a production assistant. He rose quickly and by January 1946 he was writing, directing and producing television programs for the network. He helped to originate, and has produced the *Playhouse* since its inception on October 3, 1948.

Recently, Mr. Coe and six of his top writers—Robert Alan Aurthur, Paddy Chayefsky, Tad Mosel, Horton Foote, N. Richard Nash and David Shaw—incorporated as "Playwrights '54" to create a special half-hour dramatic series for television. Patterned after the Playwrights Company in the theatre, the new company represents the first time a group of writers control their own TV show, including a pension and insurance system for writers that is unprecedented in television.

Now executive producer of NBC-TV's *Producers Showcase,* Fred Coe has won many awards including the Sylvania Award, the George Foster Peabody Award and the Look Award for distinguished service to the television public.

139

NATIVE DANCER

FADE IN: *The clock atop the Paramount Building. Day. Pan slowly down building to street level, Broadway, and dolly in towards the drug store on the corner of 44th Street.*

DISSOLVE THRU TO: *Drug store interior. The long fountain at which people are eating. Behind the fountain with her back to us is Shirley, the short order cook. Her equipment includes a large griddle, an electric toaster which she feeds incessantly, and which pops up incessantly, and a sandwich board. She is terribly busy at the moment trying to fulfill the various orders that Frances, the waitress behind the counter, keeps shouting to her.*

FRANCES

One toasted American. Two egg salad on rye up. Hold the butter on one. Where's my bacon and tomato?
SHIRLEY (*cutting the just-finished bacon and tomato sandwich in half*)
Bacon and tomato. Pick up.
FRANCES (*picking it up*)
One fried egg on whole wheat toast.

SHIRLEY
Gee.
FRANCES
Is my toasted American working?
(*During this camera has panned down to Shirley's feet which are clad in ballet slippers. For while she works Shirley also practises a few positions. After this shot is established, pan up again*)

SHIRLEY

No harder than I am.

FRANCES

Well, it'd be a lot easier on you if you
did your ballet lessons on your own
time.

SHIRLEY

My teacher says every minute counts
if you want to be a great dancer.

FRANCES

Sure, what does he care? He doesn't
have to eat here. Shirley, the customers are beginning to complain
about the service.

SHIRLEY

Tell them I'm on my toes.

(and she is)

FRANCES

Boy, if determination is all you need
to become a ballet dancer, you're the
next Pavlova.

SHIRLEY

I saw her dance once. Mama took me
when I was a little girl. She seemed
to just—float, Frances. You know
what I mean?

FRANCES

Like a balloon.

SHIRLEY

Like a bird. After that I knew the
only thing I ever wanted was to be
like she was.

FRANCES

In the meantime you got a toasted
American coming up and two egg
salads on—

SHIRLEY (seeing a man come up to
the fountain)

Oscar Miller!

FRANCES

Who?

SHIRLEY

That's—Oscar Miller.

FRANCES

Friend of the family's?

SHIRLEY

Oscar Miller is only the biggest ballet
producer in the world. Frances, let
me wait on him.

FRANCES

Look, Shirley, you're four orders behind now and—oh, go ahead.

SHIRLEY

How do I look?

FRANCES

Fine. Now hurry up.

(Shirley tries to walk down to where
Miller is seated in the grand, classic
manner of a ballerina. She more than
overdoes it. Miller watches her, puzzled. Being as gracefully theatrical as
she can, Shirley leans over the counter
toward him)

SHIRLEY

What is your pleasure, Mr. Miller?

MILLER

A glass of water, please.

SHIRLEY

But of course.

(She spins artistically around to get
a glass which she fills from the tap.
All her movements are very elaborate.
She sets the water before him. He
watches her closely as he pops a pill
into his mouth and takes a sip of
water. She gets a napkin for him as
though the whole movement has been
badly choreographed)

SHIRLEY
Headache, Mr. Miller?

MILLER
Toothache.

SHIRLEY (*striking a pose of dismay*)
Ahhhhhhhh . . .

MILLER
Thanks for the water, Miss.

SHIRLEY
Kochendorfer.
(*He exits quickly leaving Shirley in a rather ridiculous pose. Frances comes up behind her carrying plates of sandwiches in both hands*)

FRANCES
Well, did he sign you up for the Ballet Russe?

SHIRLEY
He must've been in awful pain not to notice me.
(*Frances goes about serving the sandwiches to the customers while Shirley picks up the napkin Miller used and cherishes it as though it is a beautiful rose. Frances re-enters frame*)

FRANCES
I need two salami and eggs.

SHIRLEY
Someday—when I'm his premiere danseuse—I'll remind Oscar of this. He won't remember it but I'll remind him by showing him this napkin. . . . What did you order?

FRANCES
Two salami and eggs. . . .

SHIRLEY (*putting the paper napkin in her bosom*)
We'll both have a good laugh about it—

FRANCES
On rye.

SHIRLEY (*sighs*)
Someday.

FRANCES
Never mind. I'll get it myself.
(*She leaves frame and Shirley—in her dream world. Now Dr. Max Binder climbs up on the stool across the counter from her. He wears an overcoat, no hat, and we can see his white doctor's jacket with its high neck under the unbuttoned coat*)

MAX
Hello, Shirley.

SHIRLEY (*still entranced*)
Hi—
(*Now really sees Max and comes back to earth*)
Hi.

MAX
Think I can have a cup of coffee?

SHIRLEY (*the short order cook again*)
Sure.
(*She pours a cup. Max watches her idyllically*)
How's the doctor today?

MAX
As long as he can always come down ten floors and have you here to serve him a cup of coffee, he can't complain.

SHIRLEY
I guess I'll be here for some time yet
—(*Serves him the coffee*)
You want something else?

MAX
Yes.

SHIRLEY
A piece of Danish, maybe?

MAX
I want you to marry me.

SHIRLEY (*This is an old story.*)
Ma-a-a-x.

MAX
Listen, is there any law that says you can't be a ballerina if you're married to a dentist?

SHIRLEY
Max, people are looking at us.

MAX
I would like to know what's so incompatible about it. It would be different if you didn't love me. But you do.

SHIRLEY
I know, Max. Only my aim in life is to dance, not to get married.

MAX
Married women don't dance? You marry me and you can dance until doomsday. I'll send you to ten dancing schools.

SHIRLEY
We've been all through this and you promised me yesterday not to bring the subject up again.

MAX
I love you, Shirley.

SHIRLEY
Max.

MAX
All right, I'll change the subject. Will I see you tonight?

SHIRLEY (*shaking her head*)
Tonight is rhythmics. You know that.

MAX
Tomorrow night?

SHIRLEY
Tomorrow's Thursday?

MAX
Yes.

SHIRLEY
I take Interpretive on Thursdays.

MAX
Friday.

SHIRLEY
I'm sorry but I can't, Max.

MAX
You were always free on Fridays.

SHIRLEY
I start a new course . . . Modern.

MAX
You mean the only times I'll ever see you again is when I come in here for a cup of coffee?

SHIRLEY
And Legal Holidays. There's no school on Legal Holidays.

MAX (*disgusted*)
That's fine.

SHIRLEY
Don't hate me, Max.

MAX
Just when my practise is starting to grow. I'm a good dentist, Shirley. I'm going to make a very respectable income.

(*Frances moves into frame carrying a wire basket of glasses*)

FRANCES
Pardon the intrusion but I need a double chocolate malted.

SHIRLEY
Okay.

(*Frances moves out of frame and Shirley starts to make the malted*)

MAX
I'm even getting a few celebrities for patients. I had Oscar Miller in my

chair just a half hour ago.

SHIRLEY

Oscar Miller!

MAX (*proudly*)

Yop.

SHIRLEY

Is he a patient of yours?

MAX

And will be for a long time. His teeth are in a terrible condition.

(*Frances returns*)

FRANCES

So where's the malted?

SHIRLEY (*vaguely*)

What? . . . Oh.

FRANCES (*taking the metal container out of Shirley's hand*)

Never mind.

(*she exits*)

MAX

I'd better be getting back upstairs.

SHIRLEY

Max. . . . About tonight. Can a girl change her mind?

MAX (*delighted*)

Really?

SHIRLEY

I'll meet you out front at six-thirty.

MAX

Where'll we go? You just name it.

SHIRLEY

Ohhhhh—anywhere.

(*DISSOLVE QUICKLY TO: Sign "Madam Slovenskia's School of Dancing"*)

(*DISSOLVE THROUGH TO: A rehearsal room where there are many hopeful ballerinas individually going* about *their dancing. Finally camera dollies in and finds Shirley in a work outfit working on the bar. Max is seated near her, holding his hat and coat, watching her, admiring her. Throughout this scene Shirley continues her exercises—though not very well*)

MAX

Shirley.

SHIRLEY (*in the midst of a complicated routine*)

Just a minute . . .

(*she finishes*)

How did that look to you?

MAX

Anything you do looks beautiful.

SHIRLEY (*chiding him*)

Oh, Max . . .

MAX

Only don't you think we ought to go? It's after nine.

SHIRLEY (*going back to work*)

I've got to perfect this.

MAX

All the restaurants'll be closed.

SHIRLEY

Watch me and tell me if it's better.

MAX

I wanted to take you out real fancy tonight. I thought we might even take in a show. Can't you even skip one night of dancing school?

SHIRLEY

Not with my big audition coming up. I want to be at my best for Oscar Miller.

MAX (*surprised*)

Are you going to audition for Oscar Miller?

SHIRLEY
That's up to you, Max.
(*She dances away leaving Max
stunned and puzzled as we*)

(*DISSOLVE TO: Living room of a
Brooklyn apartment house. 11 P.M.
Pictures of ballerinas on the walls,
otherwise the room is quite typical.
Mrs. Kochendorfer, a woman of fifty,
is alone mending a ballet costume
with needle and thread. She holds it
up to examine it, is satisfied, and
starts to put away sewing things. The
door in the foyer opens*)

MAMA
That you, Shirley?
SHIRLEY (*off*)
Yeah, Mama.
MAMA
You're late tonight.
SHIRLEY (*off*)
I thought you'd be asleep.
MAMA
I just finished sewing that so-so for
you.
SHIRLEY
Tu-tu, mama.
MAMA
Tu-tu. You'll take it with you to-
morrow.
SHIRLEY (*off*)
Max is here, Mama.
MAMA
Max? . . . Doctor Max?
(*Crosses to foyer and sees Max and
Shirley. Shirley has her coat off. Max
hasn't. Mama extends her hand to
Max*)

So quiet? I didn't even know some-
body was here.
MAX (*glum*)
Good evening, Mrs. Kochendorfer.
MAMA
Come in. Take your coat off. I'll make
coffee.
MAX
No, thanks very much but I got to go.
MAMA (*sensing something*)
You two had a fight?
(*Shirley and Max avoid her ques-
tion*)
SHIRLEY
Mama, I'm too tired to go all over it
again.
MAMA
Go splash cold water on your face.
You'll feel better, Doctor Max will
tell me. Go.
SHIRLEY (*to Max*)
Will you stay?
MAX
I'll wait till you come out.
SHIRLEY
I won't be long.
(*She exits into hall leading to bed-
room*)
MAMA
So what's the argument now, Doctor?
MAX
What's always the argument?
MAMA
Career versus wedding bells, huh?
MAX
Worse. Mrs. Kochendorfer, your
daughter is going to work herself into
a state. I tell you this as a medical
man. She can't go on working all day
in the drug store and practising ballet
all night.

MAMA
This is news you're telling me? I worry plenty about my Shirley.

MAX
Tonight, for instance. We made a date—

MAMA
She made a date on a school night? I'm very surprised.

MAX
She had her reasons all right. I was going to take her out to an expensive restaurant. Maybe even to a Broadway show. You know where we went? To her dancing school. You know where we ate? Nedicks. Two hot dogs was her dinner. She's ruining her health.

MAMA
Haven't I told her? Haven't I tried to stop her? She's got this ballet bug in her head and it's like moving the mountains to talk to her. But this has been going on for years, Doctor Max. Why, tonight all of a sudden, should you and Shirley have a fight about it?

MAX
Because tonight the situation has come to a head. She wants me to use my influence to get her an audition with Oscar Miller.

MAMA
You've got influence with Oscar Miller?

MAX
He's one of my patients.

MAMA (*very impressed*)
My!

MAX
But I don't like to ask favors of my patients. It doesn't look nice.

MAMA
That's the only reason, Doctor? It doesn't look nice?

MAX (*sheepishly*)
No . . .

MAMA
Look, Doctor Max. Nothing is going to stop Shirley from trying. Not you. Not me. Not even Oscar Miller. She'll get her chance to show what she's got some day. She'll make her own chance. So why delay the agony?

MAX
Agony is right.
(*Shirley enters, visibly refreshed*)

SHIRLEY (*to Max*)
Wouldn't you like to take your coat off?

MAX (*rising*)
I was just waiting to say good-night.

MAMA
Why don't you stay and have a sandwich? I'm going to make one for Shirley anyway.

SHIRLEY
I'm not hungry, Mama.

MAMA
Don't tell me what you're not, Miss Two-Hot-Dogs-For-Dinner.
(*to Max*)
I've got some nice chicken from dinner left over. How about it, Doctor?

MAX
Shirley can tell you—I'm a pushover for a chicken sandwich.

SHIRLEY
He eats them all the time at the drug store.

MAMA (*to Shirley*)
A man like this. The day after I took you to see Pavlova I should've had

my head examined.

(*She exits into kitchen. There is an embarrassed pause between Shirley and Max*)

SHIRLEY

I'll take your coat.

MAX

Oh . . . thanks.

(*She helps him off with it and hangs it in the closet. Comes back and picks up the tu-tu that Mama had draped over a chair.*)

SHIRLEY (*examining it*)

Mama did a beautiful job on this. It was all torn.

MAX

Your mother is a wonderful woman.

SHIRLEY

Did you discuss—our problem?

MAX

I mentioned it, yes.

SHIRLEY

Bet I can guess what she said. She said: "Don't let anything she does now upset you, Dr. Max. She'll get over this ballet business once and for all and then you can settle down in a nice house in Flatbush. With lots of children."

MAX

Is that bad?

SHIRLEY

Not if that's what you want.

MAX

How do you know it isn't what you want until you try it?

SHIRLEY

Marriage isn't like buying a coat, Max. Once you accept it there are no returns in five days like in Klein's.

. . . But I guessed right about what Mama said, didn't I? That's all I get from everybody. Discouragement.

MAX

Your mother thinks I ought to try and get you that audition with Oscar Miller.

SHIRLEY

Mama said that!

MAX

Why prolong the agony, she said.

SHIRLEY

Then why won't you do it, Max? Even Mama knows how much it means to me. It could be the beginning of something wonderful for me—everything I've ever wanted. You have no reason to say no.

MAX

No reason? I love you. Is that a reason? And you say you love me. That's another reason. And that house in Flatbush and all the kids. More reasons. I don't know anything about it but to me you're a great dancer, Shirley. Oscar Miller will take one look at you and good-bye my love and the house and the kids and you. You have no right to ask a man to arrange for his own heartaches. Don't you see, Shirley, I'm trying to hold onto you as long as I can.

SHIRLEY (*in tears she throws her arms around him and buries her head on his shoulder*)

All right, Max. That's enough. . . . I—I'll never mention Oscar Miller's name to you again.

MAX (*moved*)

Shirley—darling—

SHIRLEY
I'll just have to get an audition with him some other way.
(*Max goes limp. He walks over and gets his coat*)
Where are you going, Max?

MAX
He's coming in to have an inlay fitting tomorrow. I'll speak to him then.

SHIRLEY
But what about your chicken sandwich?
(*Max leaves. Shirley stands there brokenly until Mama comes in from the kitchen with the sandwiches*)

MAMA
I didn't know if you take ketchup or not so I— Where's the Doctor?

SHIRLEY
He went home, Mama.

MAMA
He wouldn't get you the audition so you sent him away?

SHIRLEY
No, Mama—he's going to talk to Oscar Miller tomorrow.
(*She bursts into tears and Mama cradles her in her arms. Mama strokes her head*)

MAMA
My head examined I should've had . . .
(*FADE OUT:*)

FADE IN: A dentist's office. Day. Max is in his white jacket, apart from his patient, mixing a tiny cement solution. He seems very uneasy. In the chair is Oscar Miller, his mouth open, stuffed with all sorts of dental paraphernalia.

MILLER (*says something that cannot be understood*)

MAX
What was that, Mr. Miller?

MILLER (*repeats the incoherent phrase*)
(*Max comes over and removes the saliva drain*)
I said I'm in something of a hurry.

MAX
This won't take long.

MILLER
Got to be at NBC by four o'clock. They're doing one of my ballets on television tonight.

MAX
NBC? You don't say. Open wide, please.
(*starts to work in Miller's mouth*)
Mr. Miller?

MILLER
'Ah?

MAX
How does a man like you go about finding new talent?

MILLER
Agrsns!

MAX (*taking the drain out of his mouth*)
How's that?

MILLER
Auditions.
(*Max puts drain back in his mouth. Examines the tooth carefully*)

MAX (*getting the drill ready*)
You must get plenty of people bothering you for auditions all the time, eh?

MILLER (*meaning yes*)
'Ah-ha.

MAX
This may hurt a little.

(*He starts to drill the tooth. Miller writhes a little. Max stops the drill a moment*)
Because there's a girl I know . . .
(*drills some more. Stops*)
I think she's a real talent, Mr. Miller.
(*more drilling*)
Not that I know too much about it, you understand.

MILLER
Ah-ha.

MAX
But I think she's good . . . too good. I wouldn't even impose on you like this if I didn't think she had something on the ball. You know what I mean?

MILLER
Ah-hah.

MAX
Open wider, please.
(*He drills some more*)
So I was wondering if I could bring her around sometime to see you.

MILLER
Anrtynr.

MAX (*taking the drain out*)
How's that?

MILLER
I said sure, anytime.
(*Max puts the drain back in and starts to drill*)

MAX (*mournfully*)
Thanks, Mr. Miller. I sure appreciate it.

(*Dolly in tight on the drill buzzing and DISSOLVE TO: CU of malted machine buzzing behind the counter of the drug store. Pull back and*

Shirley is there not paying much attention to the malted. Her eyes are fastened towards the front of the store, obviously looking for somebody. Her feet, as always, are doing ballet exercises. Frances comes up behind her)

FRANCES
Isn't that malted ready *yet?*

SHIRLEY (*still looking off*)
Huh?

FRANCES
Never mind.
(*She takes the metal container off the mixer and tries to pour it into a glass. Nothing flows out. Frances looks into the container*)
Now, really, Shirley.

SHIRLEY
What's the matter?

FRANCES (*shaking the inverted container a few times until a solid chunk of malted comes out in her hand. She can hold the whole thing like a glass*)
I would say you let it whip a mite too long.

SHIRLEY
I'm sorry, Frances. I guess I'm so anxious to see Max that I— I'll make another one.

FRANCES
Never mind. You stay right where you are—on cloud seven.
(*She leaves. Shirley is contrite. She turns and sees Max seated at the counter*)

SHIRLEY
Max!

MAX
A cup of coffee, please.

SHIRLEY
Did you see him? Did you ask him?

MAX
Black.

SHIRLEY
Max, don't torture me. Since last night I've been going crazy. I can't stand it another minute.

MAX
The way you feel about being a big ballet dancer, that's about how much I want you.

SHIRLEY
I'll get your coffee.
(*She goes about serving him coffee*)

MAX
He said okay, Shirley. You can have the audition.

SHIRLEY
You mean it?

MAX
I wish I didn't.

SHIRLEY
Oh, Max, I could kiss you.

MAX
I don't want your kisses for a reason like this.

SHIRLEY
When, Max?

MAX
When you want to kiss me as a husband, that's when.

SHIRLEY
I mean—when is the audition?

MAX
Oh—the audition? He said any time. Any time at all.

SHIRLEY
You didn't make a definite appointment?

MAX
He was in a hurry today. Some television show he's doing on NBC tonight. I didn't get much chance to talk to him.

SHIRLEY
Wait'll I tell Frances. Don't go 'way.

MAX
Don't you think you'd better wait until you see how you make out in the audition before you start telling everybody?

SHIRLEY
I got to tell her I'm leaving, don't I?

MAX
Where you going?

SHIRLEY
NBC.

MAX
Now?
(*Camera dollies in very tight on his face as Max's expression changes from shock to resignation*)

MAX
When else?

(*DISSOLVE TO: Film. RCA building and NBC sign*)
(*DISSOLVE TO: Studio 8G during a break in camera rehearsals. We see cameras around and stagehands, light men, etc., on a long shot*)
(*Dolly in and pick up Oscar Miller on the floor looking up at the lights on the ceiling. With him are the stage manager and a man from the agency whose name is O'Leary*)

MILLER
There's got to be more lights up there

or we don't do the show. It's ridiculous. The Swan Lake number does not take place in a coal mine.

STAGE MANAGER

Yes, Mr. Miller.

(*He exits. Max now sidles up to him hesitantly. Miller is still looking up at the ceiling*)

MAX

Hello, Mr. Miller.

MILLER (*preoccupied*)

Hello, hello . . .

MAX

Guess you're surprised to see me here, eh?

MILLER

Nothing surprises me around this place any more.

(*now he sees Max*)

The dentist!

MAX

Knew you'd be surprised.

MILLER

Did I leave some of my bridgework in your office?

MAX

Oh, no—nothing like that.

MILLER

By the way—this is Mr. O'Leary. Dr. Binder.

MAX (*shaking hands*)

Hi, Mr. O'Leary.

MILLER (*shouting up at the ceiling*)

Put lots more lights up there. It's got to look sunny.

MAX

Incidentally, Mr. Miller—I brought Shirley Kochendorfer with me.

MILLER

That's nice—who?

MAX

The girl for the audition.

MILLER

You don't expect me to audition her now?

MAX

I'd certainly appreciate it, Mr. Miller. Shirley's very excited about it.

MILLER

Look, my dear friend, as a dentist I like you very much. But as an agent —don't bother me, please.

MAX

I'm not asking for myself, Mr. Miller. If it was up to me she'd never put on another pair of ballet shoes in her life. But she's lived her whole life for this moment, Mr. Miller.

MILLER

What kind of a name is that for a ballerina anyway? Shirley Kochendorfer.

MAX

She's willing to change it legally. She'll do anything.

(*Stage Manager re-appears*)

STAGE MANAGER

It'll take about ten minutes to fix that lighting, Mr. Miller.

MILLER

Well, fix it and let's get on with the rehearsal.

(*Stage Manager leaves*)

MAX

You could use those ten minutes to maybe discover a great star.

MILLER

Is she ready now?

MAX (*pumping Miller's hand*)

I'll never forget this, Mr. Miller.

Never. Tell the orchestra to play—
(*He races across the studio to where Shirley is waiting, a coat over her costume*)
Now, Shirley!

SHIRLEY
He said it was all right?

MAX
Yes.

SHIRLEY
Oh, Max, I'm so nervous . . .

MAX
You'll knock 'em dead.

SHIRLEY
I love you, Max. I really do.
(*She kisses him and a moment later the music begins*)
(*Shirley goes to the center of the studio and does her audition dance*)
(*During it keep cutting to Max who enjoys every step and to Miller whose reaction is quite the opposite. Near the end of the dance:*)

(*DISSOLVE TO: The living room in Brooklyn. Evening. Sound: The door-bell is ringing constantly. Mama emerges from the kitchen with baking flour on her hands*)

MAMA (*crossing to front door*)
All right, all right, I'm coming.
(*she opens the door and Max bursts in*)

Doctor Max?

MAX (*he is visibly upset*)
Is she here?

MAMA
Shirley? Of course not. Tonight is Thursday. She's interpreting.

MAX
No she isn't. Didn't she phone or something?

MAMA
Something happened to Shirley?

MAX
I don't know. Now, please, Mrs. Kochendorfer, don't get excited.

MAMA
Look who is talking! What happened, Doctor Max? You've got to tell her mother.

MAX
This afternoon she had her audition with Oscar Miller.

MAMA
Already?

MAX
You know Shirley. When she makes up her mind to do something. She couldn't wait. It had to be right now.

MAMA
That's Shirley, all right. But tell me, how was the audition?

MAX
I thought she was wonderful.

MAMA
You're not exactly an expert. What did Oscar Miller think?

MAX
He thinks she ought to forget she ever even heard of Pavlova. In plain English he said she was terrible!

MAMA
Yeah, and?

MAX
Mrs. Kochendorfer, you don't seem to understand. He told Shirley she'll never be a good dancer. I wish I

could've died right then and there.

MAMA

And that's what's making you so upset? I could have told you long ago that Shirley had everything a ballet dancer needs except one thing. Talent.

MAX

And he didn't pull his punches. He told all this to Shirley right to her face. Like he was deliberately trying to hurt her . . . Wait'll I get him in the chair next time, I'll—

MAMA

So where's Shirley now?

MAX

I wish I knew. We were both standing there talking to Miller and the next minute she's gone. Disappeared. I don't want to alarm you, Mrs. Kochendorfer, but a girl in her state of mind should not be alone tonight.

MAMA

It's possible she went back to her dancing school to work some more on her . . .

MAX

I went to the dancing school. To the drug store. Any place she might possibly be. Then I came here, thinking maybe she came home.

MAMA

Sit down, Max. You look tired.

MAX

What are we going to do?

MAMA

You're going to sit there and worry and I'm going in the kitchen. I've got a cake in the oven. Upside down.

MAX

The whole world is upside down.

MAMA

Relax, Max, please.

(*She goes into kitchen. Max paces nervously until he hears the front door close. He crosses to the foyer and sees Shirley. She can't look at him*)

MAX

Hello, Shirley.

SHIRLEY

I didn't expect to find you here.

MAX (*the lame joke*)

I got bored drinking champagne at the Waldorf Astoria so I thought I'd drop over.

(*Shirley crosses into living room. He follows*)

SHIRLEY

Mama here?

MAX

In the kitchen . . . You like upside down cake?

SHIRLEY

I just ate a little while ago.

MAX

Two hot dogs at Nedick's?

SHIRLEY

Scrambled eggs at Schrafft's.

MAX

That's nourishing.

SHIRLEY

Max, I'm sorry.

MAX

What's to be sorry about?

SHIRLEY

Everything.

MAX

You're not going to let one man's opinion stop you, are you? That's not the Shirley I know. How many stars are there who were once turned down by big producers? Hundreds! Oscar Miller isn't the last word, you know.

SHIRLEY

Maybe not. But he was right about one Shirley Kochendorfer.

MAX

Will you stop it, please?

SHIRLEY

He was, Max. Why kid ourselves now? I'm no dancer and I never will be.

MAX

He was just sore because he didn't want to have an audition today in the first place. He was nervous about his television show, too, which made him extremely irritated. I mean—the way he insulted your dancing was like he wanted to be as mean as he could.

SHIRLEY

He was being kind, Max.

MAX

Kind? If that's kindness I'm going to be awfully kind to him the next time I get him in that chair. I'll—

SHIRLEY

He wanted me to quit, Max. That's why he did it. He saw a girl who had no business in ballet and he wanted to spare me the years of drudgery I would've gone through for nothing. He was really pleading with me not to throw my life away on a thing I could never have . . . I ought to write him a thank you note.

(*She is sniffling*)

MAX

Aw, come on, Shirl. There are mil-

lions of wonderful girls who aren't ballet dancers. It's nothing to cry about.

SHIRLEY

I'm not crying about that.

MAX

Something else?

SHIRLEY

Uh-huh . . . Us.

MAX

There's nothing sad about us any more . . . Is there?

(*She nods her head affirmatively, unable to speak*)

You mean you still don't want to marry me?

SHIRLEY

I do, Max. I do.

MAX

Shirley . . .

SHIRLEY

But I can't—now.

MAX

Shirley!

(*Phone rings*)

SHIRLEY

You'd always have it at the back of your mind that I married you on the rebound. She couldn't be a dancer so she married the second fiddle.

MAX

If I'm the third fiddle, I don't care . . .

(*Phone rings*)

SHIRLEY

It just isn't fair to a wonderful man like you. Be smart, Max darling. Drop me like a hot potato. Find yourself a girl who's good enough to deserve a prince.

(*Phone rings again*)

(*Mama enters from the kitchen on her way to phone*)

MAMA

You don't hear the phone ringing in here? Hello, Shirley dear . . . (*Picks up phone*) Hello . . . Yes, this is the Kochendorfer residence . . . Shirley? Yes, she's my daughter . . . Who is this please? . . . Hold the line . . . (*to Shirley*) It's a gentleman for you, Shirley.

SHIRLEY

Who is it?

MAMA

A Mr. O'Leary.

SHIRLEY (*puzzled, not recognizing the name*)

O'Leary? I don't know any—

MAX

Don't you remember, Shirl? He was that fella from the agency who was at the studio today.

SHIRLEY (*to Max, wearily amused*)

Maybe he called up to tell me how bad the audition was, too.

MAMA

He's hanging on, Shirley.

SHIRLEY

I can't speak to anybody now, Mama. Ask him what he wants.

MAMA (*into phone*)

Mr. O'Leary, are you there? Would you mind telling me what it's all about? My daughter is indisposed at the moment . . . I see . . . Yes . . . Could you hang on again, please? (*covering the mouthpiece*)

He says his agency has a cigarette company for a client and he wants to know if you'd be willing to go on TV as the dancing legs of a cigarette package?

MAX (*to Shirley*)

What did I tell you? Oscar Miller isn't the only pebble. You're on your way, Shirley.

MAMA

Should I tell him that, Shirley? You're on your way?

SHIRLEY

I'll speak to him.

(*she takes phone from Mama*)

Mr. O'Leary, this is Shirley Kochendorfer speaking . . . Yes, my mother gave me your message and I can't tell you how much I appreciate your offer, Mr. O'Leary. Only I'm afraid I'm unavailable . . . Have I got a better offer? I suppose you might call it that . . . No, not from another network. From a prince who's going to give me a house in Flatbush and lots of kids and . . .

(*By this time the camera has panned down slowly from Shirley's head to her feet and we find out that while she has been speaking she has been doing her ballet exercises in very small movements*)

(*Fade out*)

The End

TOP DRAMATIC SHOW OF THE YEAR

"ONE ACT" PLAY

KRAFT TELEVISION THEATRE

The Thinking Heart

THE THINKING HEART
Excerpt—Act II, Last Scene

BY

GEORGE H. FAULKNER

KRAFT TELEVISION THEATRE

DIRECTOR . . . . FIELDER COOK

SCENIC DESIGNER . . . . . ROBERT BRIGHT

CAST

ABRAHAM LINCOLN . . . . ANDREW DUGGAN

TINKER . . . . JACK ARTHUR

CHANDLER . . . . WILLIAM McGUIRE

NARRATOR . . . . ANTHONY ROSS

SPONSORED BY KRAFT FOODS COMPANY

TELECAST: FEBRUARY 11, 1954
NBC TELEVISION NETWORK

Note: This excerpt is the closing scene of Act II of a full one hour program, as originally telecast. The dramatic "telegraph office scene" is a complete one-act play in itself and will probably be used again as such on the air.

THE THINKING HEART

Georgy H. Faulkner was born on August 14, 1903 in Winooski, Vermont. Graduating from Colgate University, he worked for several newspapers in and around New York. Later, he did publicity for Paramount Pictures and in 1929, joined the newly formed radio department of the J. Walter Thompson Company. Here, he participated in many of the early radio successes of the agency. For six years, he wrote, cast and helped produce the *Rudy Vallee Variety Hour*. In 1939, he left JWT to free-lance, with notably successful results.

Since then, Mr. Faulkner has maintained a steady list of outstanding credits. For example, he is responsible for the writing of more than 25 programs for DuPont's *Cavalcade of America*. He has written numerous plays for the *Kraft Television Theatre* among which was "The Thinking Heart."

He has also written literally hundreds of plays for such programs as *Armstrong Circle Theatre, American Portraits, Theatre Guild's U. S. Steel Hour,* and others. He has recently turned out a full-length book, *Gentlemen and Rebels,* published by Little, Brown & Co.

THE THINKING HEART

Music: Martial in tone, hits in full
Crossfade to film shot of marching
men in Civil War uniforms, narrative
image Number 12
Crossfade to narrator over marching
men

NARRATOR

The color of the ground was in him,
   the red earth;
The smell and smack of elemental
   things:
The rectitude and patience of the
   cliff:
The good-will of the rain that loves
   all leaves:
The courage of the bird that dares
   the sea:
The gladness of the wind that shakes
   the corn;
The undelaying justice of the light . . .
Action followed thought and feeling.
And action led to bloody war. For
Lincoln, war meant torment. And
waiting . . . waiting . . . waiting . . .
In the Federal army telegraph office
at Washington . . .
Fade out above
Fade in, close-up of a chattering tele-
graph key, then our view broadens
to encompass the office of the Union
army's chief telegraph operator, in
the War Department Building. It is
late at night. The key chatters, under.
Other similar Morse-code keys are
heard in an outer office, off screen,
muted, throughout scene, occasion-
ally. We see Charles Tinker, the chief
operator, at the table on which the

instrument is chattering. Then we see Lincoln. He is lying on a decrepit horse-hair sofa which is placed under a high Washington-like window. Perhaps there is an indication of bitter weather outside. The sofa is too short. Or Lincoln is too long. His feet are hiked up at one end, and he is asleep. He has a woolen shawl over him. He is awakened by the noise of Tinker's key . . .

LINCOLN

Mr. Tinker!

TINKER (*rather old, in uniform but with collar open*)

Yes, Mr. President?

LINCOLN

Is it from General Burnside?

TINKER

No, sir. Routine. From Harper's Ferry. A Colonel Ferris asks for more blankets. Says it's cold in Virginia.
(*The key stops. Tinker sends "Message Received"*)

LINCOLN

Reckon I could loan him *this*.
(*Throws woolen shawl off*)
But then I guess he'd need a couple more—
(*Lincoln sits up, peers down at his coat lapel. Very carefully, with exaggerated interest, he takes a case of spectacles out of his pocket, puts on the glasses, looks down at his lapel. He carefully seizes, between his thumb and forefinger, an insect . . .*)

LINCOLN (*announces, solemnly*)

Charlie—I have taken a prisoner.

TINKER

Here, sir?

LINCOLN (*rising and carrying his captive for examination to the telegraph desk, which is lighted by a kerosene light*)

No, *here*. Poor little critter! Know what they call him, Charlie?

TINKER (*dubiously*)

Looks to me like—

LINCOLN (*interrupts*)

That's what *you* think. I looked it up, because I have encountered blood relatives of this little tike ever since I can remember. This persistent and persnickety mite is called *cimex lectularius,* by folks who know how to pronounce it.

TINKER (*peering, over spectacles*)

I still think he looks like a bed-bug.

LINCOLN

That's what he is, Charlie, that's what he is. But he's the runt of the litter, I expect. Sort of a citified *cimex.* Back on the Sangamon, in Illinois, his like grow to three inches long, not countin' the horns and tail.

TINKER (*playing up, this is an old game for two fairly old men*)

I hear tell, Mr. Lincoln, that down N'Orleans way they have such-like bugs that can carry off a pair of fire tongs, two to a tong.

LINCOLN (*going along with it*)

Mr. Tinker, back in Hardin County, Kentucky, where I was born, we had fellers like this that used to *chew up* fire tongs, regular. And then spit out tupenny nails. We used to train 'em to tack shingles onto roofs . . .
(*The two men look at each other, under the oil lamp, across the desk.*

And they burst into laughter. The
laughter dies rather quickly, as both
realize the reason for Lincoln's vigil
tonight . . .)

LINCOLN (*regarding bug closely*)

If it weren't so cold out, Charles, I'd
loose little cimex through the window.
As it is—

(*He lets the insect go with an upward
lift and fling of his arms*)

—go back to your bed, bug . . . com-
panion of my bosom!

TINKER

Mr. Lincoln, I have complained to
Secretary Stanton a hundred times
about that old couch of yours—

LINCOLN

Mr. Stanton has other things to worry
over.

(*Suddenly serious*)

There hasn't been anything at all
from Fredericksburg since I fell
asleep?

TINKER

Nothing, Mr. President. Burnside has
crossed the Rappahannock. He is attacking—that is, he *was* attacking,
this afternoon. Nothing since.

(*Lincoln slumps, tiredly, into old,
broken-down, easy chair opposite
Tinker's table-desk. This chair was
reserved for him. Like the old sofa*)

LINCOLN

Seems to me I spend about five times
as many hours here in the War Office
as I do anywhere else in town.
Where's Mr. Stanton?

TINKER

Gone home, sir. He'll be back at
dawn.

LINCOLN

Poor old curmudgeon! He doesn't
like me, much. And, between you and
me, Charlie—I don't so much like
him.

(*We see Charlie's face. It is evident
that Charlie agrees with Mr. Lincoln's
opinion of Secretary of War Stanton*)

LINCOLN (*tired, tired*)

But he's a *worker*. My land! Such a
worker! And he usually talks good
sense. Have you ever noticed how
often people don't seem to do that
any more, Charlie?

TINKER (*a little warily*)

Yes, Mr. Lincoln. I . . . I have.

LINCOLN

Stanton may be pig-headed. But even
when he's wrong, he has reasons. In
a pig-headed sort of way.

(*He realizes he is talking perhaps too
much to a subordinate of Stanton*)

I . . . I guess I'm . . . pretty well
tuckered out, myself. I don't talk
much . . . good sense, late at night.

TINKER (*positive affirmation, intense
loyalty*)

To me, Mr. President, you *do*.
Shouldn't you . . . go home, sir?

LINCOLN

Not before I get some word from
General Burnside at Fredericksburg.
Meantime . . . well, I like it here.
Mr. Tinker, it's a pleasure to sit in
this old chair and listen to those keys
rattle out there—and know I'm
among men who *work* for a living
. . . not just talk, talk, talk . . . as
they do over yonder on the hill . . .

(*The key starts to chatter*)

LINCOLN
Tinker!

TINKER (*after listening for a second or two*)
Nothing, sir. Message for General Halleck. Concerning promotions. Chandler will take it down, outside. And reply.
(*The key stops*)

LINCOLN
Do I . . . do I get in your way here, Charles?

TINKER
No, sir. We like to have you in here with us.

LINCOLN
I know you do. I'm sure of that, and it—well, it comforts me. This is just about the only place in Washington where I can let loose and act as if I were back home in Springfield—or out on the circuit, lawyerin' again . . .
(*Lincoln leans back in his chair and starts to put his feet up on Tinker's desk-table. The key opens up . . . Lincoln pulls his feet down, all attention. The message is very brief. It stops*)

TINKER
Sorry, sir. Nothing. Have you had any supper, Mr. President?

LINCOLN
No, Charlie. Things have sort of piled up on me all day long, over yonder. Maybe you could do something about a bite to eat?

TINKER
I have, Mr. President. Sent an orderly half an hour ago for sandwiches and coffee. Guess I better go see what's happened to him.
(*Tinker gets up, starts to leave*)

LINCOLN
What about the key?

TINKER
Chandler's desk outside is a duplicate, sir. A duplicate key. If anything comes through from Fredericksburg, he can give it to you. But I'll only be a minute—you need *food*, Mr. President.

LINCOLN
Charlie, I swear telegraphers are my favorite folks. They know I've got human *insides* in spite of all the evidence to the contrary *outside*.
(*Calls*)
Don't be long, now . . .
(*Tinker exits. Lincoln regards the telegraph sender and receiver*)

LINCOLN
Ambrose Burnside! Deep in your
 whiskers!
Why are you silent, why are you
 dumb?
And why did I choose *you*, from all
 the others?
I know. Yes, I know so well, too
 well—
Because the politicians whispered in
 my ear
"He's McClellan's friend, the *West
 Point* friend:
Be kind to friends of George Mc-
 Clellan,
For McClellan still has partisans . . .
 and power" . . .
(*He strikes desk in momentary anger*)
Why! Why! I needed a *man*

Not a friend of a friend of railroads
  in New York.
I've been weak again, for the hun-
  dredth time
And now I fret, and now *we* suffer—
And those poor devils there beyond
  the river . . .
(*He turns from the desk, goes to
window, looking out on a desolate
winter landscape*)
On the Rappahannock, now, it's over
  and done.
There on the Virginia hills beyond
  the stream
Hundreds have died and still are
  dying slowly—
And it's cold in Virginia, December
  cold.
I've seen the battle-ground on fresh
  and tidy maps
With never a smirch of dry, brown
  blood . . .
There's a hill called *Marye's Hill,*
Up beyond the river, and in the mar-
  row of my bone
I know young men are taken hardly
  there,
Dribbling a lively, unlived youth
  away
Between living and dying, *between
ice and flame*—
(*With a start, Lincoln draws back
from the window, starting back as if
he has seen a ghost. He begins pacing
the floor . . .*)
Ice and flame? Why flame—and ice?
Why should I so often think on
  opposites
In such a bitter, stabbing thrust of
  thought?

Why must that eternal desperate
  paradox—
The damnable mystic mirror image
Of all things made in earth or
  heav'n—
Clutch me tight in ever-double clamps
  of iron
And shake my mind until it reels
In sick wide captive spirals down the
  night:
Fire and ice . . . life and death . . .
  good and evil—
If they *are* the same, my work's a
  random cheat
And the savor of God's unholy God-
  less jest
Is the taste of ashes on a burning
  hill . . .
I'll not believe it. 'Twas Jack Kelso's
  doom—
(*He paces up and down for a mo-
ment*)
I remember now. The last despatch.
It was clear and *dry* below the
  stream,
Burnside said. How often have I seen
  the like
Where other hills meet other rivers:
The winter fields, still high in grassy
  sedge,
But sere and yellow-grey and dry—
Like tinder ready for the careless
  match.
Such fields will *burn,* and burning
  must . . .
(*We hear, and then see, close-up.
Quickly, dramatically, in a sudden
purposeful shift of camera emphasis,
the telegraph key going in a vehement
chatter. The soliloquy is abruptly*

broken off. Lincoln goes to Tinker's desk. He is piteously helpless . . .)

LINCOLN (*leaning over chattering key, desperately*)

What are you saying! What is it? What is it? *Chandler!* Chandler, come in here!

(*Chandler, another operator, younger, enters. Goes to Tinker's desk. The key stops, momentarily*)

CHANDLER

It's from Burnside, sir. I caught the first of it, outside.

LINCOLN

Yes, young man?

CHANDLER

Bad news, sir, I'm afraid.

(*The key starts again. Stops quickly*)

LINCOLN

From General Burnside, himself?

CHANDLER

No, sir, an aide, Colonel Hardwick. He just identified himself.

LINCOLN (*controlling his voice*)

Read it to me as it comes, Chandler, if you will?

(*Key starts again, stops*)

CHANDLER (*without emotion, like a television air force type*)

General Burnside reports, sir, he is utterly defeated.

(*Pause. Key sounds*)

Attack on Marye's Hill repulsed, sir, with heavy loss by artillery fire from sunken road.

(*Key . . . Pause*)

Meagher's Irish Brigade destroyed on Marye's Hill.

(*Key . . . Pause*)

Attempts to relieve Meagher rendered

futile by fire in dry sedge-grass on the hill . . .

LINCOLN (*close-up. Unspoken thought*)

The flame, the flame! I *saw* the flame! From the window, there—

(*Key chatters, briefly*)

CHANDLER (*almost bored*)

Burnside has retreated across the Rappahannock, sir, to the north.

(*Key*)

Weather is worsening. Very cold. Freezing sleet.

(*Key*)

River crossing makes necessary abandonment of wounded on Marye's Hill. Losses exceed twelve thousand men. Comprehensive report in morning, sir.

(*Key stops*)

(*We see Lincoln, who has been bending intently over telegraph desk. He straightens up*)

LINCOLN (*aloud, but as if to himself*)

Those who were burned in the flame on the hill, and yet lived for a while— why, then, this night they'll freeze to death . . . there on the hill . . . on Marye's Hill in the ice . . . fire and ice . . . fire and ice . . .

TINKER (*off screen*)

Mr. President, sir!

LINCOLN (*wearily, after a pause, turns to door*)

Yes, Charlie?

TINKER (*coming on*)

I've brought the sandwiches, sir . . .

(*Sees Lincoln's face*)

You—you've had the news?

LINCOLN (*struggling for control*)

Yes. I . . . I don't think I'll want anything to eat, Charlie. Thank you. (*Music is under. Lincoln takes up his shawl from the side of couch. The camera watches him as he walks slowly off, putting the shawl over his shoulders and clutching it about him,* *huddled over. He turns at door*)

LINCOLN

Thank you, Charlie. Thank you.

Black-out
Music resolves

End of Act

TOP NEWS SHOW OF THE YEAR

THE CAMEL NEWS CARAVAN

"Today's News Today"

THE CAMEL NEWS CARAVAN

"TODAY'S NEWS TODAY"

Produced for Camel Cigarettes by NBC

NEWSCASTER . . . . JOHN CAMERON SWAYZE

PRODUCER . . . . FRANCIS McCALL

TELECAST: JULY 28, 1954

CAMEL NEWS CARAVAN

The Camel News Caravan IS ONE OF THE most popular news program on television today. It has achieved its high ratings (a weekly audience of more than 40,000,000) as a result of its crisp, fresh presentation of the news events and its frequent use of visual material and demonstration techniques.

A news program which makes a specialty of presenting "live" pick-ups and exclusive film shots of important news events, *The Camel News Caravan* has been on the air since 1949. It takes 75 persons to put on a single newscast and under the direction of John Cameron Swayze, its commentator, the program has achieved an enviable record of exclusive filmed news events. Among them was the first interview with Robert Vogeler after his release from a Hungarian prison; the Yugoslavian parliament in session; the Pope's Easter sermon and others.

John Cameron Swayze has been busy making telecasting history since the summer of 1948 when he covered the three national political conventions in Philadelphia. Since then, he has won more than 25 awards and citations including the *Look* Magazine Award and the Michaels Award.

He was born in Wichita, Kansas in 1906 and graduated from the University of Kansas. Swayze's first job with the old Kansas City *Journal Post* moved him into radio as a result of a tie-in with KMBC to broadcast news bulletins. In 1940, he left the newspaper for a full time job in the KMBC news department. In 1947, Swayze moved to New York for a news-round-up position with NBC and a year later he landed a spot on the television quiz program, *Who Said That?*

Soon after, came *The Camel News Caravan,* a nation-wide network show which skyrocketed Swayze to fame and fortune. He now writes a newspaper column, published five times a week and has invented and is marketing a game which is expected to reach the popularity of "Scrabble" and "Monopoly." Swayze is married to Beulah Mae Estes and has two children, 19 year old John Cameron, Jr., a student at Harvard and a daughter Suzanne, who is 15.

WNBT
WEDNESDAY
7:45-8:00 PM
ANNOUNCER: *Opening.*
SWAYZE: Ladies and gentlemen, a good evening to you! The Presidents of the United States and the Republic of South Korea made top news in Washington today with separate statements on the Asian problem. David Brinkley has those stories for us at NBC NEWS, WASHINGTON.
BRINKLEY: At his Wednesday news conference President Eisenhower told reporters this country will not be truculent with the Chinese Communists, but he said we will defend our rights and he said the US Navy planes that shot down the two Chinese had a right to be where they were. This was taken here to be a kind of warning to the Chinese to be careful and also as a word to those of our allies who think we've been too belligerent and quick on the trigger. The President said our planes were there on legitimate business looking for the British survivors and that they would defend themselves and stay there until they have finished. Otherwise he served public notice that candidates for Congress who want his support had better vote for his program. This was a new Eisenhower policy over that of the last election when he said he supported all Republican candidates for office. Otherwise here today Syngman Rhee, President of South Korea, had the unusual honor of being invited to address a joint session of Congress in the House Chamber. His wife came with him, sat in the gallery to listen, members of the Washington diplomatic corps were there too. He had a prepared speech but departed from it occasionally;

once was when he said in an emotional way that while he is a Korean by law and by birth, by sentiment he is an American. Rhee's English is a little difficult and the members of Congress had some trouble catching all of what he said, but they got most of it like this: (Rhee in heavy accent) What he said was there ought to be what he called a counterattack on Communist China and said it would be successful if carried out by an Asian army of more than two million men, backed up and supported by US planes, guns and ships. In short, he called on this country to join in a full-scale war on China. He said he knew this would be a momentous decision for us to make but said unless the Chinese mainland is taken away from the Reds the free world ultimately will lose the war against Communism. After Rhee had spoken most members of Congress expressed admiration for him as a man and a patriotic leader but no enthusiasm for his call to arms. For example, Senator George of Georgia said it was a great fighting speech, that if all our allies had the same spirit we'd be in good shape. But as for war with China he wouldn't express any opinion. When he finished Rhee was loudly applauded but the applause was for him personally and not for his call to World War III. Now back to Camel News Headquarters in New York.

SWAYZE: In another part of the world, less than a day after Egypt and Britain settled their ancient feud about the Suez Canal, it's reported the United States played a key role in the agreement.

NARRATOR: At Kings Rest House near the pyramids final details of the agreement were worked out over a dinner that lasted five hours. Egypt's Premier, Gamal Abdel Nasser signed for his country where ratification is assured because rule is by a small military junta. British initials were affixed by War Secretary Antony Head to an agreement providing British military withdrawal from the Suez Canal Zone in 20 months with a return permitted in case of attack on the Arab states or Turkey. The agreement was speeded up by US promises to boost dollar assistance for Egypt. Winston Churchill stakes the fate of his government on its ratification tomorrow.

Commercial Announcement.

SWAYZE: Today President Eisenhower said he would be greatly disappointed if Congress failed to pass a half dozen bills in his legislative program. He named them as tax, farm, foreign aid, anti-Communist, housing and social security. Almost as he spoke the House did pass the big tax revision bill, including a cut in taxes on incomes from dividends. The measure, which reduces revenues $1,363,000 goes to the Senate tomorrow. And the House passed the foreign aid bill after cutting it a little more than 800 million dollars. Likewise in Washington senatorial critics of their colleague from Wisconsin spoke out sharply again today. And for this report we return to the nation's capital.

BRINKLEY: Today Vermont's Senator Flanders said he is determined to go ahead this Friday with his resolution to censure Senator McCarthy in spite of attacks that have been and will be made on him. Here's what he said:

FLANDERS: Let me say that I am confidently expecting attacks on myself and the supporters of my resolution, perhaps between now and July 30, certainly on July 30th. There are gumshoe tracks all around me and fingerprints on all the doorknobs. I don't have to send for an expert to trace the source of these gumshoe tracks and the fingerprints. But I'll not be diverted from my purpose of getting on Friday a vote of censure on the Junior Senator from Wisconsin. I intend to produce my own Bill of Particulars. Other senators have theirs and I hope they will state their own particulars with regard to the Senator from Wisconsin. But we should always remember that we are not merely condemning a particular action on a particular date, but that we are also dealing with an "ism." The depredations of McCarthyism launched from the perch of the chairmanship of the government's operation committee have affected the lives of all of us. McCarthyism has invaded the religious, military, educational, cultural life as well as the political affairs of our country. It is all-inclusive in its effect and must be deplored in an all-inclusive manner.

BRINKLEY: The vote will be this Friday, July 30th. Now back to New York.

SWAYZE: Senator McCarthy himself left Washington today for New York and tonight's big testimonial dinner honoring Roy Cohn. Our cameras were on hand to cover the Senator's arrival.

NARRATOR: He landed this afternoon on the way to the Hotel Astor. There, before 2,000 people tonight, Senator McCarthy will deliver the main address at a testimonial dinner for Roy Cohn, sponsored by the Joint Committee Against Communism. Accompanied by his wife and staff members Frank Carr and James Juliana the Senator faced an immediate barrage of questions that ranged from his role at tonight's dinner to his reaction to Senator Flanders.

REPORTER: Tonight's the big dinner and some of us are going on the air before the dinner. Can you tell us what words you're going to have for Mr. Cohn?

MC CARTHY: No, I don't think I can tell you now—I haven't prepared the speech yet.

REPORTER: Well, could you tell us just exactly how important you think Roy Cohn was to the committee?

MC CARTHY: Extremely important.

REPORTER: Are you gonna have a replacement soon, do you think?

MC CARTHY: It'll be impossible to replace Roy. We'll get a man to take his place, yes, but it'll be impossible to replace him.

REPORTER: Senator, how about the Flanders thing on Friday?

MC CARTHY: No reaction at all. I haven't listened to Flanders, I don't know whether I will.

REPORTER: Do you expect to be present on Friday?

MC CARTHY: I don't know if I'll take the time to listen or not. I may . . .

REPORTER: Senator, tonight you know for the dinner tonight some 5,000 applications have been turned back.

MC CARTHY: I understand so.

REPORTER: Do you think that's because you're speaking there or you think it could be for Roy Cohn?

MC CARTHY: No, I think that was strictly a tribute to Roy Cohn.

SWAYZE: In Europe, where prospects for a unified defense seemed to be dwindling, the Communists are adding more men and more equipment to their growing East German military organization.

NARRATOR: And the man who heads the Red German army is the same man who surrendered to the Russians at Stalingrad. Hidden away by the Kremlin until very recently, former Field Marshal Friedrich Pollus finally emerged from obscurity at a carefully staged East Berlin news conference. American newsmen were excluded but the US now sees and hears the famous marshal as he appeared at that conference on film from behind the Iron Curtain. (VOICE IN GERMAN ON FILM) His statements themselves were far from startling, mostly to the effect that Germany must not be influenced by the US. His appearance was headline material because it gave to the Communist-run East German forces a name famous to all Germans. Friedrich Pollus emerges to head more than 100,000 known as the People's Police, but organized as the nucleus for the rearmament of Red Germany.

SWAYZE: In Arkansas Senator John L. McClellan has apparently won renomination. However, his margin is a thin one and his chief opponent, former Governor Sid McMath, has not yet conceded. At midday McClellan has claimed victory by 5,000 votes but what the final margin will be is a guess. McClellan blamed his thin majority on his having had a part in the Army-McCarthy hearings.

Commercial Announcement.

SWAYZE: Now it's time once again for our daily report from the Camel Weatherman. Here he is—Clint Youle at NBC in Chicago.

YOULE: Getting a little unhappy. We sure missed Chicago's forecast today. We had an unexpected shower and we cooled off, but it's only temporarily. Be hot again tomorrow from west and central Texas right diagonally clear on up, say, about as far as New York and Washington area and tomorrow there'll be some showers in the Detroit-Cleveland area, a few in through Pennsylvania and New

York and to upper, oh, say interior New England. It'll also be kind of humid in with this hot area. And there'll be some heavier rains in through here and a tropical storm is coming in, not quite a hurricane, but a pretty good-sized thing. It'll give some good rains and the storm will die out as it gets in. Some showers up in through there. Quite warm with clear skies along the west coast. That's it, now back to New York and the Camel Scoreboard.

SCORE: In the American League, it was New York 7, Chicago 5 after repeated delays. And Detroit beat Philadelphia 10-2. In the National League New York smashed St. Louis 10-0 with all other games in both leagues at night. And that's the major league picture on tonight's Camel Scoreboard.

SWAYZE: Hopscotching the world for headlines: United Nations, New York: The United States told the United Nations today that it will continue to build its military establish-ment along the lines of atomic weapons as long as the Communist world continues its aggressive policy. Niagara Falls: A section of the well-known Prospect Point fell today into the chasm of the Niagara River gorge. It has long been a popular observation point on the brink of the American Falls. It was reported that no one was hurt.

Ottawa: Canada has agreed to be a member of the supervisory group for the Indochina armistice. The other two member nations are India and Poland.

London: Prime Minister Churchill has shaken up his Cabinet, making some new appointments and doing so following the resignation of Colonial Secretary Oliver Lyttelton.

Washington: They may abandon Ellis Island as an immigration station. It has been recommended.

(*US Savings Bond Announcement*) That's the story folks. Glad we could get together. This is John Cameron Swayze saying good night.

TOP PANEL SHOW OF THE YEAR

GOODSON-TODMAN PRODUCTIONS

What's My Line?

WHAT'S MY LINE?

A Mark Goodson-Bill Todman Production
in association with the CBS Television
Network

EXECUTIVE PRODUCER . . . . GIL FATES

DIRECTED BY . . . . FRANKLIN HELLER

COORDINATOR . . . . BOB BACH

PROGRAM MANAGER . . . . . FRANCES TROCAINE

PANEL

DOROTHY KILGALLEN

STEVE ALLEN

ARLENE FRANCIS

VICTOR BORGE

MODERATOR: JOHN DALY

SPONSOR: STOPETTE SPRAY DEODORANT

TELECAST: JANUARY 31, 1954

WHAT'S MY LINE?

EASILY THE MOST POPULAR PANEL SHOW on the air, *What's My Line?* is seen by more than 10 million viewers every week and has hit the "top ten" in popularity ratings for nearly four years (unusual for "ad lib" shows).

On this show, a panel of expert game players is allowed a limited number of questions with which to cross examine a contestant (who can only answer "yes" or "no") in an attempt to uncover his occupation. The program won the 1950 Michael Award of the Academy of Radio and Television Arts and Sciences as the best panel show on the air.

The humble beginning of *What's My Line?* is almost forgotten. Someone asked the producers, Mark Goodson and Bill Todman, if, at parties, they ever tried to guess the occupations of the other guests. This led to the idea that they might be able to build a quiz game around occupations. After long conferences,

187

they arrived at a format which would include an individual, taken off the street, and have the televiewer guess his occupation. This evolved into a panel of experts questioning a selected contestant.

The show was planned originally as a serious program. However, during auditions, it was discovered that the questions were full of potential laughs, and so it was switched and played for comedy. Since then, *What's My Line?* has skyrocketed to popularity and has become the forerunner of almost all other television panel shows.

Bill Todman was born in New York in 1916. He went to Johns Hopkins University in preparation for a medical career but soon discovered his interest in writing and the theatre. He worked in a department store, an advertising agency and finally headed its radio department. Later, he became a free lance writer. It was on one of his shows, *Battle of the Boroughs,* that Todman met Mark Goodson who had been hired as emcee.

Four years of free lancing passed, however, before they were to get together as the greatest "package producing" pair the country has seen. During this time, Todman earned his living as a writer, director and producer of radio programs.

Mark Goodson was born in Sacramento in 1915. He worked his way through the University of California at Berkeley and won his Phi Beta Kappa key. In his senior year, he got a job directing a local radio show and after graduation went with KJBS in San Francisco. He later moved to KFRC as staff announcer.

For that station, Goodson handled numerous quiz shows and later moved to New York, in search of a job. In 1941, he was hired as emcee of the quiz show, *Battle of the Boroughs,* where he met Bill Todman. It was not until 1946, that the team sold their first quiz show, *Winner Take All* to CBS. The program was an almost instant success. Other shows followed, most of which have been both financial and popularity achievements. Best known include: *Its News To Me, I've Got A Secret, Beat The Clock, The Name's The Same* and *The Web.*

WHAT'S MY LINE?

ANNOUNCER

Time now for everybody's favorite guessing game *What's My Line?* Yes, time now for *What's My Line?* Now let us hear our award winning *What's My Line?* panel. First, the popular columnist whose "Voice of Broadway" appears in the Journal American and papers coast to coast, Miss Dorothy Kilgallen.

DOROTHY KILGALLEN

And on my left, the brilliant young humorist who conducts his own very funny television show nightly Monday through Friday, on another network, Mr. Steve Allen.

STEVE ALLEN

Thanks very much. I now want you to meet one of the loveliest ladies of radio and television who has her own show on another network. We are all working at a great pace these days. Arlene Francis.

ARLENE FRANCIS

And on my left substituting for Bennett Cerf tonight, a vastly entertaining gentleman who is packing them in at his own one-man show at the Golden

Theatre in New York, Mr. Victor Borge.

VICTOR BORGE

On my left, that well known news commentator and moderator, Mr. John Daly.

JOHN DALY

Good evening ladies and gentlemen and welcome to *What's My Line?* Once again tonight we have some friends in from around and about the country who brought with them some very interesting occupations and the panel will have to tussle with the occupations—Victor Borge, getting his baptism of fire. We hope that they will have a lot of trouble so that our guests will carry home some prizes although the more important thing is that they have some fun. We will also have a famous guest challenger a bit later on. But right now it's time for our experts to meet the first challenger whose job has to be spotted. Will you sign in please, Sir.

(*Guest signs J. L. May on blackboard*)

JOHN DALY

Come over here with me. Well Mr. May don't stand so far away. What does J. L. stand for?

MAY

Julius L. May.

DALY

Where from, Sir?

MAY

New York City.

DALY

New York City, well I don't think there are any strangers over there as far as you're concerned, but you may be a stranger to them. Will you go over and say, "Hello" to them, please. (*May walks to panel to shake hands*)

KILGALLEN

Good evening.

DALY

All right Mr. May, will you come over here now please and sit down next to me. I think perhaps you know at this point the panel gets one free guess as to what your line may be. We always begin the free guessing with Miss Kilgallen.

KILGALLEN

I think he is in the tailoring business.

DALY

Mr. Allen.

ALLEN

I think he is in charge of bird seed at the old flow plant here in town.

ARLENE FRANCIS

I think he is a tea bag tester.

VICTOR BORGE

I think he is a floor walker.

DALY

No, I am afraid not. Now we'll let our viewers at home have a further look at Mr. Julius May and at the same time we will tell them what his line is. (*Card saying: Printer of Parking Tickets*)

Mr. May or Mr. Julius May, if I may —I think perhaps you know the rules here. Everytime I flip a card you have given the panel a "no" answer. When you have given the panel 10 "no" answers you have got it all in the bag. All set?

MAY

All right.

DALY

Mr. May is salaried. With that, let us begin the general questioning with Steve Allen.

ALLEN

Pardon me, Mr. Julius LaRosa May. (*Arlene Francis laughs*) Thank you, Arlene. Is there a product connected with what you are doing?

MAY

Yes.

ALLEN

The sort of thing that I might come into contact with?

DALY

Is it the sort of thing *you* might come into contact with? Yes, yes indeed.

ALLEN

I can never tell why, every time I ask that question, it always seems amusing. However, trying to figure it out I might say, if you were to wear this on Fifth Avenue would people laugh?

DALY

If you were to wear this on Fifth Avenue would the people laugh? If *you* were to wear it, I think they would.

ALLEN

Could this be anything that might be associated with a woman?

DALY

Yes, this could be associated with a woman.

ALLEN

Is it something a man might give to a woman?

DALY

Yes.

ALLEN

Are they or is this as the case may be fairly expensive?

DALY

Could it be fairly expensive? Well, I would say this. I think it is only fair, and I think Mr. May would agree with me, it could be expensive. Yes, don't you think?

(*Looking at May*)

MAY

Absolutely.

ALLEN

Is this something a woman might pick up on Fifth Avenue around Tiffany's or Cartier's neighborhood?

DALY

Is this something a woman might pick up on Fifth Avenue around Tiffany's or Cartier's neighborhood?— Yes.

ALLEN

If a man gave a woman one of these could she wear it around her neck?

DALY

Mr. May makes the point that she could wear it around her neck. Yes.

ALLEN

Let me come right out and straighten the whole thing out. Is this anything in the jewelry line at all?

DALY

No, that's one down and nine to go. Miss Francis.

FRANCIS

Is it possible that Mr. May may deal with something other than human beings?

MAY

How do you mean that?

FRANCIS

You know what is other than a human being, John. Could he have anything to do with animals?

DALY

No. Two down and eight to go. Mr. Borge.

BORGE

Is it something Steve Allen can get in contact with? Something I can get in contact with also?

DALY

Yes.

BORGE

As well as Steve?

DALY

Yes. Steve.

ALLEN

I'll split it with you, Victor.

BORGE

Is it something a lady can wear around the neck?

DALY

Yes, it was answered already. Preferably, she would not.

BORGE

Would it be below the, uh, below the lower neck?

DALY

Well, Victor, I think I will have to give you a "no" on that. It cannot be worn below the lower neck. Three down, seven to go.

KILGALLEN

All right, I want to know if Arlene and I can come in contact with it, then we'll get the whole panel going with this thing.

DALY

Yes.

KILGALLEN

Would I enjoy coming in contact with it?

DALY

I am afraid not. Four down, six to go. Mr. Allen.

ALLEN

Would I also not enjoy it?

DALY

Would he also not enjoy coming in contact?

MAY

I think not.

DALY

Yes, you would not enjoy coming in contact with this thing.

ALLEN

Now let us keep it off our necks. It is unpleasant in some way?

DALY

He thinks it might be unpleasant.

MAY

In most cases, yes.

DALY

As a matter of fact he is having a hard time thinking of a case where it would not be unpleasant.

ALLEN

Is the idea of punishment associated with this product?

DALY

I think we would better say yes.

ALLEN

Something you wear around your neck? That's a noose. Do you find this associated with prisoners, they're in jail?

DALY

No, I don't think so. That's five down and five to go. I am going to give you another minute to try and guess it. Miss Francis.

FRANCIS

Do you say, Mr. May that all of us could come in contact with it, but we would not be likely to come in contact with it?

MAY

I cannot say a single soul on that panel would not be likely to come in contact with it.

DALY

That's six down four to go. Mr. Borge.

BORGE

Is it something that is worn?

DALY

No, seven down three to go and thirty seconds. Miss Kilgallen.

KILGALLEN

Is this something that in order to be used must be imposed by one person upon another?

DALY

I think that is correct.

KILGALLEN

Would anyone ever strike a person with it?

DALY

Would anyone ever strike a person with it?

KILGALLEN

Yes, or otherwise belabor.

DALY

That would be eight down two to go. I don't think you are even close to what this might be. Mr. May prints parking tickets. Mr. May you won the full prize.

MAY

I am giving my money to the March of Dimes.

DALY

Yes sir, the full prize is yours and will go to the March of Dimes. Well panel, a rather inauspicious beginning but a lot of fun. Let us see what you can do with the second challenger. Will you sign in, please, Ma'm?

(*Guest signs in on blackboard*)

DALY

Amy E. Shortie Hiller. You are not so short, you are not so short at all as a matter of fact. Is it Miss or Mrs.?

HILLER

Miss.

DALY

And where are you from?

HILLER

Houston, Texas.

DALY

Sounds very much like all of Texas has moved to New York this weekend. Well, we have got some folks here from New York. Would you like to say hello to them?

(*Guest walks to panel*)

I think perhaps you know that after the panel has had a chance to meet you, we give the panel one free guess as to what your line may be. We always begin with Dot.

KILGALLEN

I think she's a steer roper.

ALLEN

I think she's a rope steerer and we have heard these jokes before.

FRANCIS

I think she teaches ballet.

BORGE

I think she's awfully cute.

(*Gorilla Hunter*)

DALY

We'll let our viewers have another look at Miss Hiller of Houston, Texas. And now Miss Hiller the panel has got to take it from here and I will flip the card every time they give a no answer. Miss Hiller is self-employed. Let us begin the general questioning with Mr. Borge.

BORGE

Oh my goodness! Is there a product involved?

HILLER

Yes.

BORGE

Thank you. Is this a thing? Could it be found in the home?

HILLER

Yes, yes it can be but it is not normally found in the home.

BORGE

Can it be found outside the home?

DALY
Yes.

BORGE
Can I wear it outside when I go out?

HILLER
I am afraid not.

BORGE
Could I take it with me?

DALY
We said you couldn't wear it, Victor, so I'd better give you a "no."

BORGE
As a matter of fact, my question was can I take it with me when I go out?

DALY
Yes, but you didn't say that, so that is one down and nine to go. Miss Kilgallen.

KILGALLEN
Would this thing be unwieldly to carry in the hand?

DALY
Yes.

KILGALLEN
Does it ever move around?

DALY
Yes.

KILGALLEN
Is this anything that is or has been living?

DALY
Yes.

KILGALLEN
Is it in the animal kingdom?

DALY
Yes.

KILGALLEN
Is it a four legged animal?

DALY
Yes.

KILGALLEN
Is it usually larger than a breadbox when it is full grown? Are there a lot of these things in Texas?

DALY
No. I think they grow a lot of everything in Texas.

ALLEN
You have something to do with a four legged animal that is very scarce in Texas. I think it was very clever of me to figure that out. Is it an animal that might be more at home in another part of the world?

HILLER
Yes.

ALLEN
In the tropical section of the world perhaps?

HILLER
Yes.

ALLEN
Is it a wild animal sort of thing like lions and tigers?

DALY
It belongs in the wild category.

ALLEN
Is it a cat of any kind?

DALY
No. Three down and seven to go.

FRANCIS
Is this an animal that interested Darwin?

DALY
Yes, I believe he had some interest in it.

FRANCIS
This animal, is it part of the monkey, orang-utan or gorilla family? What a family!

DALY

I would think it might be. Wouldn't it?

FRANCIS

Well, does it come in one of the categories I mentioned?

DALY

Well, I never looked under one of the categories you mentioned. I would say yes.

FRANCIS

Can this animal be taught to do amusing things?

HILLER

Yes.

FRANCIS

I take it we'll not go through them all. It still could be orang-utan or is it perhaps in the monkey family?

DALY

Is it perhaps in the monkey family? You've used the definition yourself. Four down six to go. Mr. Borge.

BORGE

Is it established that it has four legs?

DALY

Yes.

BORGE

A monkey doesn't have four legs. It has two legs and two arms.

DALY

For the purpose of this program, we will consider all three of these species have four legs.

KILGALLEN

Well, is it in the gorilla family?

DALY

Yes.

KILGALLEN

Then Miss Hiller has something to do with gorillas.

DALY

Yes.

KILGALLEN

Does she raise or train them?

DALY

I am afraid that you're not quite right. Mr. Allen.

ALLEN

She's a nice girl. I don't know what she does if she doesn't train them. She sells them.

DALY

That makes it six down and four to go. Miss Francis.

FRANCIS

She buys them.

DALY

Seven down, three to go.

BORGE

She eats them.

KILGALLEN

You mean she imports them?

DALY

She hunts them. She goes on trips and hunts them. Miss Hiller are you going out anytime again soon?

MISS HILLER

Well, I hope to go.

DALY

Can I give you some hunters to take with you? I'll give you Mr. Borge and Mr. Allen. Well, you get the full prize and thank you for being a wonderful guest on *What's My Line?*

(Panel is blindfolded)

In just a moment we will meet tonight's mystery guest. Now we come to the special feature of our program, the appearance of our mystery celebrity. My friends on the panel, as well as the audience, here, all of you will recognize our guest immediately, so we give the panel members blindfolds.

Will you come in, mystery challenger, and sign in, please. (*Guest signs Dick Widmark*) Panel, as you know in the case of our mystery challenger we get right down to general questioning which we will begin with Miss Arlene Francis.

FRANCIS
Are you associated with some branch of the entertainment industry?

DALY
Yes.

FRANCIS
Have you been in pictures?

WIDMARK
Yes Ma'm.

FRANCIS
And judging from your voice you have been in the motion picture industry a long time. Are you a character actor? Are you a Western star?

WIDMARK
I'd sure like to be, Ma'm.

FRANCIS
I think you could make it. What did I get on that?

DALY
Well actually, our guest covers so wide a scope in Hollywood that you just keep on trying and you will cover all the ground.

FRANCIS
All right. Would you be considered the leading man, the star of the picture?

WIDMARK
I guess so.

FRANCIS
Have you been in radio?

WIDMARK
Yes, Ma'm.

FRANCIS
And the theater?

WIDMARK
Yes, Ma'm.

FRANCIS
Were you in any other of these mediums before you were in pictures or since you went into pictures?

DALY
That cannot be answered yes or no, Miss Francis.

FRANCIS
That's what I figured. Maybe you'd be carried away. Were you in radio or theater before you entered the pictures?

WIDMARK
Yes, I was.

FRANCIS
Oh well . . . were you a star in either radio or theater?

DALY
Mmmmmm. That makes it one down and nine to go. Mr. Borge . . . we have just a little more than three minutes to go.

BORGE
You have two legs?

DALY
Yes, Mr. Borge.

BORGE
Thank you. Is it established that you play dramatic parts only?

WIDMARK
Sometimes.

BORGE
Do you play them only sometimes?

WIDMARK
That's what a lot of people told me.

BORGE
I see then that you always do comedy parts.

WIDMARK
Very rare.

BORGE
But you do them and the answer is "yes" up until now? But I cannot see a thing and I don't know what to write.

DALY
We only have about two minutes and fifteen seconds to go.

KILGALLEN
When you were in the New York theater were you in dramatic plays rather than musicals?

WIDMARK
Yes.

KILGALLEN
Were you ever in a play in which there was a scene in the hospital?

WIDMARK
No.

DALY
Two down and eight to go . . . Mr. Allen.

ALLEN
Is there a product connected with what you are doing? Now, let me see. Are you over forty?

WIDMARK
No.

DALY
Three down and seven to go. Miss Francis.

FRANCIS
Oh, you're a young man. Are you employed in any picture currently on Broadway?

WIDMARK
No, Ma'm.

DALY
Four down and six to go. Mr. Borge.

BORGE
Are you playing in any picture that doesn't play on Broadway? Have you very recently had a hit?

WIDMARK
No.

DALY
Five down, five to go. Miss Kilgallen.

KILGALLEN
Have you ever played a bad man? Have you ever played a gangster?

WIDMARK
Yes . . . well, some.

KILGALLEN
Did you ever have a distinguishing characteristic . . . that was imitated by little kids all over the country?

WIDMARK
Yes, Ma'm.

KILGALLEN
Have you ever pushed an old lady down the stairs?

WIDMARK
Yes, Ma'm.

KILGALLEN
Are you Dick Widmark?

WIDMARK

Yes, Ma'm (*applause*)

(*Blindfolds come off*)

DALY

Dick, I know that you are here to help the March of Dimes. But I believe there is another reason why you are here.

WIDMARK

Yes. I am here on behalf of the March of Dimes and to open a new CinemaScope 20th Century Fox Production called, *Hell and High Water* . . . and by the way, John, one of the stars of the picture, *Hell and High Water* is in the audience tonight . . . Miss Bella Darby.

DALY

Oh, how nice. Please stand up. Thank you very much. It was nice of you to come and to bring such a pretty lady with you . . . and before our panel says "good night," may I remind you to tune in again Sunday at 10:30 p.m., Eastern Standard time, when once again we remind you to play *What's My Line?* For other localities, check your local listings for date and time of our weekly series.

Next week, David Wayne will be here to substitute for our missing panelist. This is John Daly, saying "good night."

KILGALLEN

Good night, Steve.

ALLEN

Good night, Victor and good night Arlene, wherever you are.

FRANCIS

I'm here. Good night and it was wonderful to have you on the show, Victor. Come back and see us again.

BORGE

Thank you very much. Good night, John.

DALY

May I say thanks to you and I hope you come back real soon. Good night, ladies and gentlemen and thanks for being with us on

What's My Line?
(*fade out*)

TOP POLITICAL PANEL SHOW
OF THE YEAR

MEET THE PRESS

Governor Herman Talmadge of Georgia, Guest

MEET THE PRESS

Governor Herman Talmadge of Georgia, Guest

PRODUCER: LAWRENCE E. SPIVAK

PANEL

EDGAR ALLAN POE   New Orleans Times Picayune

ROBERT RIGGS   Louisville Courier Journal

MAY CRAIG   Portland, Maine, Press Herald

LAWRENCE E. SPIVAK   Mercury Publications

MODERATOR: NED BROOKS

SPONSORED BY PAN AMERICAN WORLD AIRLINES
TELECAST: JUNE 6, 1954
NBC TELEVISION NETWORK

MEET THE PRESS

A PROGRAM WHICH HAS PRODUCED MORE NEWS than any other television program in America, *Meet the Press* has won almost every important award including the coveted Peabody Award.

Meet the Press is an unrehearsed and uncensored press conference, subjecting national and international personalities to the penetrating questions of some of the country's ablest journalists. It brings to millions of viewers the drama inherent in the "give and take" which occurs when the press seeks an answer to important questions.

The program has made history in numerous instances. *Meet the Press's* interview with Whittaker Chambers is credited with having started the chain of events which led to the arrest and conviction of Alger Hiss. Because of what he said on *Meet the Press,* Gerhard Eisler was picked up by the FBI and convicted of perjury. The program is credited with having played an important part in the nomination of both Eisenhower and Stevenson in 1952.

Meet the Press has made an important contribution to journalism and proves, once again, the tremendous educational possibilities of television.

We have chosen a significant 1954 *Meet the Press* program script for

TOP TV SHOWS OF THE YEAR. The telecast on June 6, 1954 presented as its guest the Governor of Georgia, Herman Talmadge, a leading defender of segregation, and this interview took place immediately after the Supreme Court had handed down its historic decision ending racial segregation in the public schools.

Lawrence E. Spivak, producer and permanent panel member of *Meet the Press,* was born in New York City and is a graduate of Harvard University. Before becoming editor and publisher of the *American Mercury* Magazine, which he sold in 1950, he was business manager for *Antiques* Magazine and was director of circulation for *Hunting and Fishing* Magazine.

Mr. Spivak pioneered in the publication of paper-covered books. His Mercury Books, selling for 25¢, preceded the publication of current popular paper-covered books by more than two years. It was he who sold the Army on the idea of issuing special overseas editions for the troops and he did the first series for them. In the last year of the war, 50 million books were published. Until very recently, Mr. Spivak owned and published *Ellery Queen's Mystery Magazine, Fantasy* and *Science Fiction* Magazine and Mercury Mystery Books.

In 1946, together with Martha Rountree, Mr. Spivak founded *Meet the Press.* Today he is sole owner and producer and permanent member of the panel.

Mr. Spivak maintains homes in both Washington and in New York. He is married to the former Charlotte Bier Ring, a psychologist. He has two children, Judith, who is married to William Lee Frost in the Foreign Service, and Jonathan, a newspaper reporter.

MEET THE PRESS

ANNOUNCER: Now Ladies and Gentlemen, *Meet the Press,* the Peabody Award winner. Ready for this evening's spontaneous, unrehearsed press conference are four of America's top reporters. Their questions, please remember, do not necessarily reflect their point of view. It's their way of getting a story for you. Here now is the moderator of *Meet the Press,* Mr. Ned Brooks.

BROOKS: Good evening and welcome once again to *Meet the Press.* The recent Supreme Court decision directing an end to racial segregation in the public schools has touched off a new controversy in the south. The ruling has some far-reaching implications affecting as it does the school systems in 17 states, having a total enrollment of about 11 million pupils. For nearly 60 years the states have been permitted under a previous Supreme Court decision to maintain separate schools for white and Negro pupils as long as the facilities were

equal. The Court now says that under that doctrine, Negro pupils are barred from equal opportunity for education. Our guest tonight is Governor Herman Talmadge of Georgia, who is leading the fight to retain separate school systems. In spite of the Court ruling, Governor Talmadge says he will continue segregation in Georgia as long as he holds his present office. Now, Governor Talmadge, if you're ready, I think we'll let Mr. Spivak have the first question.

SPIVAK: Governor, in a message to the state of Georgia in January of '53, you had this to say, and I'd like to quote it. "Provisions of separate but adequate and equal school facilities is a requirement of our Georgia constitution for the children of both races. For the first time in its history, our state is making an honest all-out effort to live up to this section of our constitution." Now isn't that confirmation of what the Supreme Court said, that the doctrine of separate but equal does not work?

TALMADGE: My statement is correct, Mr. Spivak, but the Supreme Court said lots of things to my mind it shouldn't have said. It overruled all existing precedent that this nation has ever seen and uprooted the Constitution of the United States, repealed the 10th Amendment of the Constitution of the United States, and occupied the field of public education. Georgia today with the resources that she possesses, is doing more for education, both white and colored, than any state in the Union.

SPIVAK: Governor, may I come back to my original question?

TALMADGE: Sure.

SPIVAK: Didn't what you said in '53 confirm what the Supreme Court said on the question of the doctrine of separate but equal? You had 58 years in the State of Georgia since the Plethy v. Ferguson decision about separate but equal schools. Yet you yourself said "for the first time in our history an honest effort is being made to live up to this section of our constitution."

TALMADGE: I wasn't Governor for the 58 years preceding. I'm carrying out the Constitution of Georgia.

SPIVAK: You will admit though that the separate but equal doctrine has not worked up until that time.

TALMADGE: We haven't had adequate educational facilities in 58 years for white people nor colored people. We do have for both now.

POE: I'd like to ask you if the Supreme Court should say specifically that Georgia must comply with this decree, what would you do then?

TALMADGE: Well I might have to go into a little detail to answer your question. Number one, the Constitution of the State of Georgia empowers the state to levy taxes only for segregated schools. The minute we have non-segregated schools, our state and local governments would be without authority to levy taxes. Number two, the appropriations to the General Assembly made by the General Assembly of Georgia for school purposes contain a provision that those appropriations cease the minute we have mixed schools in our state. Number three, as Governor of the State of Georgia, I am director of the State's Budget, and as Budget Director, I am going to enforce the law. We will not have mixed schools in Georgia as long as I am Governor of the state.

POE: Governor, I presume you concur then with Justice Jackson that there will be about a generation of litigation going on in this country.

TALMADGE: I would say at least a generation, probably more.

CRAIG: Governor, the Supreme Court is set up by the Constitution to interpret law. Do you set yourself above the Supreme Court?

TALMADGE: I might give you some better authority than myself, Mrs. Craig. The preceding Supreme Courts held that separate but equal facilities were valid under our Constitution. On those courts sat such Justices as Fuller, Field, Gray, Brewer, Brown,

Sharris, White, Peckham, Taft, Holmes, Van Devanter, McReynolds, Brandeis, Sutherland, Butler, Sanford, Stone and Rawls, all of whom upheld the separate but equal doctrine.

CRAIG: What's that got to do with it? They're dead and gone now. You're dealing with the present Supreme Court and present decision. Can you set yourself above it?

TALMADGE: I might quote you another outstanding authority. Here's what former Supreme Court Justice Cardozo had to say, and he's recognized by everyone as one of the most able jurists the nation ever had. I quote from his book: "Judges have of course the power though not the right to ignore the mandate of a statute, and render judgment in despite of it. They have the power, though not the right, to travel beyond the bounds set to judicial enervation by precedent and custom. Nonetheless, by that abusive power they violate the law."

CRAIG: I feel you're evading me. Justice Cardozo did not participate in this decision. This was a unanimous decision of all the nine justices, only two of them appointed by a Republican, and they have said segregation must go. Now I ask you how you set yourself above the Supreme Court?

TALMADGE: Let me answer that question in this way. I admit the Supreme Court has ruled and under the Constitution of our United States, having made that decision, it becomes the supreme law of our land. But I must recite to you that there are many precedents in history where tyranny has been resisted by the people and when you just by simple judicial decree try to wash away the customs of the centuries, the people will not accept it.

CRAIG: You have said that you would fight for your way of life. You don't mean armed rebellion against the United States, do you?

TALMADGE: I hope it will not come to that.

CRAIG: Are you prepared to do that?

TALMADGE: No, we're not going to call out any troops in Georgia except to enforce our law as long as it remains law, and I'm going to uphold my law. No Federal Court can make me spend money contrary to the laws of Georgia.

RIGGS: You said there would be no mixed classes held. Your term expires next January.

TALMADGE: Expires next January. Under the Constitution of Georgia, I am ineligible to seek reelection.

RIGGS: Is it true the court has set a time—this couldn't come to a head during your administration?

TALMADGE: They're calling for us to come up to visit them in October. We're not coming.

RIGGS: By the time you got there, you'd be out of office.

TALMADGE: I'd be out of office next January.

RIGGS: I judge from your reply you're faced with a situation where there would be no schools at all in Georgia.

TALMADGE: It's entirely possible. The people of Georgia are going to maintain separate schools in our state, come what may.

RIGGS: It's your opinion that the people of Georgia, if they choose between non-segregated schools and no schools at all, will take no public schools at all.

TALMADGE: They would take no public schools at all and subsidize the children to go to private schools. If we have no public school system, we wouldn't have any law requiring any schools. But the thinking of all of us in Georgia is that we should certainly continue education. In order to continue it under that method, we would grant a subsidy to all school children, white and colored, who went to private schools.

RIGGS: Suppose you had a private school using public money and not allowing—

TALMADGE: Private school wouldn't use public money. The tuition fees would be granted by the state to pay admission to private school.

RIGGS: If you spent state money to a private school, you are—

TALMADGE: You are using it to support tuition fees in going to private schools. The state of Georgia pays tuition fees to many private schools now. We pay them to Harvard and other schools all over the country.

RIGGS: Supposing you were paying this tuition only for white children

and a colored parent sued you?

TALMADGE: If Georgia money is spent for tuition fees, it will be spent for white and colored children.

RIGGS: But not in the same school.

TALMADGE: No sir.

RIGGS: Suppose a test case did come from your state, a certain person brought the test case and the Supreme Court ordered your state to put this person in school?

TALMADGE: We wouldn't have any school to put him in.

BROOKS: Did I understand you to say Georgia is not going to avail itself of the opportunity to present to the Supreme Court any new material or new ideas on this decision?

TALMADGE: I don't know of any reason why we should. Georgia is not a party to the suit. I don't see why we should become a party to the suit by invitation, particularly after the suit has been lost. I have never believed in accepting invitations to my own execution.

SPIVAK: Governor, one of the arguments you raise is that this decision is unconstitutional or illegal. Isn't it true that the Supreme Court has many times reversed itself? Can you rightfully say that you will obey one decision and not another?

TALMADGE: I'll say this, Mr. Spivak. In rendering this decision, they reversed five previous decisions of their own Supreme Court.

SPIVAK: Haven't they often done that?

TALMADGE: They've reversed 13

decisions of their own federal courts, 59 decisions of state and territorial courts. Now if our court has degenerated to a body that no lawyer can anticipate and determine what law will be, but can only say what the law was the last time the Supreme Court ruled, then we are in a serious predicament in this country.

SPIVAK: Isn't it true that the last rule is the one that applies?

TALMADGE: Yes, that's the rule.

SPIVAK: You said you don't think the Supreme Court decision is legal. If you don't think it is legal, why do you plan to make legalistic moves in your state to get around the decision?

TALMADGE: We are not, of course, going to secede from the Union. If the Supreme Court says something is the law, of course right or wrong, it's the law until corrected. But the people themselves are the court of last resort and they have constitutional and judicial and legislative remedies and we're going to pursue that.

SPIVAK: You are accepting this decision, then, as the legal decision of the Supreme Court?

TALMADGE: We do not recognize it as a legal decision. We know that it is a decree of the United States Supreme Court, yes.

SPIVAK: And as such you're accepting it?

TALMADGE: We are not accepting it.

SPIVAK: Why do you go about, then, making legalistic moves to evade it if you're not accepting it?

TALMADGE: Because, Mr. Spivak, we realize that it's the Supreme Court of the United States and we cannot openly defy a decision of the United States Supreme Court, so it will be necessary for us to get our house in order to meet any future decisions of that court.

SPIVAK: Suppose the court, after you supposedly have gotten your house in order, suppose the court says to you: "this is an evasion, this is a lot of paper stuff, this is illegal." What are you going to do then?

TALMADGE: Of course, Mr. Spivak, reading the decision of this court, when it gets into sociological theories and proceeds to legislate for the people of our country, and when it says it's going to exercise executive power to enforce that decree, they could do anything. But I am convinced that as long as the people of my state, and at least 90% of the white and colored people want their schools left alone just like they are, and as long as that sentiment continues in our state, no amount of any judicial brain washing will ever change it.

SPIVAK: The Supreme Court hasn't said you have to have non-segregated schools. The Supreme Court has simply said that it is illegal, that you must not have a law about it. If the white people and the colored people of your state want to go to separate schools, why don't you repeal your laws and let them do it?

TALMADGE: We **are** going to let them do it. In fact, we're going to insist on it.

SPIVAK: Insisting and letting, Governor, is quite a different thing. Are you going to do it voluntarily? Are you going to allow them to go to their separate schools voluntarily, or are you going to insist that they go?

TALMADGE: We are going to exercise every sovereign authority that the state possesses to see that they do go to separate schools.

POE: Governor, the state of Mississippi a few weeks ago passed, the legislature passed a 1954 law providing for the individual assignment of pupils on the basis of health and welfare; it didn't mention color. Could this be a legal answer?

TALMADGE: It's been recommended by some in the state of Georgia. But the decision of the same Supreme Court stated that you cannot classify students by color in schools. That was their ruling, in public schools. Ultimately our state might have to choose between a segregated public school system and private schools, and if we have to make that choice, we're going to retain a segregated system of schools.

POE: From a political standpoint, I might ask, which, the Republicans or the Democrats, are getting credit for this decision?

TALMADGE: Well, I don't think either one of them are escaping entirely. Of course, we know the United States Supreme Court bench is composed of seven Democrats and two Republicans, eight appointed by a Democratic President, one appointed by a Republican President. But the Chief Justice who wrote the decision was appointed by a Republican President, and then, surprisingly enough, some way he managed to get the Court to give a unanimous verdict. So I think the Republicans will carry the burden of the criticism in the southern states.

CRAIG: Governor, we've been talking about the legal aspect. But isn't it true that your real objection is to the social mixture of races?

TALMADGE: Well, Mrs. Craig, there are a number of reasons. First, we think that each state certainly has the right to operate its public school system as it sees fit. Also in our state we have three and a half million people, two thirds of them white, one third of them colored. All of them want to retain their civilization and their culture. The while people want to retain their civilization; so do the colored people. They want to retain their respective churches. They want to retain their respective schools. And for centuries our two peoples have not associated with each other socially, nor do we expect to do so at the present time.

CRAIG: Governor, I'm a South Carolinian by birth and I have some way of judging. I have never met any colored person that preferred segregation. However, I will not dispute your opinion. I want to ask you this. Don't you think that segregation, whether you like it or not, is un-American and un-Christian, and undemocratic?

TALMADGE: First, let me say that the colored people of Gloster County, Georgia, two weeks ago voted 600 to nothing to retain their present segregated school system. Second, when it comes to Christianity, as I read my Bible, the Good Lord made all of us. He made some of us white, He made some of us black, He made some of us red, He made some of us yellow. He put the white people in Europe, He put the black people in Africa, He put the red people in the Americas, He put the yellow people in Asia. And I believe if He had wanted one race and one color, He would have created one race and one color. And I think when He segregated them, that that's good enough for me.

CRAIG: How can we seek allies around the world among the black, brown and yellow peoples to fight for freedom against Communism if we ourselves do not practice it in this country?

TALMADGE: Mrs. Craig, we had allies before we started tampering with our Constitution and trying to bribe people all over the world and since that time, why we have lost our allies. One reason we have lost them is because the yellow people are running the white people of Asia. They're segregating us.

CRAIG: Are you willing to let all of Asia go to the Communists?

TALMADGE: Mrs. Craig, I don't think it's a question of whether I'm willing or not. It looks like to me our government has pretty well deter-mined that policy already. Unless I'm surprised, the whole of Asia is going Communist at an early date.

CRAIG: Don't you think we owe a debt to the colored people? They have no other home but this country.

TALMADGE: The colored people in the south get along better than the colored people anywhere on the face of the earth. I'm not interested in trying to please Communists at home or abroad.

RIGGS: Governor, the week after the school ruling by the Supreme Court, it took another action in a San Francisco case that seemed to say there could not be segregation in public housing. The case isn't quite clear, and there's some argument about it. But if it means no segregation in public housing, would you be opposed to further public housing?

TALMADGE: I have been reading with interest lots about that in the city of Chicago. It seems a colored family moved in a white housing project out there some months ago. Since that time, it has taken 4,000 policemen in the City of Chicago to protect one colored family. Imagine what it would be with all of the millions of white and colored people in the south if you had a similar situation.

SPIVAK: Governor, a thing I find it hard to understand is this: So many southerners I know have no objection to having colored servants cook their food, colored nurses for their children, no objection to living in close intimacy with the colored people, and yet when it comes to having little children in the same school with the white children, you suddenly say: "this is bad, this is wrong."

TALMADGE: Mr. Spivak, that's something for everyone to determine himself. In my state the laws and the customs and habits and thinking of the citizens will prohibit any sort of forced mixing of the races in the schools. We are not going to have it, come what may.

SPIVAK: Is it that the southerners of Georgia believe that integration is good on a master-servant basis, but bad on a basis of equality of opportunity? If you can associate with them in a relationship of servant and master, why can't little children sit in the same schools and be taught by the same teachers?

TALMADGE: Well, I'll answer that question again. The people of Georgia don't want it and won't have it, and won't permit it under any conditions. Of course we've had a master-servant relationship with the colored people in our state for many years. On the other hand, we have some very fine colored citizens. We have inferior white citizens. We have inferior colored citizens. We have inferior yellow citizens. We have inferior red men. I wouldn't say any one race specifically is inferior because all of them have superior and inferior individuals. But you cannot by judicial decree, Mr. Spivak, change the habits, customs, thoughts and lives of people that have developed for centuries.

SPIVAK: Governor, if that is so, if you have those habits and if you have that natural law of association, I ask you again why is it necessary for you to have laws to force people to segregate? If they want to segregate, if they will do it voluntarily, why don't you let them do it and not force them to?

TALMADGE: I wouldn't say 100% of the white people want segregated schools nor 100% of the colored people, but the overwhelming majority of both races do want segregated schools.

SPIVAK: Are the people of Georgia any different fundamentally from the people of a great many other states? Isn't it true that in a great many states of the Union segregation has been ended? There has been no blood, there's been no great evil, New York has no segregation, and I think some 16 or 17 other states have laws against it. What about that?

TALMADGE: You'll find different problems in the same state, let alone the 48 states. That's the reason when our forefathers drafted the Constitution of the United States, they provided for local self-government. They knew that the problems might be different in Maine from what they would be in Georgia. They knew they might be different in Arizona from what they might be in Oregon. They therefore very wisely framed the 10th Amendment of the Constitution of the United States which reads as follows: "All authority not specifically granted to federal government nor prohibited to states, is hereby reserved unto the states and the people." Now that's plain English and it means just what it says, and anybody can understand it.

SPIVAK: Isn't it true the 14th Amendment came after the 10th Amendment and it said that you cannot deny to any person within your jurisdiction the equal protection of your laws?

TALMADGE: The 14th Amendment was adopted at a time when we had 37 states in the Union. The majority of them had segregated schools at that time; when my own state adopted the 14th Amendment, it set up a public school segregated system at the same time. That's no indication as to the intent of the framers of our Constitution. The Supreme Court so held until two weeks ago.

RIGGS: Are there any schools in your state, private or public, high or low, which do not have segregation?

TALMADGE: No, there are no schools in Georgia which have non-segregation.

RIGGS: Your people have never tried it, have they?

TALMADGE: Our people have never tried it.

RIGGS: They don't know whether they'd like it or not.

TALMADGE: They certainly do know they don't want it. They wouldn't accept it.

CRAIG: When you use the phrase "white supremacy," do you not thereby say all colored people are inferior?

TALMADGE: I have never used the term "white supremacy" in my life.

CRAIG: Do you believe in it?

TALMADGE: I believe that the white civilization is much older than the colored civilization. It has accomplished much more.

BROOKS: I'm afraid we're going to have to leave it there. I'm sorry to interrupt, but our time is up. Thank you very much, Governor Talmadge, for being with us.

(*Next week's guest will be Senator Ralph Flanders, Republican of Vermont*)

TOP SCIENCE SHOW OF THE YEAR

THE JOHNS HOPKINS SCIENCE REVIEW

Conquest of Pain

CONQUEST OF PAIN—ANESTHESIOLOGY

The Johns Hopkins Science Review Presented by
The Johns Hopkins University and WAAM-TV
in Baltimore in cooperation with the DuMont
Television Network

GUEST: Dr. Donald F. Proctor, Professor of Anesthesiology, Anesthesiologist-in-Charge, The Johns Hopkins Medical Institutions

PRODUCER . . . . LYNN POOLE

In Association with . . . . ROBERT FENWICK
AND JOHN LOCKWOOD

DIRECTORS . . . . KENNARD CALFEE
AND HERBERT CAHAN

ART DIRECTOR . . . . BARRY MANSFIELD

NARRATOR . . . . JOEL CHASEMAN

WRITER . . . . LYNN POOLE

TELECAST: SEPTEMBER 29, 1954

For the Editor's comment and background pertaining to *The Johns Hopkins Science Review* and its producer, Mr. Lynn Poole, please refer to page 5 under *Toys and Science* (Top Children's Show of the Year).

CONQUEST OF PAIN — ANESTHESIOLOGY

VIDEO	AUDIO

8:00:00
FILM
Operating Room-LS

MD at surgeons working . . .

JOEL: You are looking into an operating room at The Johns Hopkins Hospital.

The sensitive hands of skilled surgeons **are working** together so that a human being may be restored to a healthy, normal life.

Begin pan over to the anesthetist, and down to apparatus

As the surgeon's knife cuts through the chest the patient feels nothing. But . . . imagine the horrible, excruciating pain the patient would endure were it not for modern anesthetics developed by medical science in its . . .

8:00:30
Zoom in title

CONQUEST OF PAIN
Music up and under
THE JOHNS HOPKINS SCIENCE REVIEW . . . presented by the Johns Hopkins Institutions and WAAM in Baltimore in cooperation with the Dumont Television Network.
Music up and under
Johns Hopkins has been famed for seventy-seven years for its contribution to science and the humanities.

VIDEO	AUDIO
	Here in their many university and hospital laboratories, Hopkins scientists are constantly probing into the secrets of science, which when solved, are translated into benefits to be enjoyed by you.
	Each week we look over the shoulders of today's scientists and catch a glimpse of the result of their research. On this, our 229th program, we see how medical scientists won their battle for the
TITLE	CONQUEST OF PAIN
	Music up and under
	And here to introduce this weeks' program, from the Johns Hopkins University is Lynn Poole.
8:02:00	
POOLE BEGINS FOUR MINUTE SEQUENCE	POOLE: Greetings, ladies and gentlemen and welcome to another Johns
8:32:00	Hopkins Science Review. May I ask a personal question? Have you, or any member of your family, ever had an operation? If so, you know how painless it was. But . . . have you ever thought about the excruciating pain, the horrible torture you would have been forced to endure if you had not been given an anesthetic? Anesthesia is something you count on. We take it for granted that anesthetics have always been used. We are wrong about this . . . anesthesia as we know it is a shockingly recent development.
CARD 18th CENTURY	Think back to the 1700's . . . the 18th Century.
PHOTO OF BALLOON	JOEL: Montgolfier had invented a balloon to carry men above the earth.
PHOTO OF STEAMBOAT	Watt and Hornblower had developed

VIDEO	AUDIO
	a workable steam engine, and men started plans for the first steamboat.
PHOTO OF GAS LIGHTS	Homes were now lighted by gas lights . . . science was moving forward swiftly . . . but
PHOTO OF OPERATION	Human beings were suffering brutal torture when doctors had to cut into their diseased bodies.
CARD 19th CENTURY	Jump ahead a century . . . to the 19th Century.
PHOTO OF PHOTO STUDIO	Photographs were being taken.
PHOTO OF SEWING MACHINE	Clothes were being made on a new sewing machine.
PHOTO OF RAILROADS	In 1831 the first steam locomotive carried passengers from Albany to Schenectady.
PHOTO OF VICTORIA	In 1837, 18-year-old Victoria became Queen of England.
PHOTO OF TELEGRAPH	In 1844, Samuel F. B. Morse sent the first message by telegraph from Washington to Baltimore . . . a message which said: What Hath God Wrought?
PHOTO OF OPERATION	This was the 19th Century. Listen to what was written at that time:
MD on man in old-fashioned bed	JOEL: "Before the days of anesthetics a patient preparing for an operation was like a condemned criminal preparing for execution.
Dolly in to CU on face	"He counted the days till the appointed day came. He counted the hours of that day till the appointed hour came.
Man rolls eyes and listens intently	(Clop of horses hoofs) "He listened for the echo in the street of the surgeon's carriage. (Door gong sounds) "He listened for his pull at the doorbell; for his foot on the stair;

VIDEO	AUDIO
Follow feet across	for his step into the room;
Pan up to bag on bed, instruments taken from bag	for the production of his dreaded instruments; for his few grave words and his last preparations before beginning.
Pan over to face of patient	"And then he surrendered his liberty, and revolting at the necessity, submitted to being held or bound and helplessly gave himself up to the cruel knife."
	As one patient said: "Suffering as great as I underwent cannot be expressed in words . . . but the black whirlwind of emotion, the horror of great darkness and the sense of desertion by God and man, bordering close on despair . . . I can never forget."
Super card "1840"	This was 1840!
Dissolve out bedroom and card	
Bring in photo of PRIESTLY	For decades scientists had feverishly sought a drug that would kill pain . . . Joseph Priestly had found laughing gas.
Photo of Davy	Sir Humphrey Davy had experimented with Priestly's gas.
Photo of Serturner	Friedrich Serturner had developed morphine.
Photo of Morton and Frost	Dentists sought a pain killing agent for tooth extraction . . . and on September 30, 1846, a dentist, Dr. W. T. G. Morton of Boston extracted a tooth from the mouth of Eben Frost . . . using rectified sulphuric ether, and the tooth was pulled without pain.
Photo of operation	On October 16, 1846, Dr. Morton gave this ether to a patient at the Massachusetts General Hospital . . .

VIDEO	AUDIO
	Dr. John C. Warren, chief surgeon, performed the miracle . . . a completely painless operation!
LIVE	For the first time in the history of man a patient did not suffer agony during an operation . . . This was only 107 years ago. This was truly the great conquest; the conquest of pain.
CU and pan apparatus	Throughout the past century, the development was swift . . . New drugs, new techniques, new methods were invented in order that you and I feel no pain during operations, so that we may take an anesthetic without fear . . . and with safety.
	What are the modern anesthetics . . . how are they administered? For these and other answers let's turn to the Professor of Anethesiology and Anesthesiologist-in-Charge of the Johns Hopkins Medical Institutions . . . Dr. Donald F. Proctor.
Pan up to Proctor	
8:06:00	PROCTOR: Since sleep is an experience we all undergo at more or less regular intervals throughout our lives, it seems strange that the secret of anesthetic sleep remained undiscovered until 107 years ago. But the fact of the matter is that to this day we know very little about the ordinary sleep that we all experience each night; the manner in which anesthetic sleep is produced is still, in large part, a mystery.
Person asleep in chair	Actually ordinary sleep is to some extent anesthetic, is that, without normal appreciation of sensation. When we are sound asleep we are not so

VIDEO

AUDIO

Dissolve to person on table anesthetized

Live on Proctor

Diagram

likely to respond to sounds or touch as when we are wide awake; but even in very deep natural sleep, painful stimuli will awaken us and be remembered.

In light anesthetic sleep we may respond in some manner to pain, but we are not awakened by it, nor do we recall it afterwards. In deeper levels of anesthesia we give no evidence of any appreciation whatsoever of even the most painful of stimuli. Yet the beating of the heart, breathing, and other essential bodily functions continue more or less undisturbed, just as they do during natural sleep.

Since 1846 many drugs in addition to ether have been found capable of producing this anesthetic sleep when they are breathed in adequate concentrations. Chloroform, Nitrous Oxide, Ethylene, Cyclopropane, Ethyl Chloride, Vinethene, Trichloroethylene and the element Xenon, are some of them. All of these anesthetics gain access to the body through the lungs. They are mixed with the air the patient breathes and, by the patient's own breathing, carried into the body. Through the lungs they pass into the blood and are carried to all the tissues of the body. They seem to have little effect upon these tissues with the exception of the brain. In some manner they alter the function of the brain producing something like a very deep sleep. In other words consciousness is eliminated while the other physiological processes continue.

VIDEO	AUDIO
	This condition continues as long as a proper amount of the anesthetic is mixed with the air the patient breathes. When this mixture is discontinued, the anesthetic leaves the tissues, passes out through the lungs, is blown off, and the patient awakens.
Reverse Diagram	The remarkable facts about these events are:
	1. The known inhalational anesthetics (those we breathe) have widely differing chemical structures ranging from the simple element Xenon through Nitrous Oxide to Cyclopropane.
Chemical Formulae and Names	2. These drugs enter the body, produce their effect and are blown off without undergoing any chemical change. They are temporary visitors to the body and no one knows in exactly what manner they produce their blessed effect.
	3. The changes they produce in the body are only transient. When the anesthetic has been completely eliminated from the body, a matter of minutes in many instances, consciousness returns as completely to normal as upon awakening from normal sleep. There are two other principal groups of anesthetic drugs, the barbiturates, and the local anesthetics.
Diagram	The barbiturates can be introduced directly into the blood instead of passing through the lungs, thus producing their effect with great rapidity. These drugs are destroyed in the body and excreted in a different form; but here again their effects are only transient.

VIDEO

AUDIO

The principal differences noted by the patient, between an anesthetic with one of the gases or vapors and one with an intravenous barbiturate such as Pentothal, are the rapidity with which one is overcome by sleep, the lack of the noises and dizziness so characteristic of the breathing of ether and the anesthetic gases, and less of a tendency to nausea on awakening.

Local anesthetics such as Cocaine, Novocaine, Pontocaine, Xylocaine and many others stop the activity of the nerves with which they are brought in contact, but again only for a transitory period.

Application and Model

They can simply be painted on the mucous membranes, such as the nose or mouth or throat. Painted on the skin they have no effect. They can also be injected into or near nerves leading to the area to be anesthetized, or into the spinal fluid to anesthetize the entire lower portion of the body. The commonest uses for these drugs are in dental anesthesia and spinal anesthesia; but almost any surgical operation can be performed painlessly with local anesthesia if desired. Although a great deal of time and work has been spent in the development and study of these drugs, an equally productive investigative effort has been devoted to ways and means of protecting patients from untoward events occurring during surgery and the devising of machines and equipment for the exact administration of

VIDEO	AUDIO
	anesthetics and the support of respiration.
Movie—Gas Machine and Flow Meter	Today thanks to the success of the many investigators of these problems, we are able to administer exact amounts of oxygen with the anesthetic. We are able to adjust the amount of anesthetic given to exactly that required for the safe performance of the indicated surgical procedure. We have available numerous tools and methods to assure against any possibility of suffocation during anesthetic sleep; and the proper employment of these methods enables the surgeon to work for hours within the chest or the heart or lungs without any interruption to normal breathing. These same methods also find application in the resuscitation of victims of drowning; of drug poisoning, and the maintenance of life while patients are recovering from diseases producing deep unconsciousness or paralysis of respiratory muscles as in Polio.
MD on operating table	Some patients who are faced with the necessity for a surgical operation, because of some unpleasant past experience, a story they have heard about someone else, or some personal fear, have a deep dread of the anesthetic. Although the anesthetist's chief job is to facilitate the performance of the required surgical procedure, he is usually able to accomplish this and at the same time choose a drug and a method of administration which will be not only satisfactory but even

VIDEO	AUDIO
	pleasing to the patient.
Live: Proctor	The patient who has a horror of Ether may not be required to take Ether at all. The patient who dreads losing consciousness can often be operated upon under local or spinal anesthesia. The patient who simply doesn't want to know anything that goes on can usually be heavily sedated and go to the operating room already largely impervious to his surroundings.
	Perhaps most important of all is the fact that the patient can know that the anesthetist is interested in his minor fears and discomforts and is able before and during the operation to concentrate upon their alleviation.
Patient Suffering, As in Opening	In 1845 the patient could choose only between no surgical treatment of his disease and horribly painful surgery. After 1845 the patient could choose between surgery with pain or surgery with Ether and no pain.
Live: Proctor	Today no patient need suffer pain during surgery and the choices are multiple: local or general, spinal, intravenous, inhalation of gases or vapors. Each of these methods is accompanied by a strong wall of protection against all conceivable hazards —the machines for careful measuring of gases, the tanks of oxygen, drugs for controlling blood pressure, blood transfusions, are but a few of the ingenious devices developed since 1846 for the maintenance of life during anesthesia and surgery.
	The anesthetist wishes to know each patient's wishes, fears, and experi-

VIDEO	AUDIO

ences related to anesthesia, and he will endeavor to provide anesthesia with these in mind.

On the other hand the anesthetist asks the patient to bear in mind that the final choice of anesthetic and method will come in consultation with the surgeon after careful consideration of all factors involved. The patient can rest assured that this final choice will always hold his safety first but his comfort a close second.

Patient's Room

JOEL: Sometime on the day before this film was taken the anesthetist talked with this patient. At that time he studied the patient's medical history and physical examination, asked about past experiences, fears or dislikes and, later, discussed the problem with the surgeon.

At the present time, about an hour before scheduled time for the operation, the patient is receiving an injection. This contains a sedative, Morphine, which will enable the patient to face the strange experiences ahead of him without undue apprehension. It also contains atropine which will prevent flooding of the respiratory tract with secretions during anesthesia.

0:42

Corridor

Now, about 45 minutes later, the patient is arriving in the anesthesia room which adjoins the operating room.

At this point the anesthetist, whom the patient met last night, takes over. The patient is transferred from the stretcher to an operating table, and now the anesthetist is attaching a

Cuff

blood pressure cuff which will remain

VIDEO	AUDIO
1:06	in place throughout the operation.
	The blood pressure is measured, the pulse counted and these findings are recorded on a chart.
Chart	Such measurements and other important occurrences will be recorded on this chart every few minutes from now on.
1:20	
	Notice that the anesthetist has brought to this room quite a variety of equipment designed for the administration of the anesthesia and for the protection of the patient in the event of some unexpected difficulty.
Picking up objects	There are syringes of Pentothal, which will be used as the major anesthetic; there is a Curare-like drug to produce profound muscular relaxation; there is a flexible, hollow rubber tube for insertion into the trachea or windpipe, and a laryngoscope for exposing the larynx.
	In the center of the picture you see the gas machine which is carefully
2:00	checked and tested before each use.
Tourniquet	Now a tourniquet has been applied to the patient's arm, a needle is passed into a vein, and a solution of
Venal Puncture	sugar in water is started flowing.
	This intravenous injection is to make up for the fact that the patient has had no food or fluid for eight hours.
Syringe	Through the same needle will pass blood if the patient should require it, and at present the anesthetic is being
2:25	injected by the same route.
Patting Face	During all of this time the anesthetist has kept up a quiet conversation with

VIDEO	AUDIO
	the patient explaining what he is doing, and quietly reassuring him that he will have no discomfort.
Bag	As the patient goes to sleep he is given pure oxygen to breathe so that he will have adequate stores of this essential gas during the minute or so required for passing the tube into his
2:46	trachea.
	The oxygen is passing from the gas machine into the black rubber bag, which is in turn connected to the patient by a soft rubber mask fitting
Laryngoscope	over his nose and mouth.
	The patient is now sound asleep and a small dose of a Curare-like drug produces profound muscular relaxa-
3:06	tion for the ensuing few minutes.
	By lifting the tongue with a lighted tube, the laryngoscope, the larynx or
Tube	opening into the windpipe is clearly seen, and the endotracheal tube is
3:16	readily passed into the trachea.
	This tube is now connected to the gas
Bag again	machine. Oxygen flows into the bag from the machine and as the patient breathes in and out of this bag carbon dioxide is removed by soda lime con-
3:30	tained in the shiny metal canister.
	His respirations are at present depressed by the anesthetic and the Curare and the anesthetist assists his breathing by rhythmic pressure on the rubber bag.
	As the patient does not require 100% oxygen (there is only 20% oxygen in the air we normally breathe) by
Machine	turning a dial on the gas machine,
Flow meters	enough nitrous oxide is added to the

VIDEO	AUDIO
	mixture to reduce the oxygen to 50%. This permits the maintenance of anesthesia with less Pentothal.
4:00	The blood pressure is again being measured.
Nurse	And now, as we enter the operating room we see the surgical nurse, in her sterile gown and gloves, who has prepared the instruments for the operation.
Clean-Up 4:15	The surgeon's assistant is cleansing the chest wall with disinfectants.
Chart	The anesthetist has rechecked his equipment and now notes on his chart the events which have occurred up to this time.
Incision	This patient is undergoing an operation upon the lung. The surgeon's incision passes between the ribs and into the chest cavity.
	Not so very many years ago such an operation would not have been possible. Techniques developed in the past 60 years enable the anesthetist today to breathe for the patient as long as it is necessary for the surgeon
4:47	to have the chest open.
	Thus the surgeon is permitted to exercise his skills for the correction of a wide variety of diseases of the lungs, the heart and the great blood vessels. The anesthetist is continually checking the patient's condition and by now his chart provides a clear picture of the patient's course and a guide for the subsequent management of the
5:09	anesthesia.
Bag and Lungs	Watch the rhythmic pressure of the anesthetist's hand on the rubber bag.

VIDEO	AUDIO
	The patient's chest is now open, and you can see the corresponding inflation and deflation of the patient's lungs.
	This process is continued throughout the time the chest remains open thus providing ventilation of the lungs, adequate oxygen for the body's needs, and permitting the administration of whatever anesthetic is given through the lungs. As the gas passes to and fro through the soda lime with each breath, carbon dioxide is continually given off as a result of the patient's metabolism.
5:49	The principal reason for the passage of the endotracheal tube was to insure a reliable open airway between the anesthesia bag and the lungs.
	The operation has been halted for a few moments so that these pictures of the movements of the lungs could be made.
6:06	And now the camera has been moved above so that you may get the same view of the operating room as is obtained by the medical student from the observation area.
	The surgeon and his team have by now nearly completed the operation. The entire body of the patient is covered with sterile drapes except for the area of the incision, and the head.
	A screen separates the head of the patient and the anesthetist from this sterile area.
	The anesthetist continues to inflate the patient's lungs about 20 times each minute. At the same time his

VIDEO	AUDIO
	checks of the blood pressure and pulse are done at least every five minutes. While the surgeon is concentrating on the delicate job of completing the operation, it is the anesthetist's responsibility to follow the patient's general condition as well as to maintain adequate depth of anesthesia.
7:00	As the operation nears completion, the amounts of Pentothal injected are reduced so that the patient gradually approaches a state of consciousness. His own respiratory effort should be adequate, and he should be able to cough, move about, and respond to commands as soon after the end of the operation as possible.
	In other words during the operation a state of anesthesia has been maintained to permit the performance of the surgical procedure; and during this time minute-to-minute care is taken to see to it that the vital functions continue in spite of the anesthesia and the operation. Now we wish the patient to return as quickly as possible to his normal state in which his own physiological processes can be counted on to do their own
7:43	normal job.
	Secretions have been suctioned away from the patient's air ways and the endotracheal tube has been removed. The patient is awakening and coughing.
Removing Tube	
	When he is conscious enough to be aware of pain he will be given sedation sufficient to deaden these sensations, but not to return him to the

VIDEO	AUDIO
8:00	deep sleep of anesthesia.
	Back in his own room he receives special nursing care during the period in which he recovers from the immediate effects of the surgery.
	In a day or so he will be up and about and within two weeks fully recovered
8:15	from the surgical procedure.
	In this and similar ways in The Johns Hopkins Hospital nearly fifty patients every day are anesthetized for the performance of a wide variety of surgical operations. Thanks to the work of a multitude of scientists during the past 107 years this safe sleep has completely replaced the consciousness of pain while the surgeon employs his corrective instruments.
	Medical men won the battle for the Conquest of Pain.

SEQUENCE OUTLINE OF PROGRAM

Sequence Subject	Time	Begin
Film Sneak Peek—Operating Room CU of Patient and Apparatus	30 sec.	8:00:00
Standard Opening	1 min.-30 sec.	8:00:30
Poole—Intro. and Historical sketch of anesthetics	4 min.	8:02:00
Proctor—Demonstrations of pharmacology and apparatus of anesthetics	4 min.	8:06:00
Proctor—Types of anesthetics, methods of administering, and patients' choice	4 min.	8:10:00
Poole—Transition to film and developed demonstration of the giving of an anesthetic	1 min.	8:14:00
Proctor and Narrator—Over film following patient from hospital room, through operation and back to recovery room	10 min.	8:15:00
Proctor—Summary	1 min.	8:25:00
Poole—Conclude and intro. preview of next week	1 min.	8:26:00
Preview (30 seconds) and close		8:27:00

TOP WOMEN'S SHOW OF THE YEAR

NATIONAL BROADCASTING COMPANY

THE HOME SHOW

THE HOME SHOW

A production of the National Broadcasting Company, by whom all broadcasting rights of this material are reserved.

PRODUCER . . . . DICK LINKROUM

STAR AND EMCEE . . . . ARLENE FRANCIS

WRITERS . . . . BERYL PFIZER

NANCY ANN GRAHAM

HAZEL ARNETT

CLAIRE BARROWS

PHYLLIS ADAMS

JACK FULLER

ROBERT RUTHMAN

MAURICE ROBINSON

TELECAST: JULY 26, 1954
NBC TELEVISION NETWORK

THE HOME SHOW

A COMPARATIVE NEWCOMER TO THE NBC family of "magazine" type shows, *Home* made its debut on March 1st, 1954. This daytime program is pitched to women, primarily housewives, and provides a format much like many of the popular women's magazines on the newsstands.

Home covers such fields as family affairs, fashions, beauty, interior decoration, architecture, gardening, child care, and related subjects.

Despite strong competition from TV "soap operas" and radio shows, *Home* has captured a huge listening audience, with thousands of enthusiastic letters flooding into the studios every week.

Arlene Francis, Emcee and star of *Home,* was born in Boston, Mass., the daughter of Aram Kazanjian, a distinguished Armenian-American portrait photographer. On completion of her schooling, she attended classes at the Theatre Guild and eventually was signed for numerous radio daytime serials.

Miss Francis made her Broadway debut soon after and appeared in such plays as *The Doughgirls, The Women,* and *Late Love.* In Hollywood, she appeared in the movie version of *All My Sons* and currently, is appearing as a regular panelist on the video show, *What's My Line?* (see page 189). She is also hostess on *Talent Patrol* and has guest-starred on many major TV programs.

She is married to Martin Gabel, the actor-producer. They have a seven-year-old son, Peter.

THE HOME SHOW

Opening
CU: Automatic Adding Machine
HUGH (*VO*)
Do you know what this is? It's one of the many things you'll see today on HOME . . . so watch!
Logo
Music   •
HUGH (*VO*)
NBC presents the 104th daily edition of HOME, starring Arlene Francis.
ARLENE
Good morning. How is everyone this morning?
According to a story in the paper a little while ago an Employment Bureau in Los Angeles reports that men are more willing than women to hire out for housecleaning, floor waxing and odd jobs around the house.
I'm sure that men are very good at these household jobs. Much better than women probably. They should be—after all, for years they've been sitting around watching the women do them!
I'm only kidding, I know lots of men who help their wives with the household chores—some even have to stay home and do all the housework, because all the golf widows aren't women— Lots of *women* just can't stay away from the golf course and Eve Hunter's going to show us the clothes these women wear . . .

AUDIO	VIDEO
EVE HUNTER: The keynote is comfort . . . (*music in*) and it's par for the course in golf wear this summer. Thanks to the widest variety of styling ever, women can tee off in culotte	*MS Eve Hunter. She leans on golf stick*

AUDIO

or coverall . . . Bermuda short or classic dress. And teamed with this styling is the cool comfort of cotton in undistracting colors. So now let's hie ourselves off to a golf course where the keynote is comfort.

Our first lady golfer wears a green chambray sundress and white pique top for cover. Note the tee strap on the left and the ball bag on the right.

By McMullen, this outfit retails under $25.

The classic reddish-orange of a madras shirt is teamed with coffee linen . . . in the form of a culotte skirt. The shirt by Florence Walsh sells for less than $8. And the culotte by Rockland under nine.

Feminine frills ruffle the pale blue man-tailored shirt that's paired with these olive twill shorts. Made by Loomtogs the shirt costs about five and the shorts $6.

And guaranteed comfort for that hole-in-one, is this orange sailcloth all-in-one. It has pockets ready to carry balls and tees and a back pleated for action. The price? Just under $9. Now cocoa brown sailcloth stitched in white steps up to the tee. Keyed

VIDEO

Dissolve to set with RP of clubhouse in background, green in foreground matched with grass mats on platform, two golf bags on wheels stand upstage. On left, Model sits on bench, on right, Model works ball wash stand, in center, Model sets up to tee off

Model #1, Gloria, tees off. ¾ shot of dress with jacket
CU jacket
Waist shot front and back as removes jacket
ECU tee shoulder strap
ECU pocket on skirt
MS Gloria exiting
Model #2, Betty, tees off. Full shot of outfit
Waist shot, then pan down skirt front as unbuttons to reveal culotte, and up back without losing silhouette
¾ shot Betty exiting
Model #3, Lee, tees off. Full shot of outfit
Waist shot, then pan down shorts

¾ shot Lee exiting
Model #4, Gloria, enters in ¾ shot. Takes stick out of bag
Pan down front and up back without losing silhouette. Catch back pleat
Gloria goes over to ball wash stand
Model #5, Betty, enters in full shot
Bust shot, then cut to full shot of skirt

AUDIO	VIDEO
for the course from crew neck to action-free skirt, this dress costs about $8.	*front and back*
	Betty takes club out of bag, then sits on bench
These last two fashions were by Rockland Sportswear, and they, like the first three, are available in stores right now from coast to coast.	
And now they're knee high in plaid . . .	*MCU Eve seated on bench—golf set*
That's the headline news for golf fashions this fall. Skirts and shorts have gone knee length and plaid mad . . . the horse blanket type running maddest. And fabrics, for the most part, have a natural fiber base. And now, fashions that are knee high in plaid . . .	*Camera pulls back to three models putting*
Red wool jersey tops red and green wool plaid, the plaid being that horse blanket variety we just mentioned.	*Model #1, Lee, stops putting*
Worthy of note, too, is the greater width of the short leg. By Loomtogs, these separates are priced around $6 for the shirt and $11 for the shorts.	*Waist shot, then pan down shorts, without losing silhouette*
And now for a classic—and yet not so classic—sweater and skirt. The	*¾ shot Lee resuming putting*
	Model #2, Betty, stops putting
lemon Shetland cardigan is newly cut short, as is the kilt . . . now diminutively named a "kiltie." Both are by Florence Walsh, the sweater selling for less than $11 and the kiltie under	*Waist shot*
	FS kiltie, front and back
fifteen.	*¾ shot Betty resuming putting*
Something brand new for the lady golfer is this romper shirt and short swing skirt. The former is faded blue denim and the latter banker's grey flannel. By Raissa Masket, they are sold separately or together for less	*Model #3, Gloria, stops putting*
	FS of outfit
	Bust shot front and back
	CU romper leg

AUDIO	VIDEO
than $15 apiece.	*FS Gloria resuming putting*
And now how about taking a look at	*¾ shot Eve now standing*
what I'm wearing. My man-tailored	
shirt is olive green . . . and my lady-	*Waist shot*
tailored skirt grey flannel. If you look	*Pan down skirt without losing outline*
a little closer you'll see some more of	
that plaid gone mad—this time in the	
back panels of my four inverted	*CU pleats*
pleats. Florence Walsh thought this	*MS*
one up.	
And so we end our peep into the fall	
golf scene. You'll find these fashions	
in stores from the middle of next	
month on.	

(Music up and out)

MAIL FROM HOME

ARLENE

Thank you, Eve.

I've been reading some letters—and I have some Mail from Home I'd like to show you. This is sort of special mail, from people we feel are very special around the HOME—children. Some children seem to be a big help to their mothers—even when it comes to watching television. We've gotten several reports from mothers saying that their children copy down Kit Kinne's recipes for them . . . Mrs. Margaret P. Mann sent me the recipe her son Craig copied down for her the day Chef Phillip made Lobster Newburg . . . And I'm sure it's delicious . . . It says Nion, Veget, Ad Le Bread Crumd R Ad I L (THAT MUST BE ADD ONE LOBSTER)

Id Watr Doud . . . That's very nice, but I'm afraid it would turn out to be Suki-yaki . . . And here is a letter from Miss Nancy Ellis who sent us her own recipe . . . It says: LEMONADE
    PUT LEMON INTI
    PUT SUGAR INTI
    PUT WATER INTI
FROM NANCY ELLIS IN BALD-WIN, KANSAS—AGE 6 . . . Thank you, Nancy, I'm sure that's a very good recipe for Lemonade. There are lots of television stars and executives growing up, too. Bob Jones of Gilberts, Illinois wrote this letter: Dear Arlene: I love HOME very much. I never miss a moment of it because you show the studio at station breaks. I have a

Television Studio and my call letters are WNBJ-TV. J is for Jones.

WNB Jones-TV. I'm sure that's a very good station, Bob. And I may just change this Station to NBF . . . N B Francis!

Miss Pamela Sue Elliot of Davenport, Iowa wrote:

Dear Arlene:

Arlene, would you write me a letter about anything you think I would like? I have never had a television star write me a letter. I watch your program every morning. I think your program is very good. I am unhappy when your program goes off the air. (I AM TOO, PAM) then she writes . . . I would like to see Hugh Downs cry. I am nine years old. I am going into fourth grade.

Well, we try to oblige any request . . . but how on earth can we make Hugh Downs cry? (*Hugh enters*) Hugh, do you feel sad enough to cry today?

(*Hugh sings first line of "Cry."*)

Or maybe you could sing a line of that song Johnny Ray used to sing . . .

HUGH

If your sweetheart sends a letter of good-by . . . It's no secret you'll feel better if you cry . . .

ARLENE

That's not good enough, Hugh . . . we want *real* tears . . . Go on over in the corner and think about something sad . . .

Pam, we're trying. And I will write you a letter about something I think you will like . . . dolls, ice cream cones, pretty dresses and little ten-year-old boys . . .

You know, HOME could do a little matchmaking among the younger set, too. Some time ago our Color Mobile Unit showed us Landmier Farm in Illinois, and the Landmier Family, including daughter, Judy. I got a letter shortly after that program from Paul Venancio of 216 Reservoir Avenue, Middletown, R. I. And he said:

Dear Arlene Francis:

Would you please send me the address of the Landmier Farm that Home toured on the television screen June 23, 1954. I would be interested to write to Judy Landmier, age 11. I appreciate this very much.

Well, we're passing the message on to Judy . . . Paul Venancio of 216 Reservoir Avenue, Middletown, R. I. wants to hear from you, Judy . . . Gosh, I feel just like Cupid. We're going to do a little matchmaking now while we have a station break, then we'll be back with Dish of the Day . . .

DISH OF THE DAY

(*Celebrity Tie In*)

(*CU Dish of the Day*)

ARLENE

Agnes Moorehead gave us a suggestion for our Dish of the Day today. It's OLIVE SWISS STEAK . . . a delicious variation of this ever-popular method of preparing inexpensive cuts of beef.

(*Overhead hands adding ingredients to browned steak in pan*)

Miss Moorehead tells us that to prepare the dish you flour pieces of flank steak and brown in hot fat just as you would in any Swiss Steak recipe. Then sprinkle with salt and pepper . . . top with sliced stuffed olives, chopped green pepper and sliced onions . . . and cook slowly in diluted tomato soup until tender . . . this takes about two hours.

ITALIAN FAMILY

ARLENE

Today we're bringing you the second in our series called "Life Abroad," films which help us understand how our foreign sisters live and work and raise their families and manage their homes. We're going to Italy today to meet the Iannelli family. They live in a small fishing
(*Roll film*)
village not far from Rome—called Fiumicino, a town of 14,000 souls.
(*Start film—view of village, mother on roof*)
This then, is Fiumicino—and here is Mrs. Iannelli, Orlanda, who is 31 years old and the mother of three children who we will soon meet. It's early morning and she is hanging up the family wash. The Iannellis live in a small house which they rent for $10 a month. We can get an idea of how that compares with rents we pay when we consider that the total family earnings come to a little under $100 a month.
(*Mother enters house, fills thermos*)

(*CU Dish of Day*)
And the result is well worth the time . . . *Olive Swiss Steaks A La Agnes Moorehead.* We'll look forward to trying your dish, Miss Moorehead, and to seeing you do your usual fine acting job in the current Universal International Technicolor Release, *Magnificent Obsession.*

Time now for Orlanda to fix her husband's lunch. This, by the way, is a typical Italian kitchen. That coffee cost $2 a pound.
(*Husband enters, drinks coffee, leaves for work*)
Here comes Pasquale Iannelli, the head of the family and sole proprietor of his own fishing boat. He pays his hands by sharing the catch.
A quick cup of coffee and he's off for work, taking a new coil of line with him. Let's leave the house with Pasquale and see where he works.
(*Water front and fishing boats*)
This is where Pasquale starts out every day to make his catch and earn the family income. He's 39 years old and considered fairly prosperous in the town. Even when catches are small, his family never wants for seafood.
(*Children enter kitchen for breakfast*)
And here come the little ones. That's Mariapia, aged eleven, carrying Annamaria who is two. The boy is

Dario, he is nine. Hasn't that baby got wonderful curls? After breakfast they go to school,
(*Baby eating*)
even little curly locks, who goes to the church kindergarten. She probably will be a great beauty when she grows up.
(*Mother wraps lunch, straightens boy's collar, children leave*)
Dario takes his lunch to school and mother sees to it that he will have plenty to eat. She manages very well without any of the mechanical and electrical conveniences which we feel are essential in a kitchen. None of her neighbors has them so she doesn't miss them. Dario gets a final neatening up and off he goes with his sisters.
(*Mother clears table*)
With the children and her husband out of the house, Orlanda gets down to her housework. The kitchen, which is the communal room—there is no living room in the house—gets cleaned up first. There is a dining room but it is equipped with a day bed and serves as a bedroom for the two older children.
(*Two shots of dusting and mother leaves with dress in hand*)
Here we are in the dining room. Orlanda has already straightened up and is giving the room a final sprucing with a duster. That radio is the only modern gadget in the house and provides the family with the most of its entertainment. For the rest, they enjoy family gatherings and an occasional movie. Well, it's time now to put on a street dress and go marketing.
(*She leaves house with shopping basket and walks down street*)
Not counting the fish that Pasquale brings home, the family spends $70 a month for food. That may not sound like much for a family of five, but it's more than two thirds the total income. Orlanda's first stop will be the vegetable market.
(*Crosses street to vegetable stand and makes purchases*)
As in the case throughout practically all Europe, there is no Super Market or giant food store where all purchases may be made. Even so, it has only vegetables in season, since there is no refrigeration to keep fruits and vegetables fresh. Nor is there refrigeration in the homes of the village. Today Orlanda buys cabbage, potatoes and tomatoes, all averaging about 8 cents a lb. Incidentally, the paper bags and sacks that we take for granted when marketing simply don't exist.
(*She walks down street and enters another store*)
Next stop is the grocery store. While Orlanda does her marketing, here are some prices to compare with our own. Cheeses run about 90 cents a lb.; lard, 35 cents a lb.; bread, 10 cents a lb. Today Orlanda is buying bread and pasta. Pasta is, of course, a staple of the family diet and averages about 15 cents a lb.
(*Bins of pasta and pan down to bread*)
Our system of keeping foods under

glass is reserved for delicacies.
(*She selects pasta*)
Stores in Italian towns have the rich aroma of the foods they sell and they're all out in the open where they can be seen. I'll show you what I mean right now.
(*Lard*)
Here's the lard on display.
(*Cheese*)
And here's that good cheese that grates so well.
(*She pays for purchases*)
And now that this phase of the daily marketing is done, Orlanda is off to the dairy. How would you like to have to make the rounds this way every day? Orlanda doesn't mind, because she knows no other way.
(*Enters doorway, we see sign over doorway*)
At the dairy Orlanda buys milk at 12 cents a quart and eggs at 73 cents a dozen. The sign beside the doorway says "milk and eggs" and shows the day's prices.
(*She leaves store and puts packages in basket*)
Next stop will be the dry goods store. Clothing comes high. Men's suits cost about $40, shoes $8 and dresses $10 to $15. So Orlanda does a lot of knitting. She's going to buy yarn now.
(*She picks up a hank of yarn*)
This will make a sweater for her husband.
(*Winding yarn into ball*)
Back at the house, Orlanda winds her yarn into a ball, then she joins her daughter,

(*Mother and daughter in kitchen*)
who has already started the family dinner. Soon Pasquale will be home from his day's fishing expedition.
(*Boat enters harbor*)
As the boats come into the harbor, each gives its distinctive toot which the wives recognize.
(*Father on deck*)
Looks like Pasquale had a good day.
(*Boats at wharf and men handing boxes of fish*)
By the time the boat is tied up at the wharf the catch has been sorted and each man gets his share ashore.
(*Pasquale leaves boat with fish*)
There is always a box of the best of the catch to take home for the family. In Pasquale's book, his family comes first.
(*He walks toward home and stops under window*)
This time Pasquale hurries along because he has a special treat for the children: shells and coral to play with. When he gets beneath the window he stops and gives a holler. That's a happy daily family ritual which the Iannellis wouldn't think of skipping.
(*Mother waves*)
His greeting is returned,
(*Father waves*)
and after a friendly wave he enters the house.
(*Mother and daughter in kitchen*)
This is the busiest time in the kitchen. The menu tonight is minestrone, fried fish, macaroni—and of course, cheese with wine. The Iannellis only have

meat about once a month.

(*Mother serving as father enters with baby—then family starts to eat*)

This is a happy family time. The father comes in carrying his little one and kisses his wife. The family's evening meal is a social occasion, full of small talk and the homey things a close knit group have to say to each other the world over, regardless of the language they are speaking in. Appetites are good and the aromatic hot food is eaten with gusto. Mmm, mmm, mmm, doesn't that look good? I often think that the expression, "Sunny Italy" refers to more than just the climate. Certainly, there's sunlight in the lives of these people who are content with their simple lot.

(*Father eating*)

After a day at sea, Pasquale's appetite needs no pampering,

(*Son and daughter eating*)

and two healthy kids like these are always hungry.

(*Family at table, then father gets shells and coral for children*)

And when the meal is over they don't leave the table. It's time for the children's surprise. From the sideboard Pasquale gets the shells and branch coral he brought home earlier and the children sit around and play with them. They say that if you hold a shell to your ear you can hear the roar of the waves, and the children know it's true.

(*Children with shells*)

These youngsters don't need fancy mechanical toys.

(*End film*)

In the long summer days, the Iannellis go to bed with the sun. They'll rise with it again tomorrow.

And didn't that dinner look good! I love good Italian food—and I bet the Iannelli's daughter is going to be a good cook! I'm sure you want *your* daughter to be a good cook—

Cooking Precis
Summer Cooking School—

Lesson #1
Tools of the Trade

Part I

OBJECT:

The object of this spot is to explain the purposes of the first five lessons of HOME's Summer Cooking School—and to give the first lesson which is devoted to teaching the beginner cook with the proper "tools of the trade" that are needed in a well-equipped kitchen—the tools she will need to cook IN.

PROCEDURE:

We will use Kit and Hugh Downs throughout the five lessons. Hugh will represent the unknowledgeable beginner—and Kit will be the teacher.

We use Arlene to introduce the spot. She says that Kit Kinne is holding a summer cooking school and Hugh Downs is her star pupil, so class will now come to order.

We use Kit in Area M with B.G. of artwork of Cooking School Sign. Also pots and pans hung on pegboard with labels specifying what they are and number needed. She explains purpose of summer cooking school and says that first five lessons will be devoted to teaching the beginner cook about the tools of the trade she will need to cook well, and the cooking terminology that will make it easier to read recipes. She says today they are going to discuss the tools that you need to cook *in*—Pots and Pans. At this point we hear a great clatter of pots and pans. We see Hugh Downs wheeling in a wheelbarrow absolutely loaded with every manner of pot and pan imaginable. He says these are the pots and pans he has brought for his lesson. Kit explains that the beginner cook should start off more modestly and build her supply of cooking utensils to fit her needs. She shows Hugh the basic pots and pans that are needed, explaining the principal use for each, and pointing out what other uses they can be put to. She shows these utensils mounted on pegboard in B.G. and lined up on counter, as Hugh takes notes. Hugh reviews basic points of lesson. She tells everyone to be on hand for next lesson, which will be devoted to the tools you cook WITH. (Spoons, forks, mixers, etc.)

COOKING SPOT

AUDIO	VIDEO
ARLENE: Today we're starting classes in another one of our HOME Summer School Courses. These courses are dedicated to the proposition that homemaking is an art and a career that requires never-ending study and interest.	*Arlene in area A*

ARLENE: Today we're starting classes in another one of our HOME Summer School Courses. These courses are dedicated to the proposition that homemaking is an art and a career that requires never-ending study and interest.

And so, for the next two weeks, Kit Kinne will be holding forth in HOME's Summer Cooking School.

The qualifications for the course are simple . . . all you need is a desire to learn to cook well. Maybe you're a new bride just starting out . . . or perhaps you're a teen-ager who wishes to get a *head* start in practicing this most important of homemaking arts . . . or maybe you're the man of the house home on vacation, and have always pictured yourself as an amateur chef but never knew quite where to start. And I guarantee that even if you've been cooking for *years* you'll still be able to pick up plenty of hints that you will find helpful in making your cooking more *fun* and more efficient.

Our teacher, of course, is Kit Kinne . . . and the first pupil to register in her class was, believe it or not, Hugh Downs, who has always had a longing to cook but never has gotten much closer to a pot or a pan than the wrong end of a dish towel.

So grab your mixing spoons and

Arlene picks up frying pan and starts

AUDIO

cookbooks . . .

Our school bell's a-ringing . . . and the class will now come to order.
Music: "Schools Days" in and under

KIT: Welcome one and all to the HOME Summer Cooking School. We'll be holding classes in our HOME kitchen here for the next two weeks.
First of all I want to tell you something that I know you'll discover once you've started cooking, and that is that cooking is *fun*—not just an unpleasant duty that must be performed to keep body and bone together. Also remember that cooking is *creative* . . . giving you an unparalleled opportunity to express yourself, display your imagination, and show off your skill as a homemaker.
If you keep these ideas in mind you'll find that you've already won half the battle in learning how to cook . . . and loving it!
And after establishing these thoughts, you'll need several other things to start cooking . . . you'll need food to cook, of course, you'll need equipment to cook in, and you'll need a basic knowledge of the language of cooking . . . the terms that you will run across most frequently in the cookbooks you are using.

VIDEO

to bang on it in "come and get it" style

Dissolve to "Home's Summer Cooking School" sign in B.G. of M
Pull back to show Kit in area M in front of B.G. of cooking school sign and mounted pots and pans.

AUDIO	VIDEO
It is these last two points that we are going to discuss this week . . . tools and *terminology,* the most logical beginning for any cooking course.	
And today we'll talk about the tools of the trade . . . the pots and pans and bowls that you will need to have to cook *in,* and we can get our lesson started just as soon as Hugh Downs gets here . . . I wonder where he can be.	*Hugh starts wheeling supply of pots and pans in with a great clatter*
Oh-oh, *that,* if I'm not mistaken, is Hugh coming now.	*CU wheelbarrow piled eye-high with all manner of pots and pans* *Pullback to show Hugh wheeling wheelbarrow into M* *Two shot Hugh and Kit*
KIT: Good heavens, Hugh, what did you do . . . rob a hardware store?	
HUGH: (*proudly*) Well, no . . . you told me we were going to assemble the pots and pans needed for cooking today, and so I thought I'd get a little ahead and get all my equipment ready. I think I'll have everything I need . . . look, I have four frying pans, five saucepans, ranging in size from two cups to six quarts, three roasting pans, six pie plates . . .	*CU* *Hugh indicates some of his pots and pans*
KIT: (*interrupting*) Whoa . . . whoa there, Hugh . . . why, don't you realize that you've got enough equipment there to stock a hotel?	
It's nice to have enough pots and pans to really do your job of cooking well, but an overabundance of pots and pans is the mark of an inefficient cook. So put your wheelbarrow aside,	

AUDIO

Hugh, and come on up here and let's
talk about the pots and pans you
really need.

HUGH: (*crestfallen*) Gee . . . and I
thought I was being so smart.

KIT: When stocking your kitchen
with utensils and facing the myriad
numbers of pots and pans on the
market there are three questions you
should ask yourself that will help you
in buying . . .

1. Does it do the job for which it
is intended, and can it serve several
functions? Now don't let yourself be
carried away by gadgets that promise
to do a hundred things in one operation . . . very often you'll find that
these multiple-purpose gadgets do
nothing well . . . but if you inspect
carefully you can see if it will serve
its purpose.

2. Does it justify storage space and
can it be stored easily?

3. Is it easy to clean?

And there's another criterion to set,
too . . . is it a good investment. Basi-
cally it pays to buy good utensils to
start with . . . cut down on the number you buy, if necessary, and add to
your supply as you can afford it . . .
but buy the best and you'll find it's
cheaper in the long run.

HUGH: Okay, teacher, I catch. But
let's suppose that I'm starting out
buying for my kitchen—I have absolutely nothing in the way of equipment—what should I get? . . .

KIT: Well, Hugh, let me show you
about twenty pieces of equipment that

VIDEO

*Hugh pushes wheelbarrow off camera
and goes behind counter with Kit*

AUDIO

I think are basics for a well-stocked kitchen. Each piece serves many purposes and yet performs each task efficiently. These are the pieces with which you should start out—you can add others as you go along. Got your notebook ready? . . .

HUGH: Ready!

KIT: Okay—well, first off you need a frying pan. If you can only afford one, well then get a large one—you can always fry an egg in a large pan, but you can't cook a chicken in a small one.

Then if you can afford it, get a seven-inch frying pan, too, or add it to your collection as soon as you can. Be sure frying pans have lids because they can double as chicken fryers and serve other cooking chores.

Then three graduated saucepans *or* a double boiler and a saucepan—you can use components of double boiler as saucepan, or you can use graduated saucepans as double boiler.

One large saucepot. This can double as a spaghetti cooker, soup kettle, pot roast cooker and the like. And I have found one of these food blanchers like this particularly versatile because with this basket inside you can also use it as a deep fat fryer and a bottle sterilizer, and a steamer and a host of other things.

Another item you will need is one large and one small strainer, which you can also use as colanders, food mills, flour sifters, etc.

Also a tea kettle and a coffeemaker

VIDEO

CU Hallite frying pan mounted on pegboard in B.G.

CU saucepans on pegboard

CU saucepot/food blancher on counter

Kit shows inside of sauce pot

CU strainers on pegboard B.G.

CU tea kettles and coffeemakers on

AUDIO	VIDEO
—and perhaps here we might even go a little hog-wild and suggest TWO coffeemakers—one small one to be used for coffee for two or three, and one large one when you're entertaining. This isn't necessary, of course, but you always get the best cup of coffee when you use your coffeemaker to its capacity, or at least two thirds of its capacity.	*shelf mounted on pegboard in B.G.*
For roasting you should have a roaster like this. You can use a cake rack as a rack in your roaster—and you can also use this kind of roaster as a cookie sheet or a sheet cake pan, or even as a tray.	*CU roaster on counter*
Other baking items that I think are necessary:	
Two round cake pans—can also be used to make scalloped dishes or as cookie sheets	*CU cake pans on counter*
One square cake pan—can also be used as baking dish, for casseroles, and the like	*CU square cake pan on counter*
Two cake racks—one square and one round (uses)	*CU cake racks on counter*
One muffin tin—can also be used to bake biscuits, small gelatin molds, individual meat loaves, etc.	*CU muffin tin on counter*
Now here are two pans that are not really essential but which are mighty handy to have and should certainly be included early in the game when you stock your kitchen, if not immediately. They are—a loaf pan which can be used for many kinds of quick breads, meat loaves, and jellied salads . . .	*CU loaf pan on counter*
And a tube pan—including this not	*CU tube pan on counter*

AUDIO	VIDEO

only because packaged mixes make angel food cake baking so easy these days, but also because this makes an excellent gelatin mold or even meat loaf pan—good for coffee cakes and chiffon cakes, too.

And now just two other items, but very important ones—a set of nested oven-proof glass mixing bowls which double as casseroles.   *CU mixing bowls on counter*

And six medium glass custard cups.   *CU custard cups on counter*
I suggest the medium size because these serve well also as small mixing bowls, storage dishes, molds, individual casseroles, soup dishes and— well, there are a thousand uses for them.

Now these are what I consider basic   *Two shot Kit and Hugh, Hugh busily* items to be stocked in a beginner's   *writing in his notebook* kitchen. These enable you to cook well and efficiently and don't take up too much storage space. Certainly you will want to add quickly items like electric toaster, griddle, pressure cooker and other modern appliances that make life in the kitchen so much easier. If you want a list of these items write to us here at HOME, and we will be happy to send them to you. So Hugh, how about reviewing the basic principles of our lesson today. . . .

HUGH: (*as a schoolboy reciting a lesson*) When stocking your kitchen with utensils ask yourself four basic questions— Does it do the job for which it was intended? Does it store easily and justify the storage space? Is it easy to clean, and, Is it a good investment?

An overload of pots and pans is the mark of an inefficient cook . . .

Start out with the bare essentials and add needed items as you go along. There are about twenty pieces of equipment that should be found in a well-stocked kitchen and each one performs many services . . . and if you want a list of these items write to us here at HOME and we'll be glad to send it to you. (*draws breath*)

KIT: Bravo, Hugh—go to the head of the class.

But just be sure to be here *on time* tomorrow when we'll be discussing the second part of our "tools of the trade" lesson and find out what other utensils one needs in a well-stocked kitchen . . . utensils to cook *with*.

And I hope all of you will be on hand, too!

Now it's time for a station break— and then the Story of the Day.

Logo
Music
Break
Flash

"HOME . . . *part two* . . . *story of the day with Hugh Downs* . . ."

Now here's Arlene with a story— from the woman's angle in Washington—Esther Van Wagoner Tufty

2-WAY: WASHINGTON—
NEW YORK

ARLENE

Today we have asked our Washington editor . . . Esther Van Wagoner Tufty . . . to do some fancy predicting as to the number of women who will be elected at the next Congressional election . . . How about it, Duchess . . . What does your crystal ball say?

TUFTY

There'll be MORE than 13 women now serving in the Congress . . . but not as many as there should be! Women have had the vote since 1920 . . . and yet so few have even TRIED to come to Congress (which needs the kind of face-lifting women could give it). Women don't know their own power . . . and forget there are a million more potential women voters than men . . .
We should be ashamed that in:
(*Ad lib*) Japan . . .
West Germany . . .
Little Finland . . .

ARLENE

Why don't more American women run for Congress? The pay is good and then there is all that Washington glamour . . . ?

TUFTY

I asked that question of the two women in Washington who should know:
(*Ad lib*) Bertha Aikens, No. 1 Republican woman . . .
Katie Louchheim, No. 1 Democrat woman . . .
Personally, I think just "being a woman" gets in the way. The WOMAN candidate doesn't have a wife . . . to make life easy between campaign speeches!
(*Ad lib*) If married . . .
If a spinster . . .
If a widow . . . (Seven of the 13 now in Congress are widows and inherited their seat in Congress from their late husbands.)

ARLENE

Duchess . . . how about that prediction . . . don't dodge!

TUFTY

Let's do a little arithmetic. Twelve of the 13 are running for re-election. (Not the Senator from Nebraska, Mrs. Eva Bowring.) Let's say they all are elected.
There are nine new Democratic women candidates and six new Republican women candidates. Suppose only half . . . no, a third of the new candidates . . . make the grade . . . Then added to the 12 incumbents . . . my guess becomes 17. And that would be the largest number of women ever to be seated in Congress!

ARLENE

We will not let you forget that prediction . . . Esther Van Wagoner Tufty . . . when election day rolls around in November.

ARLENE BOOK SPOT
Note: Bring up lights
Arlene in chair in A with book

ARLENE

Thank you, Esther. Women do have

a very important part to play in the history of our country. And I've been reading an interesting book on just that topic. It's called *These Were the Women* by Mary Ormsbee Whitton, published by Hastings House. It is the story of the women who helped make American culture—a series of brief sketches of women of all stations and conditions who illustrate woman's role in the development of American civilization from Revolutionary days down to the Civil War. There is a close-up of George Washington's mother, to whom George was dutifully devoted although he preferred to have her live under a roof other than his. There are sketches of John Hancock's fashionable Bostonian wife, Dorothy—and the less fashionable woman John Hancock did not marry, Dorcas Griffiths.

Heroines of battles, Molly Pitcher for one, and one you probably never heard of, Deborah Samson, are described. Deborah Samson was a rather pathetic girl. Her early home was so bad that the town authorities had the children removed. She was placed in the house of a respectable farmer. She was never sent to school, she put herself through grade school by hiring out to a farmer. She was a big, strong girl, and her circumstances made her into a farm laborer. In 1778 Deborah disappeared with a suit of clothes she had made for herself, and reappeared disguised as a man, calling herself Robert Shirtliffe. She joined the army and for three years

was a common soldier.

She was wounded, her identity was discovered and General Washington handed her her discharge. She then settled down to an average life as a wife and mother, her chief battle in later life was trying to live on the meager earnings of her husband.

You know, Marlene Dietrich's daring costume worn out in Las Vegas recently caused a lot of comment— She didn't set any precedents, however, because in the very early 1800's there was a good bit of similar comment about the clothing of a Mrs. Jerome Bonaparte, formerly Miss Patterson of Baltimore. Margaret Bayard Smith, living in Washington at that time wrote this. "She has made a great noise here, mobs of boys crowded around her carriage to see what I hope will not often be seen in this country, an almost naked woman . . . her dress was the thinnest sarcenet . . . there was scarcely any waist to it and no sleeves; her back, her bosom, part of her waist and her arms were uncovered and the rest of her form visible." The Washington ladies, after this occasion, warned the young Mrs. Bonaparte that in the future she must promise to have more clothes on. You'll meet all kinds of women in Mary Ormsbee Whitton's book . . . rich and poor, famous social leaders, frontier heroines, teachers, artists, writers, tavern keepers and propagandists of great causes; women who wore satin slippers and handled dainty teacups, and also women who wove their own linsey-woolsey and carried water up from the spring in wooden buckets. Good browsing—particularly those of you who have to do your reading in brief snatches. You know, that fifteen minutes when you have lunch all ready and are waiting for the kids to come in to eat. . . .

LOGO
MUSIC
BREAK

Precis
"How to Play Badminton"

PLAYING AREA: Turntable
PURPOSE: To show how badminton is a simple and inexpensive backyard game
PROCEDURE: 1. Sarah Palfrey will interview Ken Davidson, national badminton champion, and will demonstrate:
A. Size of area needed;
B. Type of equipment;
C. Cost of equipment;
D. Layout of area;
E. Principles of the game and scoring;
F. A sample rally between Ken and Sarah

(*Fade in: Film clip of family playing badminton*)
ARLENE (*VO*)
Are you looking for more fun in your backyard this summer? Here's an easy game for you to learn—and here to teach you about it is our former national women's tennis champion—Sarah Palfrey . . .
(*Cut to: Sarah standing in tennis costume in area "H," seated on the rise. Beside her is Ken Davidson*)
SARAH
Hi, there. There's no doubt about it—badminton is one of the best family backyard games in the world, and I'm very happy to have with me today the world-renowned badminton star, Ken Davidson. Welcome to HOME, Ken.
KEN
Thanks, Sarah. You know the most wonderful thing about badminton is the fact that you can have *immediate fun* with it—right away—the minute you get your set.
SARAH
That's right, Ken. I understand even the complete novice can get right into the rhythm of the game. What's the

main reason for that?

KEN

The main thing is that the bird—or the shuttlecock—can be hit back and forth slowly and easily until you get the hang of it—then you can hit it as hard as you want.

SARAH

Well, Ken—let's get right into learning the fundamentals of the game so that our viewers can follow along with us.

KEN

Good—first, be sure you get a good, serviceable family set—

(*Cut to: Pre-set display of Sportcraft Badminton Set*)

Here's a family set by Sportcraft. It's ideal for beginners, and sturdy enough to last a long time.

(*Cut to: Sarah and Ken live. They are now standing in H1*)

KEN

Now—first thing to learn is how to hold a racquet. It's very simple—like this—

(*Cut to: CU of Ken's right hand as he shows grip*)

Now—you do it, Sarah—just to get the hang of it.

(*Cut to: CU of Sarah's right hand as she does the same*)

(*Cut to: Two shot, Sarah and Ken*)

SARAH

Simple enough, Ken. What's next on the docket?

KEN

Next thing is learning to serve— which is just about as simple . . .

(*Cut to: MCU, Ken as he demonstrates serve. Hits shuttlecock wild*)

into camera)

Okay, Sarah— You're next . . .

(*Cut to: MCU, Sarah as she serves, hits shuttlecock wild into camera*)

KEN

Now the last fundamental to learn is your foot position . . . for the forehand and backhand—like this . . .

(*Cut to: MCU, Ken as he shows footwork*)

All right, Sarah—let's see you try it. . . .

(*Cut to: MCU, Sarah as she does it*)

SARAH

That looks nice and simple, Ken. Tell you what—I've got a young friend of mine here who has been watching right along—and I'd like to see him try carrying these things out on the court.

(*Ken takes boy out on court. They demonstrate three things:*)

1. Serve

2. Backhand

3. Forehand.

(*Sarah comments voice over as they do this*)

(*At conclusion:*)

SARAH

Ken—that looks so easy, I'm going to try it myself with you. Are you game?

(*He is—and they volley as music comes up and under. After several seconds of volleying, with X-dissolve to Arlene*)

ARLENE

And there is the game of badminton —a game you can have fun with the minute you start—and one which you can play in your own backyard.

TEXAS TROUSER FASHIONS

AUDIO	VIDEO
EVE: Texas Trousers make fashion news for lounging at home.	*Eve in Area F, G or H sitting in patio chair wearing Texas Trousers*
My vel-jeans are made of navy blue velvet with rhinestone buttons in the patch pockets.	*CU trouser pockets on Eve*
My blouse has a special three-way neckline.	*CU neckline of blouse on Eve*
Here's a striped cotton cover-all. It's perfect to wear in the morning while you're doing your household chores . . .	*Model #1* *Pan from head to toe*
This imported printed velvet makes a more dressy version of the Texas Trouser.	*Model #2* *Pan trousers* *Cu print on trousers*
The shirt has a ruffled front.	*Cu ruffled blouse*
Here's Arlene in her favorite blouse and trousers in printed corduroy.	*Arlene models* *Cu design on Arlene's blouse* *Pan down to print on Arlene's trousers*
All these Texas Trousers are made by Dallas Sportswear and are on sale at leading department stores all over the country.	

CLOSING

ARLENE: These are mighty good clothes for relaxing. And I know you'll love wearing them . . . if your daughter doesn't get to the closet first, because she'll love them, too. You'll probably end up giving them to her . . . but after all there is nothing a mother wouldn't give her daughter . . . her time and love as well as material things . . . Gibran said, "You give but little when you give of your possessions. It is when you give of yourself that you truly give."

AUDIO   VIDEO

Good-bye . . . See you at HOME tomorrow.

CU: Jet mixer

HUGH (*VO*): Do you know what
this is? It's one of the many things
you'll see tomorrow on HOME.

*Flash headline: Tomorrow Children
at HOME . . . Fish as Pets with Jim
Moran . . . News from Washington
. . . HOME's Cooking School . . .
Vacation by Car . . . Paris Boutique
. . . and Chef Phillip . . . all on
HOME*

HUGH (*VO*): Tomorrow, Children
at HOME, Fish as Pets, with Jim
Moran . . . News from Washington . . . HOME's Cooking School . . .
Vacation by Car . . . Paris Boutique
. . . and Chef Phillip.

All on HOME tomorrow.

LOGO

MUSIC

A DICTIONARY OF TV TERMS

Brief definitions of the special television terminology used in the scripts in this book. Adapted from the complete *Dictionary of TV Terms* published periodically by Sponsor Magazine, 40 East 49th Street, New York 17, N. Y.

Audio—That part of TV transmission pertaining to sound.

B.G. (Background)—A set, drape, drop, or any material used behind actors or foreground objects.

Boom Mike—A microphone on a long telescoping arm which may be extended or retracted, swung in a wide horizontal arc, and raised or lowered. Boom is usually mounted on a mobile platform that facilitates its movement.

Card (Title)—The card on which is printed or drawn words, credits or titles used in a television program.

Cross-fade—Where audio effect, sound, music, or otherwise is faded out while simultaneously another sound is faded in. This technique is commonly used to make transitions between dramatic scenes.

C.U. (Close-up)—Narrow-angle picture limited to object or part of one object instead of a scene. No background at all.

Cut In Shot—Camera shot of any object which is inserted into action of scene— such as a telegram, news item, a clock.

Cutting To—To move camera to a newly designated position so as to pick up a specific scene or person.

Dissolve—The overlapping fade-out of one picture and fade-in of another (electronically).

Dolly—A movable fixture or carriage, usually mounted on four wheels, which carries either camera, or camera and cameraman, and can be wheeled about during the taking of a shot.

E.C.U.—End close-up.

Emcee—Master of Ceremonies.

Establishing Shot—Long camera shot introduced at the beginning of a scene to establish the inter-relationship of details to be shown subsequently in nearer shots.

Fade In—The TV screen is dark and the picture gradually appears to full brightness.

F.S. (Follow Shot)—To follow the talent by moving the camera and dolly.

In Limbo—Scene or actor appears as in a cloud, disassociated from the main scene (or against a blank background).

In Tight—Close shot using narrow angle lens 90-135 mm.

Live—"On the spot" televising of people and/or events in contrast to transmission of film material.

Logo (Logotype)—A trade mark or similar device, usually used by business firms to identify themselves or their products.

Long Shot—Camera picking up a scene from a distance.

L.P. (Long Pan)—See definition of "pan."

M.C.U. (Medium Close-up)—Medium angle picture showing object and a limited amount of background or setting.

M.D. (Match Dissolve)—Perfect overlap or cross-fading from one scene to another where persons, objects or properties are in identical positions and illusion of one subject is created.

M.S. (Medium Shot)—Wide angle camera shot showing objects and related material.

Music Up and Under—To sustain a musical theme for a period of time, dominating one facet of drama or situation, and then to bring down the music in subordinate position to that facet.

Narrator Over—See "Voice Over."

On Camera—Talent or object is on the air—being televised—either or both sight- and sound-wise.

Pan—Gradual swinging of camera to right or left across a scene to see segments of the scene as camera moves.

Practical—Constructed TV scenery that can be used in a normal way, as a door or window that may be opened and closed.

Pull Back—To move camera away from talent or scene, usually for the purpose of enlarging the scene.

R.P. (Rear Projection)—Special technique whereby a wanted scene (photograph or drawing) is projected on a translucent screen which acts as a background for a studio set.

R.S. (Reverse Shot or Reverse Angle Shot)—To pick up the same subject or object as an existing camera, but from an exactly opposite angle. Used for emphasis and changed viewpoint.

Shot—A single continuous pick-up of the TV camera.

Super (Superimpose)—The overlapping (electronically) of an image produced by one camera with the image from another camera, both pictures being visible but appearing finally as one picture.

Title—Cards or film slides—either drawn or printed or on film—which announce the title and credits of a program. Also a term meaning any written or printed matter introduced into show or film for its own sake and not as part of the presentation.

Travelers—Loose scenes, backdrops or curtains, adjustable on pulleys.

Two Shot—Close shot of two persons with camera as near as possible while still keeping them both in the shot.

Video—(From the Latin meaning to see or I see). Usually used as a noun to denote sight broadcasting as opposed to sound broadcasting. Portion of TV signal that contains picture.

V.O. (Voice Over)—(1) Narration type recording as opposed to live sound. (2) Voice over narration where voice talent is not seen.

Wide Shot—Camera picking up a large portion of set, talent, audience, etc., from a distance with a normal lens, or from close up with a wide angle lens.

Zoom—The fast action of a smooth and continuous change of focal length with dolly-in, optical trick, Zoomar lens. Used very effectively where object starts small and zooms in to full view.